ナムイ語文法の記述言語学的研究

西田文信　著

東北大学出版会

A descriptive linguistic study of Namuyi

Fuminobu NISHIDA

Tohoku University Press, Sendai
ISBN978-4-86163-323-2

目次

図表目次　viii
略号一覧　ix

第 1 章　序論　1
1.1　ナムイ＝チベット族について　1
1.2　シナ＝チベット諸語研究史　6
1.3　チベット＝ビルマ諸語研究史　9
1.4　周辺諸言語の研究史　11
1.5　ナムイ語に関する先行研究　13
1.6　本論文で扱う方言について　14
1.7　社会言語学的状況　15
　1.7.1　調査の背景　17
　1.7.2　調査結果　17
　1.7.3　老年層の言語使用　18
　1.7.4　中年層の言語使用　19
　1.7.5　若年層の言語使用　19
　1.7.6　小結　21
1.8　本書の構成　22

第 2 章　音論　29
2.1　母音　29
　2.1.1　単純母音　29
　2.1.2　そり舌母音　34
　2.1.3　鼻音化母音　35
　2.1.4　二重母音　36
　2.1.5　三重母音　36

2.1.6 閉音節　37
2.2 子音　37
　2.2.1 単純子音　37
　2.2.2 音節頭子音結合　48
2.3 音節構造　49
2.4 声調性　50
　2.4.1 ナムイ語の声調に関する先行研究　50
　　2.4.1.1 孫宏開による研究（木里方言）　50
　　2.4.1.2 黄布凡・仁増旺姆による研究（木里方言）　51
　　2.4.1.3 刈による研究（冕寧方言）　51
　　2.4.1.4 筆者による解説（冕寧＝ゾロ方言）　52
　2.4.2 音響分析の手順　52
　　2.4.2.1 被験者　52
　　2.4.2.2 発話材料と録音手順　53
　　2.4.2.3 分析　53
　　2.4.2.4 正規化　54
　　2.4.2.5 テスト単語　54
　2.4.3 結果　55
　　2.4.3.1 持続時間　55
　　2.4.3.2 オンセットとピーク　56
　　2.4.3.3 声調値　58
　　2.4.3.4 声調の分布　60
2.5 ゾロ方言の強勢　61
　2.5.1 イントネーションのパターン　61
　2.5.2 叙述文　62
　2.5.3 疑問文　62
2.6 借用語音韻論　63
　2.6.1 語頭子音　63
　2.6.2 韻尾　64

2.6.3　声調　65

第3章　語及び名詞形態論　67
3.1　ナムイ語における「語」　67
3.2　名詞　68
　3.2.1　普通名詞　68
　3.2.2　固有名詞　68
　3.2.3　場所名詞　72
　3.2.4　時間名詞　73
　3.2.5　派生名詞（名詞化）　75
　　3.2.5.1　他動詞　75
　　3.2.5.2　能格動詞　76
　　3.2.5.3　非対格動詞　76
　　3.2.5.4　他動詞の内項　78
　3.2.6　代名詞　80
　　3.2.6.1　人称代名詞　80
　　3.2.6.2　再帰代名詞　81
　　3.2.6.3　指示詞　82
　　3.2.6.4　疑問代名詞　83
　　3.2.6.5　不定代名詞　83
3.3　数詞と数量詞　84
　3.3.1　数詞　84
　3.3.2　数に関する表現　85
　3.3.3　類別詞（classifier）　86
3.4　名詞句の形態　88
　3.4.1　性標識　88
　3.4.2　指小辞標示　90
　3.4.3　親族名称　90
　3.4.4　定／不定　91

3.4.5　数標示　92
3.5　名詞句関係形態素（格標示）　92
3.6　S/A/P を標示する形式　95
　3.6.1　S/P を標示する形式　95
　3.6.2　A を標示する形式　96
　3.6.3　LOCAL な意味役割を標示する形式　98
　　3.6.3.1　存在・出来事生起の位置を標示する形式　98
　　3.6.3.2　移動の着点を標示する形式　99
　　3.6.3.3　移動・時間的区間の起点を標示する形式　100
　　3.6.3.4　移動の通過点を標示する形式　101
3.7　その他の標示形式　101
　3.7.1　共格を標示する形式　101
　3.7.2　属格を標示する形式　102
　3.7.3　与格を標示する形式　103
　3.7.4　向格を標示する形式　104
　3.7.5　具格を標示する形式　105
　3.7.6　比較を標示する形式　105

第 4 章　動詞形態論　107

4.1　動詞の分類　107
　4.1.1　自動詞　108
　4.1.2　他動詞　109
　4.1.3　存在動詞　111
　4.1.4　二重他動詞　112
　4.1.5　自他同形動詞　113
4.2　結合価　114
　4.2.1　結合価を増加させるデバイス　114
　4.2.2　結合価を減少させるデバイス　114
4.3　形容詞（状態叙述自動詞）　115

- 4.4 繋辞（コピュラ） 117
- 4.5 人称標示 118
- 4.6 方位／方向標示 119
- 4.7 アスペクト標示 120
  - 4.7.1 前望相（prospective aspect） 121
  - 4.7.2 起動相（inchoative aspect） 122
  - 4.7.3 状態変化相（CSM of state） 122
  - 4.7.4 継続相（continuative aspect） 123
  - 4.7.5 完了相（perfective aspect） 125
  - 4.7.6 繰り返し（repetition） 126
  - 4.7.7 未完了相（imperfective） 127
  - 4.7.8 反復相（iterative） 128
- 4.8 否定標示 128
- 4.9 モダリティ 129
  - 4.9.1 義務的モダリティ 130
    - 4.9.1.1 義務 130
    - 4.9.1.2 許可 131
    - 4.9.1.3 能力 132
  - 4.9.2 認識論的モダリティ 132
- 4.10 結合価変化の手段（valency changing devices） 133
  - 4.10.1 結合価の増加 133
  - 4.10.2 結合価の減少 134
- 4.11 法（ムード） 136
  - 4.11.1 平叙（直説）法 136
  - 4.11.2 命令法 136
  - 4.11.3 疑問法 137
  - 4.11.4 禁止法 138
  - 4.11.5 感嘆法 139（exclamative）
  - 4.11.6 勧奨法 140（hortative）

4.11.7　許可法（permissive）　140
4.11.8　願望法（optative）　140

第5章　その他の構造　143
5.1　構成素順序　143
  5.1.1　名詞句構文　143
  5.1.2　動詞複合体構文　146
  5.1.3　節の構成素順序　148
5.2　疑問文　148
  5.2.1　極性疑問文　149
  5.2.2　選択疑問文　150
  5.2.3　疑問詞疑問文　150
5.3　否定文　151
  5.3.1　否定のスコープ　152
  5.3.2　二重否定　153
5.4　存在構文と所有構文　153
5.5　トピック＝コメント構文　154
5.6　漢語からの文法借用　155
  5.6.1　単文　155
  5.6.2　複文　156
  5.6.3　数量詞　156
    5.6.3.1　名量詞　156
    5.6.3.2　動量詞　157
    5.6.3.3　形容詞　157
    5.6.3.4　疑問詞の繰り返しによる前後呼応形式（Cross Clause Correlation）　158
    5.6.3.5　副詞　158
    5.6.3.6　側置詞（Adposition）　159
    5.6.3.7　接続詞　159

5.6.3.8　語気助詞（sentence-final particle）　159

親族名称図　161
ナムイ語テキスト例　163
ナムイ語語彙　169
参考文献　239

図表目次

図1.1	ナムイ語話者の分布地域	2
表1.1	川西民族走廊諸語のグルーピング	4
図1.2	四川省のチベット系諸言語の分布図	5
表1.2	言語使用のまとめ	18
表1.3	世代ごとの言語使用	20
図2.1	ナムイ語子音の音声的実現	38
図2.2	ナムイ語子音の音素一覧	38
図2.3	各音素の弁別的特徴	48
表2.1	テスト語彙（名詞）	55
表2.2	テスト語彙（動詞）	55
図2.4	引用形式における4声調の平均持続時間	56
表2.3	ナムイ語ゾロ方言のOnsetとPeak	56
図2.5	平均Z値で正規化されたF0軌跡	56
図2.6	平均Z値で正規化されたF0軌跡（2音節語）	57
図2.7	平均Z値で正規化されたF0軌跡（3音節語）	57
図2.8	平均Z値で正規化されたF0軌跡（4音節語）	58
表2.4	ナムイ語ゾロ方言の多音節語のピッチパターン	58
図3.1	方向を表す語彙	72
表3.1	ナムイ語ゾロ方言の格表示形式	94

略号一覧

1	first person
2	second person
3	third person
ADJ	adjective (stative verb)
ADV	adverbial marker
AGT	agentive marker
ASP	aspect marker
AUX	auxiliary particle for monosyllabic Chinese loan words
BEN	benefactive marker
CAUS	causative marker
CL	classifier
COM	comitative marker
COMP	comparative marker
COP	copula
CSM	change of state marker
DAT	dative marker
DEF	definite marker
DEM	demonstrative pronoun
DIR	directional prefix
dl	dual
DTV	directive particle
EMPH	emphatic sentence-final particle
ERG	erga fire
EVID	evidential marker
EXC	exclusion particle
EXP	experiential particle

PRS	prospective aspect form
GEN	genitive marker
HABIT	habitual action marker
HORT	hortative marker
INDEF	indefinite marker
INDTV	indirect directive marker
INF	inferential evidential marker
INT	interjection
INST	instrumental marker
LOC	locative marker
LNK	clause linker
MIR	mirative (just discovered) marker
NAR	narrative (hearsay) particle (often two syllables)
NEG	negative marker
NEG. IMP	negative imperative (prohibitive) prefix
NOM	nominalizer
NUM	numeral
PERF	perfective marker
pl	plural
POST	postposition
Q	question marker
RCA	relevant condition achieved
RECIP	reciprocal form
REFL	reflexive form
REP	repetition ('again') marker
REQU	request marker
sg	singular
TOP	topic marker
U	bound non-actor marker (e. g. '2 sgU' means 'second per-

son singular non-actor marker')

第 1 章　序論

本書で対象とするナムイ語[1]については、近年まで中国人研究者である孫宏開（孫宏開）、黄布凡及び劉輝強（劉輝強）の概略的な報告があるのみで、ほとんどその実態は知られていなかった。また孫宏開の一連の報告はムリ（木里）方言に関するものであり、本書で対象とするゾロ（冕寧）方言については黄布凡と劉輝強以外に先行研究が存在しない。本書は、ナムイ語ゾロ（冕寧）方言の記述言語学的文法便覧である。

本章では、本論文で取り上げるナムイ語を話すナムイ＝チベット族とその言語、歴史的・社会的背景、及び本論文の構成や方法論などについて述べる。

1.1　ナムイ＝チベット族について

ナムイ語話者は民族学で謂うところのナムイ＝チベット族である。ナムイ＝チベット族は、中華人民共和国四川省涼山彝族自治州の冕寧県・木里藏族自治県・西昌県・塩源県及び甘孜藏族自治州九龍県に居住するチベット族のうち自らをナムイと自認する民族グループのことである。

ナムイ＝チベット族は民国時代までは「西蕃」と称される民族グループの一つ、また新中国成立の1949年以降は「小西蕃」の一つと分類されたが、1950年代に行われた民族識別工作ではこれら二つの名称は蔑称であるとして改められ、現在では「藏族」（チベット族）として分類されている[2]。

1　言語名は、漢語では「納木義語」「納木依語」「納木茲語」「南義語」「納磨依語」など、英語では Namuyi, Namyi, Namuzi, Namzi 等と表記される。民族名は［na-muzi］、［namuzi］、［namuji］、［namji］等の発音がある。

2　現在のナムイ＝チベット族はその多くは彝族との雑居地域に居住しているため、言語及び文化面でも彝語及び彝族の影響を色濃く受けている。

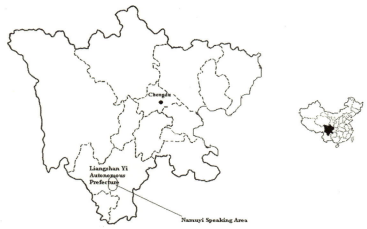

図1.1 ナムイ語話者の分布地域（中華人民共和国及び四川省の拡大図）

歴史的には、「西番」は主に大渡河以南から金沙江以北の地域に分布し、「納木依」「多須」「里汝」「爾蘇」「魯蘇」「本尼洛」「須迷」の7種の自称集団が存在する。

歴史的文献においては、以下のような記載がみられる；

「蜀中南高山有西蕃部落」（『博物志』異魯）
「至黎州……入西蕃求良馬以中市」（『宋史』巻49蛮夷4）
「冕寧聚五方之民、西蕃、猓、獏狻……雑処其地……」（『冕寧県志』）

咸豊7年（1857年）編の『冕寧県志』によると、現在のアルス語話者を「西番」、ナムイ語話者を「獏狻」と称していたらしい。しかし、同音の「摩梭」すなわちナシ族とは言語学にも民族学的にも別の民族であることに留意されたい。ナムイ＝チベット族は1984年に正式にチベット族という族称に決定した。

チベット文化圏の東端、四川省西部の山岳地帯は古来数多くの民族が移動し興亡を繰り広げてきた地域であると考えられる。この地域には金

沙江・烏江・岷江・大渡河・雅砻江などの大河が南北に貫流し、海抜高度1,500〜4,000メートルの険しい峡谷が形成されている。この地域に主に分布している「西番」諸集団の大部分を占める四川の羌系チベット族の言語である所謂「川西民族走廊諸語（Languages of the Ethnic Corridor）」のひとつであるナムイ語の言語系統は、シナ＝チベット語族・チベット＝ビルマ語派・羌語支（Qiangic, Tibeto-Burman, Sino-Tibetan）（孫 2001：160）とされるのが一般的であるが、確定するには至っていない。ナムイ語の話者人口は3,000人[3]で、多くは彝語と漢語を流暢に操りナムイ語のみを話すモノリンガルの話者は殆ど存在しない。

　ナムイ語を含む川西民族走廊諸語は、従前ヒマラヤ語支（Himalayaish）乃至は彝語支（Lolish）として分類されてきた。孫（2001：160）が羌語支の設定を確定して以来、その類型構造と同源語の共有率にもとづき川西民族走廊に分布する諸言語の大部分が羌語支（Qiangic）として設定・確定されるようになってきている。

　以下に掲げるグルーピングは、孫（2001）の系譜分類図に若干の修正を施したものである。変更点としては、言語の地理的分布に合わせた配

---

[3] 孫宏開（私信）によれば、本言語の話者人口は5,000人であるという。劉輝強（私信）によれば3,800人であるとのことである。四川省のみならず、中華人民共和国内の少数民族言語の正確な話者数は把握しがたいものがある。センサス実施時に使用言語の調査もなされるが、実態と異なる回答が出てくることも少なくないという。2000年に実施されたセンサスによれば、西昌在住の蔵族は2,000人との数値が出ている。しかるに、これらのすべてがナムイ＝チベット族であるという訳ではなく、ギャロン、白馬、アルゴン、ジャパ、クィリャン、ミニヤック、アルス、シシン、チュユなどの明らかに異なるアイデンティティをもったチベット族の人口も含まれている。同様のことは木里及び塩源での話者人口についても当てはまり、それぞれ40,000人、6,000人のチベット族は多くの回民族集団を含めて数値である。筆者の調査のよると、概数として以下の数値が得られている：西昌：800人、木里：1,200人、塩源：400人、その他の地域：300人。よって、現時点では2,700人の話者人口を有するものとする。また、Charles Kevin Stuart（私信）によれば、大水村：80人（総人口600人）、大水村：80人（総人口600人）、郷水村：800人（総人口9000人）、大水村：80人（総人口600人）、東封村：560人（総人口1100人）、沙覇村：290人（総人口1600人）、総計1,740人であるという。

列とした点、言語間の親疎関係とグループ化は孫（2001）に沿っているが筆者の考えも反映させている点、言語名に英語名も付加した点、などである。

孫の謂う羌語支は死語である西夏語を含む以下の13言語から成り立っている。

表1.1　川西民族走廊諸語のグルーピング

　繰り返しになるが、ナムイ語は四川省涼山州冕寧県、木里蔵族自治県西昌県・塩源県、及び甘孜蔵族自治州の九龍県内の一部の地区に分布する。この言語の使用するチベット族は約5,000人いる。各地でこの言語を話すチベット族は基本的に2種類の良く似た自称があり、九龍県と木里県に居住する者の自称はナムズ（Namuzi）であり、冕寧県・西昌県・塩源県などの地域内に居住している者の自称はナムイ（Namuyi）である。木里県ではプミ語を話すチベット族はナムズのことをアルスと呼び、現地のモンゴル族はムヒ（雑種の意）と呼ぶのに対して、アルスはモンゴル族のことをガヒ（雑種の意）と呼んでいる。木里県に居住する民族はナムズのことをナヒの一部であると見做している。

　ナムイ＝チベット族の間では新中国成立以前は一夫多妻制が存在したが、現在は完全に一夫一妻となっている。

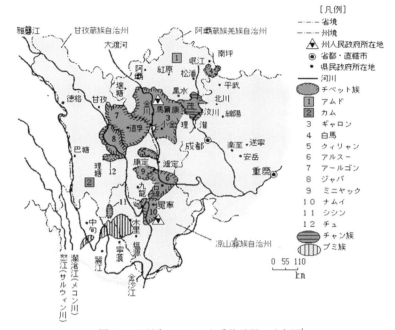

図1.2 四川省のチベット系諸言語の分布図[4]

　ナムイ＝チベット族には、自分たちの祖先は400年ほど前にラサから移住してきたという伝承が広く分布している。また、ナムイは当時の某有力者の10人兄弟の息子達のうちの5人兄弟の末裔であるとの伝承も流布している。当時はナムイ＝チベット族は漢族と通婚すべきではないとされたが、ある有力者が漢族と結婚したことでそれを快く思わない人々の間で戦争がはじまり、大規模な要塞に建設され多くの人が配置されたという伝承もある。現在では、ナムイ＝チベット族は漢族及び彝族と広く通婚している。

　涼山彝族自治州のナムイ＝チベット族の中には、「ナムイ」という語が「ナム」が「黒」、「イ」が「人」から構成されていることを根拠に、

4　松岡正子氏提供の資料による。

自分たちの祖先が彝族と関係があると信じている者が少なくない。歴史的にはボン教を信仰していたと主張する者もいるが、現在ボン教寺院は一つも存在しない。各家族で信仰する山をもち、家族が死亡すると死者の加護を目的に山羊・羊・豚などの家畜を殺し神に捧げる。

　超自然的存在の表象としてナムイ＝チベット族は、ナムイ語で ᴿmupu と称される白石祀る習慣があるが、白石を深山から採取して持ち帰り、屋根の東端に3個または5個か7個置く。その際オンドリ・ヤク・メンヨウのいずれか生贄とし、ᴴpapi と称される宗教職能者が経文を唱える。この他に、樹神及び山神が重要な宗教的存在となっている。

1.2　シナ＝チベット諸語研究史

　従前、シナ＝チベット語族の基本的な工具書としては Robert Shafer の *Introduction to Sino-Tibetan*（Wiesbaden：Otto Harrassowitz 1966-73年．合本1974年）と Paul K. Benedict の *Sino-Tibetan : a conspectus*（New York：Cambridge University Press、1972年）が用いられてきた。この二冊は、主に史的考察を主眼としており依拠したデータが時代的な制約もあり、精密さに欠け、分析の深さ・厳密さにも問題があったためこれらにかわる、漢語派（Sinitic）とチベット＝ビルマ語派（Tibeto-Burman）両者をバランスよく扱った書物の刊行が久しく待ち望まれていた。また周知の如く、漢語派に関しては夥しい数の研究書が表れてはいるが、この語族を網羅的に解説したものは存在しなかった。

　1990年代に中国で相次いで刊行された《蔵緬語音与詞匯》（《蔵緬語音与詞匯》編写組編、1991年）や《蔵緬語族語言詞匯》（黄布凡編、1992年）といった中国国内のチベット＝ビルマ系言語の対照語彙表も、北京大学から出版された《漢蔵語概論（上・下）》（馬学良主編、1991年）や《蔵緬語十五種》（戴慶廈他、北京燕山出版社、1991年）なども、中国境外の諸言語は扱われていなかったからである[5]。

　21世紀を迎えて、前世紀の記述的・歴史的研究を総括するかの如く、

漢語派・チベット＝ビルマ語派双方の情報をふんだんに掲載した、シナ＝チベット語族の専書が立て続けに三冊出版された。第一にベルン大学（出版当時はライデン大学）の George van Driem の手になるヒマラヤ諸語の大部の著作（*Languages of Himalayas. vol 1・2*、Leiden、Boston and Köln Brill、2001年）、第二に James A. Matisoff によるチベット＝ビルマ祖語に関する労作（*Handbook of Proto-Tibeto-Burman*. Berkeley、Los Angels and London：University of California Press. 2003年）である。前者は、比較歴史言語学を修めた文献にもフィールドにも強い筆者による、数百年にわたるこの分野の研究の概観と最前線を手際よくまとめたものであるが、2巻で1300ページ余りのボリューム感ある研究書である。シナ＝チベット語族は勿論のこと、印欧語族やオーストロアジア語族にも言及しているが、特に筆者の得意とするブータンやネパールの諸言語については他の追随を許さない記述となっている。参考文献として挙げられているものは、この分野の全研究を略カバーしており、後学にとってもこの上なく貴重な文献目録となっている。後者は、前世紀後半をチベット＝ビルマ諸語の研究に捧げ、多くの研究者を育成してきた筆者のチベット＝ビルマ祖語に関する研究の集大成であり、バークレーで継続中の STEDT（Sino-Tibetan Etymological Dictionary and Thesaurus Project）で収集・分析したデータを十二分に活用したものである。声母・韻尾の正確な網羅的な再構が提示されているが、声調の再構は懐疑的であるとの理由から触れられていない。最後に新進気鋭の中国語学者であるワシントン大学の Zev Handel による上古音の概説が付され、中国語研究者にとっても非常に有益なものとなっている。

5　因みに、戴慶厦主編《二十一世紀的中国少数民族語言研究》書海出版社、1998年は中国国内の少数民族語研究の背景を知るのに有益である。近年、《漢藏語同源詞研究》（丁邦新・孫宏開主編．南寧：広西民族出版社．（一）漢藏語研究的歴史回顧、2000年、（二）漢藏、苗瑤同源詞専題研究、2001年、（三）漢藏語研究的方法論探索、2004年、（四）上古漢語侗台関系研究、2011年や《漢藏語同源詞研究》呉安其．北京：民族大学出版社．2002年等が出版されたことはこの分野におけるこの上ない貢献である。

中国語音韻論の分野では李方桂・鄭張尚芳・藩悟雲・龔煌城等の研究、欧米ではBodman、Nicholas C. の Proto-Chineseand Sino-Tibetan: Data Towards Establishing the Nature of Relationship.（Frans van Coetsem andLinda R. Waugh eds.、*Contributions to Historical Linguistics*. Leiden: E. J. Brill. pp. 34-199. 1980年）や William Baxter（白一平）の A Handbook of Old Chinese Phonology.（Berlin and New York: Mouton de Gruyter、1992年）及びその改訂版ともいうべき *Old Chinese: A new reconstruction*. Oxford University Press. 2014年）をはじめロシアのスタロスティン（S. A. Starostin、*Rekonstrukcija drevnekitajskoj fonologicheskoj sistemy*、1989年）、本邦の藤堂明保・賴惟勤・三根谷徹・河野六郎・橋本萬太郎・平山久雄らの研究により大いに進展していた。

　シナ＝チベット語族は、漢語派（Sinitic）とチベット＝ビルマ語派（Tibeto-Burman）からなり、広域に分布するものである。かつて西田龍雄が「シナ＝チベット語族と称される言語グループは、そのような包括的な名称が与えられているにも拘わらず、そこに所属する諸言語相互の言語系譜的な関係が、いまだ比較言語学的に十分に証明されていない語族である」と述べたが[6]、この状況は現在でも当てはまり作業仮説の域を出ていないとする者もいる。

　シナ＝チベット諸語は族話者人口からすると印欧語族を凌ぐ最大の語族であり、中国、インド及びネパールのヒマラヤ地域、東南アジア諸国で行われており、中国、インドシナ半島、アッサム、ヒマラヤ地域に分布する数多くの言語が親族関係にあるとして与えられた名称である。それら諸言語の比較言語学的研究は不十分で、所属言語、分派関係、他の語族との関係について諸説があるが、かつて系統関係が唱えられたベトナム語・タイ諸語やミャオ・ヤオ諸語との類似は言語接触の結果であろうとされている。

6　「チベット語・ビルマ語語彙比較における問題」『東方學』第十五輯：64-48、1957年）

中国国内ではいまだ李方桂（1937）の分類が現在なお優勢である（*Languages and dialects. The Chinese yearbook*. Shanghai : Commercial Press. 1973年に Languages and dialects of China. *Journal of Chinese Linguistics*. 1：1-14. として再録）。この語族の諸言語は一般的に単音節語、声調言語、孤立語、分析的言語といわれるが、言語・方言または時代により構造的特徴は一様ではない。李方桂の挙げた如く、一般的な傾向として、（1）単音節性、（2）声調を有する傾向、（3）声母の無声化傾向、（4）語彙、（5）SVOの語順が挙げられる。上述の李の分類の根拠は類型論的特徴であるが、類型論が下位分類の有力な手がかりとなりえないのは定説となっている[7]。

　この語族に属する言語同士の系統関係に関してはいまだ十分には解明されていないが、研究の進展に伴う変遷もあり、研究者の解釈による相違も見られる。今後の研究が俟たれる。

1.3　チベット＝ビルマ諸語研究史

Klaproth, Julius Heinrich von. 1823. *Asia Polyglotta*. Paris : A. Shubart. は、チベット語・ビルマ語・漢語における語彙の類似性を初めて指摘したものであり、チベット＝ビルマ諸語研究の嚆矢となった。19世紀にネパールの英国公使として赴任し自然科学者、民族学者としても名高い Brian Houghton Hodgson が1874年に出版した *Essays on the Languages*、*Literature and Religion of Nepal and Tibet*. London : Trubner and Co. にて数多くの未記述言語を記録しており、歴史的に価値の高い資料となっている。"Indonesia" という語を欧州に広めたことで有名な James Richardson Logan は1850年出版の "The Ethnology of the Indian

---

[7] 類型論の無力さについては例えば van Driem も 'The use of typological traits as indices of genetic affiliation has consistently misled comparativists in the nineteenth and twentieth centuries.'（Sino-Bodic、*Bulletin of the School of Oriental and African Studies* 60.3：470、1997年）と述べている。

Archipelago : Embracing Enquiries into the Continental Relations of the Indo-Pacific Islanders". *Journal of the Indian Archipelago and Eastern Asia.* 4：252-347にて「チベット＝ビルマ」という名称を初めて提唱・使用した。August Conrady（1896）*Eine Indo-Chinesesische Causative- Denominativ-Bildung und ihr Zusammenhang mit den Tonaccenten.* Leipzig：Otto Harrassowitz. は漢語との系統関係を示唆し、Tibeto-Burman と Sino-Siamese からなる Indo-Chinese family 説を提唱した。

"Sino-Bodic" *Bulletin of the School of Oriental and African Studies*、University of London. 60. 1：455-488. で George van Driem は、漢語とチベット語派の漢語とチベット語の系統的近親性を重視している。つまり、シナ＝チベット語族に代わる概念としてチベット＝ビルマ語族があり、その下位分類としてシナ＝ボディックなる概念を提唱するにいたった。この仮説は、ある意味 Simon や Bodman の考え方の変異と見ることが出来るかもしれない。言語の親近性を語る際、音韻・語彙・形態統語論（morpho-syntax）を考慮に入れねばならないが、van Driem はこれらの言語群を比較する際パラダイム的視点には注意を払っていない感がある。Benedict, Paul K.（1972）、Matisoff. J. A. ed. *Sino-Tibetan : A conspectus*、Cambridge： Cambridge University Press. 同様レプチャ語に関心を払い過ぎている。更に、移民移住の歴史的観点からすると、この仮説は再考の余地が残されている。Van Driem は羌語と西夏語をチベット＝ビルマ諸語の南部ブランチに分類しているが、これは戴慶厦の、プロソディ＝システム（trochaic）及びある種の語彙項目の特異な形態（例：mi"人"）等に基づき北部ブランチと分類したのと異なっている。作業仮説としては、ただ現在はよりチベット＝ビルマ語内部のより下位のレベルの研究（即ち言語記述）がチベット＝ビルマ語の作業モデルを打ち立てるのと同様重要であると考える。Van Driem の仮説は van Driem、George（2001）、*Languages of the Himalayas : An Ethnolinguistic Handbook of the Greater Himalayan Region.* Leiden： Brill. でその全貌を伺うことができるが、van Driem, George（2003）"Tibeto-Burman Phylogeny and Prehistory: Languages、Material Culture and Genes"、in Bellwood, Peter ; Renfrew, *Examining the farming/ language dispersal hypothesis*, pp. 233-249. ではより詳細な系統関係を論じている。

他にチベット＝ビルマ語派の系統分類に関する論考としては、Bradley, David（1997）, "Tibeto-Burman languages and classification", in David Bradley ed., *Tibeto-Burman languages of the Himalayas, Papers in South East Asian linguistics, 14*, Canberra : Pacific Linguistics, pp. 1 -71., Bradley, David（2002）, "The Subgrouping of Tibeto-Burman", in Beckwith, Chris ; Blezer, Henk, *Medieval Tibeto-Burman languages*, BRILL, pp. 73 -112., Thurgood, Graham（2003）, "A subgrouping of the Sino-Tibetan languages", in Thurgood, Graham & LaPolla, Randy J., *Sino-Tibetan Languages*, London : Routledge, pp. 3 -21. などがある。

1.4 周辺諸言語の研究史

中国においては、現代のチベット・ビルマ語群言語の現地調査に基づいた、チベット語や羌語、ギャロン語を中心とした研究が民国期から行われている。而るに、1982年と84年に中国西南民族研究学会が六江流域民族総合科学考察の一環として行った雅砻江上、下流域のチベット族調査以上の規模のものはこれまでなかった。

孫宏開は長期にわたってチベット・ビルマ語群言語の調査研究を進め、六江流域の西番諸集団の共通祖語を「羌語系言語」と想定している（孫宏開　1983b）。

孫宏開は孫（1982）で初めて川西民族走廊において話される諸言語が一つのグループにまとめられることを示唆した。その後、羌語支語言という概念を提唱し、独立のグループ位置付けるに至った（孫 1983b：443、451）。孫は羌藏語を西藏語系と羌語系の2つに分け、白馬語以外の西番諸語を羌語系とし、ギャロン語とその他をそれぞれ羌語系の一支とする。この分類は孫（2001）に受け継がれ、この中で彼は北部グループと南部

グループに大きく分け、ナムイ語は Lolish の特徴をもっているように見えるが、それでも語彙や方向接辞（directional prefixes）の存在を根拠に、やはり羌語支の１言語であると結論付けている[8]。Matisoff（2003：6）もまた同様の分類に立脚している。両者の違いは、孫(2001)が Qiangic を Qiang-Jingpo group のひとつとしているのに対し、Matisoff（2003）は Proto-Tibeto-Burman から直接別れた独立の語支としている点である。

　これに対して、西田龍雄（私信）は、ギャロン語と川西民族走廊を分けて扱う点で、孫と異なる。西田（1993）では、川西民族走廊からギャロン語を除外したものを川西民族走廊言語とし、羌語・プリンミ語を除いた諸言語を西蕃諸語としてまとめることを提案している。羌藏語を３つに分けて西藏語系と羌語系の中間に西番語系をおき、西番諸語のうちのギャロン語と白馬語をそれぞれチベット語系の一支とし、その他のミニヤック、アルスなどをそれぞれ西番語系の一支とする（西田 2000：21-23）。

　これに類似した分類としては Thurgood（1985）で、そこは Qiangic の上位に Rungish を立て、ここからヒマラヤ諸語と Jiingpo 語の祖語である Proto-Nungish-Jingpo が分かれたとしている。また、Proto-Gyarung-Qiang-Tangut は Proto-Gyarung and Proto-Qiang に分岐したと見なしている。また、The Qiangic Languages は The rGyalrong subgroup 及び the Qiangic Languages に分割されている。ただし現存する西番諸言語の調査がまだ十分になされていない現段階では、これらの下位分類はまだ確定されていない。これらの言語群の基礎語彙の同源語共有率の低さ、共通の改変が見出しづらい点などが理由として挙げられる。今後の研究が待たれるところである。

8　この分類は、厳密な比較言語学的手続きを踏まれたものでなく、言語分布・類型論的特徴・同源語に基づいていることに注意されたい。彼がもっとも重視しているのは共時的形態論である。

1.5 ナムイ語に関する先行研究

ナムイ語がこの世に最初に紹介されたのは孫（1983b）においてであるが、当該論文では木里方言の概況・音韻・文法の概略が示されている。その後の孫による一連の研究は全てこの論文で提示されたデータに基づいている。黄布凡（1991）及び刘（1983、1996）は本論文で対象とする冕宁（ゾロ）方言を扱っており、共に音韻・文法が概略を知ることが出来る。社会的背景に関する研究としては何（1983）及び（1990）がある。徐菊芳（主編）（1991）及び黄布凡（主編）（1992）にはそれぞれナムイ語の基礎語彙が掲載されている。系統関係の初歩的検討である拉瑪兹偓（1994）、包括的な議論をしている孫（2001）も斯界に対する非常に重要な貢献である。中でも、拉瑪兹偓（1994）及び黄（1997）は関係詞の比率の高さを根拠に、ナムイ語は彝語及び納語と系統関係があるとしている。和（1991）はナムイの別称である「摩些」の語源を考察している。晋代の書籍《华阳国志》に見られる摩些という語彙から、ナムイとナを同源としている。揚（2006）はナムイ＝チベット族とNaishグループの関係を詳細に論じているが、これは言語学的・文化人学的・民族学的に大きな寄与である。孫宏開と並んで中国少数民族言語学会を牽引してきた戴慶厦の他動性を扱った研究、戴（2001）、今後の少数民族言語研究の展望である戴編（1998）、危機言語研究の重要性を論じた戴（2006）も本書で大いに参考とした。近年では、ナムイ＝チベット族の非物質文化研究の総括ともいうべき赵丽明主編(2013)、赵丽明、张琰編(2014)、古涛、王德和（2014）が刊行されたのは喜ばしい限りである。尹（2016）は13の一次データのテキストを含む重要な著作である。刘（2013）はナムイ語で用いられる文字・符号について紹介したものである。

日本人研究者による先行研究としては以下のものが挙げられる。池田（2000）はH. R. Davisの手になる*YÜN-NAN*に記載された西南中國の民族語彙研究の一環として、当該書でムニャ語の下に記述されたものが実

はナムイ語であったこと解明した論文である。池田（2002）では川西民族走廊地域の言語分布の簡にして要を得た纏めをしている。岡本（1999）及び庄司（2003）は中国における少数民族語政策と漢語の普及に関しての諸問題を扱っている。チベット・ビルマ系諸語における能格現象（ergativity）を扱った長野（1986）も本研究に多くの示唆を与えてくれるものである。西田龍雄の一連の研究、特に西田龍雄（1989、1993、2000）は川西民族走廊言語について多くの紙幅を割いている。民族学的背景としては、松岡（2005、2006、2008、2011）が参考となる。

欧米の研究者によるものとしては、かつての言語状況を知る手がかりとなる歴史的価値の高い Baber（1882）、Davies（1909）、Hodgson（1853、1874）、d'Ollone, et. al.（1912）、Waterhouse（2004）がある。言語記述方法論に関しては van Driem（2007）が最も参考となるべき重要な研究である。Libu Lakhi, Tsering Bum, and Charles Kevin Stuart.（2010a、2010b）、Libu Lakhi, Huimin Qi, Charles Kevin Stuart, and Gerald Roche（2010）は木里方言のテキスト・民謡を文字に起こしたものである。Guillaume & Michaud（2011）では、ナムイ語・シシン語と Naish 諸語（納西語・納語・拉热語）からなる Naic なる言語グループを提唱している。

筆者はこれらの先行研究を引き継ぐ形でナムイ語研究を継続してきた。これまで国内外の研究会や学会、学術誌等で音韻論・形態統語論及び社会言語学的問題について論じてきた。西田文信（2006a、2006b、2006c、2007、2010、2013）Nishida（2005b、2005c、2006d、2006e、2013、2015）は大幅に加筆・修正を施して本論文の各項目でも再録してある。

1.6　本論文で扱う方言について

ナムイ語の方言研究はいまだなされていないが、木里方言とゾロ方言での主な違いは、方向接辞（directional prefixes）の数の違い及び声調（tone）の違いである。

筆者は2004年以来、ナムイ語のゾロ方言の調査を行ってきた。主たる

調査協力者は、李小翠さん（1975年生まれ、女性）で現在は連合郷に在住している。本稿の例文の殆どは彼女から得たものである。例文の一部及びテキストは彼女の家族、特に彼女の祖父（1920年生まれ）に発話していただいた。全ての例文は彼女の協力のもとで文法性（grammaticality）を確認してある。なお媒介言語は漢語の標準語・四川方言及び一部彝語である。

本稿では、四川省涼山彝族自治州冕宁県連合郷[9]（東経101°42′10″〜101°50′30″　北緯28°8′0″〜28°19′58″）にて2004年から2013年にかけて断続的に収集した言語データを用いる。

1.7　社会言語学的状況

本論文で扱う方言を話すナムイ語話者の多くは彝語と漢語を流暢に操るため、三言語併用（triglossia）の様相を呈している。過去十年ほどの間、当該地域でも中国の共通語である普通話の普及が図られてきており、言語状況は大きく変貌を遂げつつある。

筆者の調査した四川省涼山彝族自治州冕寧県連合郷では、彝語と漢語の二言語併用（diglossia）教育政策が施されているが、ナムイ語のまたナムイ語による授業は皆無である。当該地域には三年生まで通う小学校が各村に計3校、一年生から六年生まで通う中心校が一校ある。もっとも重視しているのは言語教育である。教授言語は漢語で、小学一年生の80％は漢語を話し、4年生以上になると100％話す蔵族は90％漢語を話す。バイリンガル教育では、3年生よりイ文字の授業があるが、2000年より国家語言委員会が普通話普及を更に徹底させるようになった。漢語を話すチベット族は50％程度、中学進学率は89％、その後高給中学への進学率は32.2％、19.6％が中級専門学校へ進学する。学歴水準は比較的

9　海抜1820m、面積210.88平方m、最も高い大山は4443m。トウモロコシ、洋芋、稲、小麦、燕麦を生産する。戸数532戸、総人口2,428人。（20013年現在）。

高く、文盲・半文盲率はきわめて低い。教育政策は一見上手く行っているように見えるが、ナムイの人々の就学人口と進学人口が増加しているにもかかわらず、ナムイ語教育は全く施されていない。少数民族による地域振興の柱とし彼らに特別優遇政策を与える民族教育政策は、基本的に民族文字をもつ言語話者を対象に行われているが、ナムイは無文字言語であるからである。また従来ナムイ語話者の上級学校への進学率が非常に低く、ナムイ語話者の教師も殆ど存在しなかった。その代わり、ナムイ語話者の漢語理解度は彝族話者のひいては多くの漢語話者のそれよりも高いことが確認された。多民族国家を国民国家へと統合させる教育政策が皮肉にも上手く機能していると言えよう。自民族の言語・文字によって学校教育が受けられていないことに対して不満をもつナムイは存在しなかったようであるが、昨今ナムイ語話者の壮年層が連合郷の郷長へナムイ語教育への要望を提出したことは特筆に価する。

　筆者が主に調査した家庭では、曽祖父・曾祖母に育てられていたものが多くまあ親戚が近隣に居住していることから、母語であるナムイ語・漢語そして彝語を同程度に話す。ナムイ語に関してはほぼ保持されており、完全な三言語話者といってよい。若年層は父母の世代との会話には漢語を用いることが多いが、将来を考えてのためであると言う。一方、自民族言語保持にこの上なく熱心な別の家庭では、小学生・中学生の子供にナムイ語を使用させるようにしつけていた。また地域的な問題で、彝語の習得が必須であるというのは、3・40代の母親の共通見解であった。

　四川省涼山彝族自治州冕寧県連合郷は異文化適応と異文化理解が上手く行われて多民族の共生する社会を築いている。周辺地域の多民族話者をめぐる諸現象を社会言語学的側面から調査・考察するためにはより多くのケーススタディが待たれるものである。

第 1 章 序論

1.7.1 調査の背景

本研究の目的はナムイ語の使用状況を把握することであるが、ナムイ語コミュニティで実際に使用されている言語、特にコミュニティ言語話者の口語状況について、言語使用の実態を接触場面において参加者が接触をどのように評価しているか等も含めて、参与観察とインタビューを中心に記述データを作成することを目標としている[10]。

ここでは3言語(ナムイ語・彝語及び漢語)を使用するナムイ語コミュニティの言語生活を、面接調査および発話の録音資料により考察した初歩的結果を提示する。なお、本研究はGibbons (1987)、Pennington 等 (1992)、及びPannu (1994、1997) という3つの同様の先行研究に基づいている。本稿のデータは、筆者が2003年以降断続的に四川省涼山彝族自治州冕寧県連合郷(東経101°42′10″〜101°50′30″、北緯28°8′0″〜28°19′58″)にて収集したものである。

1.7.2 調査結果

筆者は、四川省涼山彝族自治州冕寧県連合郷にて地元の政府関係者、教師、及び地元のリーダーの及び彼らの家族計30名について言語使用に関するインタビュー調査を実施した。調査の媒介言語は漢語である。

言語運用能力による各言語の順位付けは以下の如くである[11]：

---

10 音声・音韻レベルの諸現象、多言語の語彙表示、コード切り替えに関与する文法的条件等々にも着目した研究を進めていく予定である。最終的にはこれまでに行われた種々の調査結果を踏まえて、通時的にデータの取れるコミュニティを選定し、上記目的に適合する調査の枠組みを構築するのが狙いである。

11 場面別の言語選択・会話能力・言語意識や自己意識、個人的属性等に関する多肢選択式のアンケート調査を実施したが、その結果をもとに作成した。内省による自己評価を評価方法とした。言語使用に関する調査を行った。基準として、(1) 話せないし聞けないを0点、(2) 聞けるがあまり話せないを1点、(3) まあまあである2点、(4) 流暢である、聞くのも話すのも問題ないを3点、を設定してとり行った。複数回答可としこれらの合計点数をもとにパーセンテージを算出した。

言語	第一言語	第二言語	第三言語
ナムイ語	12.7%	10.5%	22.4%
彝語	45.7%	19.8%	6.6%
漢語	33.7%	48.9%	21.7%

表1.2　言語使用のまとめ

　ナムイ語話者自身の感覚からすると、社会経済的な要因によりナムイ語は危機に瀕しているという意識が非常に強い。言語保持を主張する者もわずかながら存在するが、教育制度における言語政策[12]、経済的な趨勢、通婚のパターン、ラジオ・テレビ・インターネットといったマスメディアの普及、それに加えて、ナムイ語に対するネガティブな態度が言語シフト（漢語や彝語を多用）や言語喪失（ナムイ語を完全に使用しない）へと向かわせているのは否めない事実である。

　参与観察の過程で、コードスイッチングの例が多くみられたが、ナムイ語をベース言語としていても語彙は完全に彝語と漢語に置き換わっている文も多くみられ、形態面における特に漢語の使用が甚だしい。

　以下に世代別の言語使用の特徴を述べる。

1.7.3　老年層の言語使用

　ここでは1950年代以前に出生したものを老年層とする。老年層の多くは山岳農村部出身であり、ナムイ語を流暢にはほぼ保持されており、完全なネイティブである。彝語はやや困難を感じる者もいるが彼らを彝語とナムイ語とのバイリンガルと称することができる。

　中年層・若年層との会話には主に彝語を用いるが、ナムイ語が使用されなくなることに関しては時代の趨勢と受けとめとりわけ深刻には考え

---

[12] ナムイ＝チベット族の居住地域における教育は、2000年より国家語言委員会の要請で普通話教育がはじめられたことから現在ではすべて漢語によって行われている。近年彝語も含めたバイリンガル教育も施行されているが、上手く機能しているとは言い難い。

ていないようである。中年層・若年層との心理的な壁はほとんど感じないと言う。

　この世代は文章を書く時は彝語及び漢語を用いるが、ナムイ語は無文字言語であるので、表記には彝文字で類似の音を表記しようとしている者もいた。

　自由発話では、彝語の文に単語レベルでナムイ語が混在する形式も多い。

1.7.4　中年層の言語使用

　中年層（1960-70年代に出生した者）は、彝語と漢語のバイリンガリズムの様相を呈している。彼らの多くは日常生活で彝語を習得し、小学校で漢語を学習した世代である。

　彼らが児童の頃は四川の他地域の青少年との交流も活発に行われてはいたようである。漢語を操り社会的経済的地位が向上した者が多く、現在当該地域のナムイ＝チベット族コミュニティにおいて中核的な地位を占めている。

　ごく少数ではあるが、ナムイ語に関しての伝統的な韻文・散文等を数多く暗誦している者もおり、彼らはナムイ語会話に関しては老年層と比べても遜色ない。

　彼らの家庭内での会話はほとんど漢語である。若年層たる彼らの子供達には、ナムイ語は習得させるつもりはないと断言するものが多い。近年はこの世代の男性は出稼ぎで現地を離れるものも多く、そのため家族と共に過ごす時間が不足するのが最大の悩みの種だと多くの人が指摘する。工事現場の労働者は、現場監督や上司との意思疎通が必須のため、流暢な漢語を話す。

1.7.5　若年層の言語使用

　若年層（1980年代以降に出生した者）は言語面で大きく２つに大別される。１つは漢語と彝語のバイリンガル、もう１つは完全な漢語のモノ

	老年層			中年層			若年層		
	漢語	彝語	ナムイ語	漢語	彝語	ナムイ語	漢語	彝語	ナムイ語
私的会話	0.0	10.7	89.3	44.3	25.7	30.0	66.4	32.3	1.3
公的会話	64.2	30.0	5.8	79.7	20.3	0.0	87.3	12.7	0.0
公衆の面前	77.6	8.0	14.4	80.4	17.3	2.3	90.5	9.5	0.0
書記言語	77.6	22.4	0.0	86.6	13.4	0.0	96.3	3.7	0.0
報道媒体	89.2	10.8	0.0	78.7	21.3	0.0	97.2	2.7	0.0
教育言語[13]	50.0	50.0	0.0	75.0	25.0	0.0	100.0	0.0	0.0

表1.3 世代ごとの言語使用

リンガルである。この相違は両親のライフスタイルと子供の教育に関する考え方によっている。漢語と彝語のバイリンガルは中年層と同様であるが、この世代は彝語に関しては聴く・話すは問題ないものの、読み書きはほとんど不可能である。伝統的な彝文字を習得しているものはごく少数である。

　漢語のモノリンガルは２つのタイプに分かれる。１つは家族との接触時間が比較的少ない、初等教育を受けている児童であり、もう一方は経済的に裕福で、将来大都市にて立身出世を計らんとの両親の期待を受けている児童である。前者は、本来は家族との接触時間を増やしてできれば彝語やナムイ語の言語文化も教えたいと考えているが、仕事のためにいかんともしがたい家庭の子供であり、後者は、今後都市部で高等教育を受けさせるためには漢語が必須であり、彝語をあえて習得させる必要はないと考える家庭の子供である。前者は若年層の３割を占め、後者は１割を占める。

　漢語のモノリンガルには、祖父母の母語たるナムイ語、ひいては両親の話す彝語も全く理解しないものも存在するため、老年層や中年層から涼山人としてのアイデンティに関して憂慮する声も多く聴かれるが、漢語能力が有利な就職条件として働くという現実があるため、現実的な選

13　教育言語に関しては、自身が児童・生徒であった頃使用した言語である。

択を行っているのが現状である。

1.7.6　小結

　本節では、まず、涼山彝族自治州冕寧県連合郷のナムイ語話者の言語状況および言語生活を報告した。その後、ナムイ語・彝語・漢語の3言語使用を対象として Gibbons（1987）、Pennington 他（1992）および Pannu（1994）の手法の応用を試みた。

　本研究で明らかになった点は、老年層・中年層は共にナムイ語・彝語を流暢に操るが、若年層は彝語こそ家庭で耳にすることが少なくないが、ナムイ語にいたっては日常会話も覚束ないレベルであること、若年層にとって漢語が一番表現が豊かになる言語であり、且つ言語的に価値あるものと認識していること、特に若年層は無意識的にコードミクシングの形式を避ける傾向があり、なるべく純粋型で話そうとすること、等である。

　最後に、言語使用との関連で本研究を通じて感じた、四川省涼山彝族自治州冕寧県連合郷のナムイ＝チベット族の今後の課題と展望を述べておきたい。エスニックマイノリティのリテラシー問題は、特に発展途上国の教育の最重要課題として取り組まれてきたものであるが、四川省においても低所得労働者・移民にカテゴライズされる人々のリテラシーの欠如は大きな問題として捉えられねばならない。現在最もよく用いられるリテラシーの定義は、1978年ユネスコ総会で採択された、「日常生活に関する簡単かつ短い文章を理解しながら読みかつ書くことの両方ができること」という基本義に加え「機能的リテラシー、すなわち自己が属する集団および社会が効果的に機能するため、ならびに自己および自己の属する社会の開発のために読み書きおよび計算をしつづけることができるために読み書き能力が必要とされるすべての活動に従事することができること」までも含めて捉えられるようになってきている。ナムイ＝チベット族が能動的に周辺地域社会ひいては都市部と関わりコミュニケーションしていく能力を身に付けさせるためにも、若年層に対する中

年層の期待は非常に大きい。

　元来懐の深いナムイ＝チベット人が、ナムイ固有の伝統や文化保持及び漢語の価値観の理解との狭間にあって、適切なバランスを求めつつ行動していく姿を筆者は目の当たりにしてきた。今後も涼山彝族自治州冕寧県連合郷をはじめとする四川省周辺地域の言語状況に関しての事例研究を重ねていく次第である。

1.8　本書の構成

　第1章（本章）は、序論として本論文で取り上げるナムイ＝チベット族とそのナムイ＝チベット族の話すナムイ語、ナムイ＝チベット族について概説した後、シナ＝チベット諸語研究史、チベット＝ビルマ諸語研究史、西蕃諸語研究史及びナムイ語に関する先行研究を紹介する。また、本論文で扱う方言について、特に社会言語学的状況について分析を加える。最後に、本論文の構成や方法論などについて述べる[14]。

　第2章は、ナムイ語ゾロ方言の音論をまとめる。頭子音・母音・声調についてそれぞれ例を提示しながら説明した。特に音節頭子音結合、声調に関しては別立てで扱う。

　第3章は、ナムイ語ゾロ方言における語及び名詞形態論について扱う。

　第4章は、ナムイ語ゾロ方言の動詞形態論について論じる。

　第5章は、ナムイ語ゾロ方言における様々な構文について解説する。

　最後に、親族名称、テキスト、語彙一覧を附した。語彙一覧は、本書の参考となるよう、ナムイ語ゾロ方言の分類基礎語彙を示してある。

　各章の初出一覧は以下の通りである。本書に収録するにあたりそれぞ

---

[14] 記述に際しては Dixon（2009）に提示された Basic Linguistic Theory を参考にした。本書の文例、章立て、構成に関しては、孫宏開、George van Driem、David Bradley、千種眞一の各教授からご教示を頂戴した。記して感謝申し上げる次第である。

第1章　序論

れを部分的に書き改めている。

第1章　西田文信. 2004a.「書評：*The Sino-Tibetan Languages*. Edited by Graham Thurgood and Randy J. LaPolla. Routledge Language Family Series, no. 3. London: Routledge, 2003. xxii, 727 pp. $295.00（cloth）'」『麗澤論叢』15：121-132.

　　　西田文信. 2004b.「書評：*Languages of the Himalayas: An Ethnolinguistic Handbook on the Greater Himalayan Region, Containing an Introduction to the Symbolic Theory of Language*.（Handbook of Oriental Studies. Section 2 South Asia, 10）, George van Driem. Leiden, Brill Publishers, 2001, ISBN 90-04-10390-2, vol. 1, xxvi, 462 pp., viii, 916 pp., 2 vols, 193 illus.」『麗澤大学紀要』79：267-276.

　　　Nishida, Fuminobu. 2005c. A Sociolinguistic Study of the Namuyi languagein Sichuan, China. *Reitaku Journal of Interdisciplinary Studies*. 13. 1：13-21.

　　　西田文信. 2006c.「中国四川省涼山彝族自治州における言語生活～ナムイ語話者を例として～」言語政策学会第8回大会発表論文. 早稲田大学. 2006年6月18日.

　　　西田文信. 2013.「ナムイ語の使用状況について―四川省涼山彝族自治州冕寧県連合郷における調査結果から―」太田斎先生・古屋昭弘先生還暦記念中国語学論文集刊行委員会編. 『太田斎先生・古屋昭弘先生還暦記念中国語学論文集』東京：好文出版. pp. 374-382.

第2章　西田文信. 1999.「声調の音声的特徴に関する一考察」『開篇』19：159-173.

　　　Nishida, Fuminobu. 2005d. On pitch accent in the Nàmùyì language. Paper presented at the 11th Himalayan Language Symposium, Chulalongkorn University, Bangkok. 6-9, December, 2005.

西田文信. 2006b.「ナムイ語における漢語からの借用語について」『開篇』25：334-341.
　　　西田文信. 2007.「ナムイ語表記法試案」『中国研究』14：81-91.
　　　Nishida, Fuminobu. 2013. Phonetics and Phonology of Dzolo dialect of Nàmùyì. *Artes liberals*. 92：21-54.

第3章　Nishida, Fuminobu. 2006d. An outline of Nàmùyì grammar（1）. *Reitaku University Journal*. 82：67-91.
　　　Nishida, Fuminobu. 2006e.〈su〉Nominals in Namiyi. Paper presented at the 12th Himalayan Language Symposium, Tribhuvan University, Kathumandu. 27-29 November, 2006.

第4章　西田文信. 2006a.「ナムイ語動詞の他動性について」麗澤大学言語研究センター第22回セミナー．麗澤大学．2006年1月26日．
　　　西田文信. 2010.「ナムイ語の格標識」澤田英夫（編）『チベット＝ビルマ系言語の文法現象　1：格とその周辺』東京外国語大学アジア・アフリカ言語文化研究所．pp. 29-42.
　　　Nishida, Fuminobu. 2015. On Transitivity of Namuyi. Otomo, Nobuya. ed. *Studies on European and American languages and cultures*, 2：135-149.

第5章　Nishida, Fuminobu. 2006d. An outline of Nàmùyì grammar（1）. *Reitaku University Journal*. 82：67-91.

資料　Nishida, Fuminobu. 2005b. A Vocabulary of Nàmùyì. *Reitaku University Journal*. 80：213-223.

第 1 章　序論

【写真1】協力者の李小翠さんと筆者

【写真2】協力者の李小翠さんと筆者

【写真3】協力者の李小翠さんと筆者

【写真4】協力者の李小翠さんと筆者

【写真5】連合郷の景色

【写真6】連合郷の景色

【写真7】ナムイ＝チベット族の家屋

【写真8】ナムイ＝チベット族の家屋

【写真9】ナムイ＝チベット族の食事

【写真10】ナムイ＝チベット族の食事

【写真11】作成中の燻製肉

【写真12】雅砻江

【写真13】 Yamathu 地区

【写真14】 ナムイ＝チベット族の若者

【写真15】 一般的な女性の姿

【写真16】 李さんご一家

【写真17】 調査を見守る馬飼いの少年

【写真18】 連合郷の日常の光景

【写真19】連合郷小学校にて（教師の日に）

【写真20】連合郷小学校の生徒たち

【写真21】連合郷小学校の生徒たち

【写真22】山羊飼いの少年

【写真23】イ文字で書かれた政府公用車

【写真24】連合郷人民政府の看板

第2章 音論

　本章では、ナムイ語の音韻体系について述べる。本章では先ずナムイ語の音声を記述するが、その後は本書を通じて音韻表記で表す。チベット・ビルマ語派という観点からすると、ナムイ語の音韻体系はやや複雑な部類に属すると言い得る。ナムイ語には多数の子音が存在するが、本論文で対象とするゾロ方言には、44の音節頭子音（simple initial consonants）と25の音節頭子音結合（initial consonant clusters）が存在する。ナムイ語にはまた、一連の有声有気音子音が見られる。本章では以下、子音と母音の音素、音節構造、声調についての解説を試みる。母音体系については2.1で、子音体系は2.2、音節構造及び音節規則は2.3、声調とイントネーションのパターンについてはそれぞれ2.4と2.5で論じる。本言語のイントネーションまたはプロソディーについては2.6で触れる。漢語からの借用音韻論については2.7で説明する。

2.1　母音

2.1.1　単純母音

　ナムイ語には10の母音音素があり、[i] は/i/、[e] は/e/、[ɛ] は/ɛ/、[ɿ, ʅ ɯ] は/ɨ/、[y] は/ʉ/、[ə] は/ə/、[a] は/a/、[u] は/u/、[o] は/o/、[ɔ] は/ɔ/と解釈する。音韻的に母音に長短の区別は無いが、第一音節の母音は感情的色彩を付帯させる目的で延ばされることがある。例えば、ᴸatsitsi は「小さい」という意味であるが、ᴸa:tsitsi では「非常に小さい」という意味になる。ᴸa::tsitsi とすれば「非常に非常に小さい」の意を表せる。母音音素を図2.1に示した。音声学的な音価はカギ括弧（[　]）内に示した。

図2.1 ナムイ語の母音音素

音素/i/は非円唇前舌狭母音（an unrounded close front vowel）[i] で、非円唇前舌狭弛緩母音（an unrounded close front lax vowel）[ɪ] までおよぶ領域の異音を持つ。多音節単語の第一音節に置かれた場合、感情表現を表す際はしばしば [iː] で現れることがある。

ᴴchi	[tɕʰi˥]	'3 sg (s/he)'
ᶠikha	[i˥kʰa˩]	'tea'
ᴿbi	[bi˦]	'peach'
ᴸtshi	[tsʰi˩]	'dog'
-di	[di]	'TOP (topic marker)'

音素/e/は非円唇前舌半狭母音（an unrounded half-close front vowel）[e] である。場合によっては、弱く [e̞] と表現されることがある。

ᶠhe	[he˥]	'gold'
ᴿntshe	[ntsʰe˦]	'deer'
ᴸge	[ge˩]	'common yellow cattle'

音素/ɛ/は非円唇前舌半狭母音（an unrounded half-close front vowel）[ɛ] である。これはときおり、慎重な発話では、特に高齢者が話す時に、二重母音 [ai] として表現されることがある。二重母音 [ai] が通時的に [ɛ] へと発達したと筆者は推定するものである。

ᴴsholɛ	[ɕo˧lɛ˥]	'introduce'
ᶠyɛkhukhumu	[jɛ˥khu˦khu˦ mu˨]	'quickly'
ᴿmiqɛ	[mi˩qɛ˥]	'set (of the sun)'
ᴸtsɛ	[tsɛ˨]	'ride'
-lɛ	[lɛ]	'COM (Commitative)'

音素/a/は非円唇前舌広母音〔〔an unrounded open front vowel〕〕[a] で、非円唇後舌母音〔〔an unrounded back vowel〕〕[ɑ] までおよぶ領域の異音をもつ。

ᴴnga	[ŋa˥]	'1 sg'
ᶠradu	[ra˥du˨]	'collar'
ᴿhala	[ha˨la˥]	'cat'
ᴸani	[a˨ni˨]	'all'
ma-	[ma]	'NEG'

音素/ɨ/は非円唇中舌狭母音（a close central unrounded vowel）[ɨ] として表現され、特に歯茎硬口蓋子音の後でこのように実現される。これは歯茎摩擦音と破擦音の後で舌尖前部母音（an apical anterior vowel）[ɿ] として発音され、そり舌音の後で舌尖後部母音（an apical posterior vowel）[ʅ] として、また、両唇音と軟口蓋子音の後で [ɯ] として実現される[1]。母音 [ɿ] と [ʅ] はいずれも舌尖音であり、前者は舌先を歯茎音領域に近づけて、後者は舌先を後部歯茎音領域に近づけて発音する。母音[ʅ]は、舌体、特に後背側の部分が咽頭に向かって後ろに引っ張られるので、咽頭音化している。音素/ɨ/は、軟口蓋子音と両唇語頭子

---

[1] [ɿ] 及び [ʅ] は IPA ではなく、Johan August Lundell により1878年に考案されたスウェーデン語方言字母（Landsmålsalfabetet）であり、Bernhard Karlgren が漢語の舌尖母音を表記するために用いた。この言語の音声実態をもっともよく表すものとして、本書ではこれらの記号を用いる。

音の後では非円唇後舌狭母音（an unrounded close back vowel）[ɯ] として表現される。したがって、以下のようにまとめられる：

/i/ → [ɿ] / [−distributed, +anterior, −high] _____
/i/ → [ʅ] / [+distributed, −anterior, +high] _____
/i/ → [ɯ] / [−coronal] _____

ᴴmudzɨ	[muˡdzɿˡ]	'barley'
ᶠnamuzi	[naˡmu˦zɿ˩]	'Nàmùyì Tibetan'
ᴿzimi	[zɿ˩miˡ]	'female/girl'
ᴸtshɨ	[tshɿ˩]	'wash'
ᴴdutri	[duˡtʂʰʅˡ]	'wing'
ᶠsridri	[ʂʅ˩dzi˩]	'think'
ᶠdiakhɨdri	[diaˡkʰɯ˩]	'far away'
ᴿsɨta	[sɯ˩taˡ]	'discover'

音素/ʉ/は円唇中舌狭母音（a rounded close mid vowel）[ʉ] として表現され、円唇前舌狭母音（an rounded close front vowel）[y] におよぶ領域の異音をもつ。

ᴴʉqa	[yˡqaˡ]	'house'
ᶠʉphio	[yˡpʰioɹ]	'handsome'
ᴿʉχo	[yɹχoˡ]	'others'
ᴸʉ	[yɹ]	'sleep'
-nʉ	[ny]	'PERF（perfect）'

音素/ə/は非円唇中舌中央母音（an unrounded mid central vowel）[ə] である。[＋舌頂音] の語頭子音の後では、非円唇後舌中央狭母音（as unrounded close mid back vowel）[ɤ] として発音される。

ᴿphətsɛ	[phə˩tsɛ˩]	'cut'
ᴸgədzu̠	[gə˩dzu̠˩]	'blue'
ᴸgətsə	[gə˩tsɤ˩]	'respect'

音素/u/は円唇後舌狭母音（round close back vowel）[u]である。非円唇前舌狭母音（an unrounded close front vowel）/i/のように、この母音は通常、閉音節では開音節におけるよりもやや弱いが、その差は大きくはない。

ᴴvu	[vu˩]	'bear'
ᶠfu	[fu˦]	'blow'
ᴿju	[dzu˦˩]	'come'
ᴸtu	[tu˩]	'thousand'

音素/o/は円唇後舌半狭母音（a rounded close-mid back vowel）[o]である。場合によっては、慎重に話す時、特に高齢者が話す時に、二重母音[ŭo]として実現されることがある。

ᴴɕolɛ	[ᴴɕo˩lɛ˩]	'introduce'
ᶠyotshɨ	[jo˩tshɨ˩]	'goat'
ᴿyoqho	[jo˩qʰo˦]	'friend'
ᴸG'o	[ʁo˩]	'needle'

音素/ɔ/は円唇後舌半狭母音（a rounded mid-close back vowel）[ɔ]である。場合によっては、慎重に話すとき、特に高齢者が話すときに、二重母音[aŭ]として表現されることがある。二重母音[aŭ]の原型が通時的に[ɔ]へと発達したと筆者は推定する。より円唇度の高い[ɒ̹]として実現されることもある。

	i	e	ɛ	a	ɨ	ʉ	ə	u	o	ɔ
syllabic	+	+	+	+	+	+	+	+	+	+
closed	+	−	−	−	+	+	−	+	−	−
back	−	−	−	+	−	+	+	+	+	+
open	−	−	−	+	−	−	−	−	−	+
round	−	−	−	−	−	−	−	+	+	+
tense	+	+	−	−	−	−	+	+	−

表2.1 ナムイ語の母音音素の弁別的素性

^Rlɔ   [lɔ˧˩]   'addiction'
^Lχɔ   [χɔ˧]   'ten'

ナムイ語の母音音素の弁別的素性（distinctive features）の一覧は表2.1の如くである：

2.1.2 そり舌母音

ナムイ語には２つのそり舌母音、/ər/ [əʴ] と/ɛr/ [ɛʴ] がある。r音化母音（rotacized vowels）をもつ語彙は、四川省南東部に分布する諸言語の中でもナムイ語に特有のものである。

r音を有する非円唇中央中舌母音（mid central unrounded vowel）の例としては以下のものがある：

^Fvərtshi   [vəʴ˧tsʰɨ˧]   'marry'
^Hkuər   [kuəʴ˧]   'take back'

r音を有する非円唇前舌半広母音（open mid front unrounded vowel）としては以下のものがある：

ᴴhɛr	[hɛ˦]		'buy'
ꜰbɛr	[bɛ˦˨]		'snake'

2.1.3 鼻音化母音

ナムイ語には2つの鼻音化母音、/ĩ/と/ũ/がある。これらの音素は/h/とのみ共起する。/hĩ/のチベット＝ビルマ祖語（Proto-Tibeto-Burman）の*gya-であると推定する。ナムイ語における鼻音化母音/ĩ/は、Matisoff（1975）で提唱した「rhinoglottophilia」という現象によるものであり、h-の後で声門音と鼻音が繋がって発音されることによるものであると筆者は考える。

PTB	ナムイ語		
*gyat	ᴿhĩ [hĩ˧˦]		'eight'
*gya	ᴴhĩ [hĩ˦]		'hundred'

一方、/ũ/はチベット＝ビルマ祖語の接頭辞s-がついているものに見られるようだが、管見の限り以下の1例しか観察されていない。

PTB	ナムイ語		
*s-mul	ᴸhũ [hũ˨]		'fur/body hair'

ここでナムイ語とチベット＝ビルマ祖語との母音対応について少しく触れる。筆者のデータを見る限り、以下のような対応関係が確認された：

PTB	ナムイ語		
*a	＞	i	
*gla	ꜰgi [gi˦˨]		'mother'
*za	ꜰji [zi˦˨]		'son/child'
*wa	ᴸvi [vi˨]		'snow'

*ra	ᴸyi [ji˩]		'rightside'

PTB	ナムイ語		
*ya	>	ə	
*hya	ᶠrə [rəi˧˩]		'field'
*dzya	ᶠndrə [ndə˧˩]		'eat'

PTB	ナムイ語		
*a	>	a²	
*ŋa	ᴴŋa [ŋa˥]		'1 sg'
*ma	ma [ma]		'negative'
*ta	ᴸtha [tʰa˩]		'negative imperative'
*ka	ᶠqha [qʰa˧˩]		'interrogative'

2.1.4 二重母音

二重母音には次の９つがある：/ai、au、ʉo、iu、ie、iɛ、ia、uə、ua/。入り渡りと出渡り両方の二重母音がある。以下にすべての二重母音を示す。

/ai, au, ʉo, iu, ie, iɛ, ia, uə, ua/

2.1.5 三重母音

三重母音は/iau/の１つしかない。標準中国語からの借入語にのみ起きる。

ᴿphiau	[pʰiau˧]	'ticket'	「票＜Ch.」
ᴸpiau	[piau˩]	'tablaux'	「表＜Ch.」

---

2 この例は全て機能語であり、特殊な音変化を経たものであると考える。

2.1.6　閉音節

全ての鼻音語尾は、標準中国語からの借入語においてのみ起きる。

/ŋn、in、yn、uŋ、ən、an、aŋ、ian、uan、uaŋ/

例に関しては、2.6.2にて後述する。

2.2　子音

2.2.1　単純子音

ナムイ語の子音の音声、及び音韻はそれぞれ表1、表2の如くである：
そり舌音の連続があると、歯音と口蓋音の連続が起きる（Matisoff 2003：21）。語頭子音がない場合、たとえば、[a] 〜 [ʔa]（「胸」）のような声門閉鎖音がきわめて頻繁に現れる。しかし、母音性の頭子音と対立をなさないので、これは音素ではない。ここで留意すべきは、すべての子音は、非円唇前舌狭母音（an unrounded close front vowel）/i/が後に続くとき口蓋音化し、また、円唇後舌狭母音（a round close back vowel）/u/が後に続くとき円唇化を伴うということである。

以下、ナムイ語の各異音の音素及びその分布についての音声学的な説明を加える。

音素/p/は無気無声両唇閉鎖音［p］である。

ᶠpu	[pu˥]	'porcupine'
ᴿpami	[paɭmi˩]	'frog'

	labial	dental	retroflex	palatal	velar	uvular	glottal
voiceless stop	p	t			k	q	
voiceless aspirated stop	pʰ	tʰ			kʰ	qʰ	
voiced stop	b	d			g	ɢ	
voiceless affricate		ts	tʂ	tɕ			
voiceless aspirated affricate		tsʰ	tʂʰ	tɕʰ			
voiced affricate		dz	dʐ	dʑ			
voiceless fricative	f	s	ʂ	ɕ	x	χ	h
voiced fricative	v～ʋ	z	ʐ	ʑ	ɣ	ʁ	ɦ
nasal	m	n		ɲ	ŋ		
voiceless approximant			ɹ̥～r̥～ɻ̥				
voiced approximant			ɹ～r～ɻ				
voiced lateral		l					
voiceless lateral		l̥～ɬ					
approximant	(w)			j			

図2.1　ナムイ語子音の音声的実現

	labial	dental	retroflex	palatal	velar	uvular	glottal
voiceless stop	p	t			k	q	
voiceless aspirated stop	ph	th			kh	qh	
voiced stop	b	d			g	G	
voiceless affricate		ts	tr	c			
voiceless aspirated affriicte		tsh	trh	ch			
voiced affricate		dz	dr	dj			
voiceless fricative	f	s	sr	sh	x	X	h
voiced fricative	v	z	zr	j	g'	G'	H
nasal	m	n		ny	ng		
voiceless			r				
voiced			hr				
voiced lateral		l					
voiceless lateral		hl					
approximant	w			y			

図2.2　ナムイ語子音の音素一覧

音素/ph/は有気無声両唇閉鎖音［pʰ］である。

ᴿmopha	［mo˩pʰa˩］	'half'
ᴸphio	［pʰio˩］	'good'

音素/b/は無気有声両唇閉鎖音［b］である。異音は［b］と［β］である。異音［β］は、早口で話すときに、母音間で、または渡り音と母音間で起きる傾向がある。

ᴴbu	［bu˦］	'insect'
ᶠbucər	［bu˦tcə˨˩］	'intestinal worm'
ᴿbojo	［bo˩dzo˦］	'praying mantis'

音素/t/は無気無声舌尖歯閉鎖音［t］である。

ᴸtu	［tu˩］	'thousand'
ᴿtani	［ta˩ni˦］	'today'

音素/th/は有気無声舌尖歯閉鎖音［tʰ］である。

ᴸtha	［tha˩］	'tower'
ᴸthobo	［tʰo˩bo˩］	'pine'
ᴿhatha	［ha˩tʰa˩］	'time'

音素/d/は無気有声舌尖歯閉鎖音［d］である。舌先を歯の裏側に当てて発音する。

ᴴdi	［di˦］	'then'
ᴸdi	［di˩］	'sick'

-dia   [dia]   'DAT, BENE'

音素/d/は無気無声舌背軟口蓋閉鎖音［k］である。

ᴿki   [ki˩˥]   'frost'
ᴿkobo   [ko˩bo˥]   'gate'
ᴿyoko   [jo˩ko˥]   'to go into partnership'

音素/kh/は有気無声舌背軟口蓋閉鎖音［kʰ］である。

ꟳikha   [i˥ kʰa˩]   'tea'
ꟳkhiza   [kʰi˥za˩]   'light'

音素/g/は無気有声舌背軟口蓋閉鎖音［g］である。

ᴸgo   [go˩]   'beat'
ᴿgohlu   [go˥u˥]   'breast'

音素/q/は無気無声口蓋垂閉鎖音［q］である。

ᴿqa   [qa˩˥]   'hork'
ꟳqɛ   [qɛ˥]   '(sun) set'

音素/qh/は有気無声口蓋垂閉鎖音［qʰ］である。

ᴿqhotso   [qʰo˥tso˥]   'mouth'
ᴿyoqho   [jo˩qʰo˥]   'friend'

音素/G/は有声口蓋垂閉鎖音［G］である。

ᴿGɛ	[Gɛ˦]		'dig'
ᴿGo	[Go˩]		'thrust'

音素/ts/は無気無声歯茎破擦音［ts］である。

ᴿtsə	[tsə˦]		'goat'
ᴸtsolɛ	[tso˩lɛ˩]		'introduce'

音素/tsh/は有気無声歯茎破擦音［tsʰ］である。

ᴸtshi	[tshi˩]		'salt'
ᴸtsho	[tsʰo˩]		'man'
ᴸtshɨ	[tshɨ˩]		'wash'

音素/dz/は有気歯茎破擦音［dz］である。

ᴴdzo	[dzo˥]		'exist'
ᴿdza	[dza˦]		'thin'

音素/tr/は無気無声そり舌閉鎖音［tʂ］である。

ᴿtru	[tʂu˦]		'sour'
ᴸtrɨ	[tʂɨ˩]		'star'

音素/trh/は有気無声そり舌閉鎖音［tʂʰ］である。

ꟳtrhɛ	[tʂʰɛ˧˩]		'ghost'
ꟳtrhu	[tʂʰu˧˩]		'smoke

音素/dr/は無気有声そり舌閉鎖音［tʂʰ］である。

| ᴸdru | [dʐu˩] | 'waist' |
| ᴿdru | [dʐu˦] | 'origin' |

音素/c/は無気無声舌端口蓋破擦音［tɕ］である。

| ᶠce | [tɕe˦] | 'ride（a horse）' |
| ᴿce | [tɕe˦] | 'pull' |

音素/ch/は有気無声舌端口蓋破擦音［tɕʰ］である。

| ᶠcha | [tɕʰ a˦] | 'salt' |
| ᶠche | [tɕʰ e˦] | 'lead（metal）' |

音素/j/は無気有声舌端口蓋破擦音［dʑ］である。

| ᶠja | [dʑa˦] | 'correct' |
| ᴸja | [dʑa˩] | 'rice, food' |

音素/f/は無声唇歯摩擦音［f］である。

| ᴴfu | [fu˥] | 'blow' |
| ᴿfu | [fu˦] | 'incubate' |

音素/v/は有声唇歯摩擦音［v］である。これは有声唇歯接近音［ʋ］を伴なって自由に変化して起きる。

| ᴴva | [va˥] | 'to take' |

音素/s/は無声歯茎中線摩擦音［s］である。

ᴴso	［so˥］	'three'
ᴸso	［soꜜ］	'teach, learn'

音素/z/は有声歯中線摩擦音［z］である。

ᴴzɨ	［zɨ˥］	'use'
ᶠzu	［zu˦］	'nice'

音素/sr/は無声そり舌中線摩擦音［ʂ］である。

ᴴsro	［ʂo˥］	'say'
ᶠsru	［ʂu˦］	'iron'

音素/zr/は有声そり舌中線摩擦音［ʐ］である。

ᶠzru	［ʐu˦］	'grass'
ᶠzrɨ	［ʐɨ˦］	'fertiliser'

音素/sh/は無声歯茎口蓋中線舌端摩擦音［ɕ］である。

ᴸshi	［ɕiꜜ］	'tin'
ᴿshiu	［ɕiu˦］	'rust'

音素/x/は無声軟口蓋中線摩擦音［x］である。

ᴿxi	［xi˦］	'lake'

音素/g'/は有声軟口蓋中線摩擦音 [ɣ] である。

ᴸg'a	[ɣa˩]	'crane (animal)'
ᴸg'ər	[ɣər˩]	'crane (animal)'
ᴸg'ə	[ɣə˩]	'clothe. wear'
ᴸg'amu	[ɣa˩mu˩]	'help'

音素/X/は無声口蓋垂中線摩擦音 [χ] である。

| ᴸXoXoXoXom | [χo˩χo˩χo˩χom˩] | 'a douns of noise' |
| Xo | [χo] | 'plural marker' |

音素/G'/は有声口蓋垂摩擦音 [ʁ] である。

| ᶠʁoata | [ʁoa˩ ta˩] | 'in the past' |
| ᴸʁo | [ʁo˩] | 'needle' |

音素/h/は無声声門摩擦音 [h] である。

ᶠhĩ	[hĩ]	'rain'
ᶠhɛ	[hɛɣ]	'gold'
ᴿhala	[ha⁄a˩]	'cat'

音素/H/は有声声門摩擦音 [ɦ] である。この音素は頻繁につぶやき音として表現される。

| ᴿhala | [ɦa⁄a˩] | 'ghost' |

音素/m/は有声両唇鼻音 [m] である。

ᴴmo	[mo˧]	'tomb'
ᴿmo	[mo˩˥]	'horse'
ma-	[ma-]	'NEG'

音素/m/は成節子音となることがある。

| ᶠmna kha | [m̩˩ na˧ kha˩] | 'sky' |

音素/n/は有声舌尖歯鼻音［n］である。

| ᴴna | [na˧] | 'COM' |
| ᴿna | [na˩˥] | 'bean (generic)' |

音素/ny/は有声口蓋鼻音［ɲ］である。有声そり舌鼻音［ɳ］が自由変異伴いとして現れる。

| ᴿnyu | [nyu˧] | 'get (sick)' |
| ᴸnyi | [nyi˩] | 'borrow/lend' |

音素/ng/は有声舌背軟口蓋鼻音［ŋ］である。

| ᴴngu | [ŋu˧] | 'silver' |
| ᴸnga | [ŋa˧] | 'dare' |

音素/r/は有声そり舌弾音［ɽ］である。この音素は有声歯茎接近音［ɹ］として実現されることもあり、特に母音間で、強い摩擦を伴う有声舌尖歯茎震え音［r］として実現される。

| ᶠrapo | [ra˧po˩] | 'cock' |

45

音素/hr/は無声そり舌弾音［ɽ̥］である。無声歯茎接近音［ɹ̥］として実現されることもある。

ᶠahrə	[aˈɽ̥ə˩]	'shaman'
ᴿhreci	[ɽ̥etɕi˩]	'sand'

音素/l/は有声舌端歯茎側面接近音である。

ᶠluzi	[luˈzi˩]	'sand'
ᴿla	[laˈ]	'dust, plant ash'
ᴿlulu	[luˈluˈ]	'bark（dog）'

音素/hl/は無声舌端歯茎側面接近音［l̥］である。

ᴴhla	[l̥a˥]	'god'
ᶠtihla	[tiˈl̥a˩]	'this month'

音素/w/は有声円唇両唇軟口蓋接近音［w］である。

ᴴwa	[wa˥]	'interjection'

音素/y/は有声口蓋中線接近音［j］である。

ᶠyotshi	[joˈtsʰi˩]	'sheep/yak'
ᶠyiki	[jiˈki˩]	'oil'
ᴿyoqho	[joˈqʰo˥]	'friend'
ᴿyoyo	[joˈjo˥]	'self'

各音素の弁別的特徴の一覧は以下の如くである：

第 2 章 音論

	p	ph	b	m	t	th	d	n	ṇ	k	kh	g	ŋ	q	qh	ɢ	ts	tsh	Dz	tṣ	tṣh	dẓ
syllabic	−	−	−	+	−	−	−	−	−	−	−	−	−	−	−	−	−	−	−	−	−	−
consonantal	+	+	+	+	+	+	+	+	+	+	+	+	+	+	+	+	+	+	+	+	+	+
sonorant	−	−	−	+	−	−	−	+	+	−	−	−	+	−	−	−	−	−	−	−	−	−
voiced	−	−	+	+	−	−	+	+	+	−	−	+	+	−	−	+	−	−	+	−	−	+
aspirated	−	+	−	−	−	+	−	−	−	−	+	−	−	−	+	−	−	+	−	−	+	−
continuant	−	−	−	−	−	−	−	−	−	−	−	−	−	−	−	−	−	−	−	−	−	−
nasal	−	−	−	+	−	−	−	+	+	−	−	−	+	−	−	−	−	−	−	−	−	−
strident	−	−	−	−	−	−	−	−	−	−	−	−	−	−	−	−	+	+	+	+	+	+
lateral	−	−	−	−	−	−	−	−	−	−	−	−	−	−	−	−	−	−	−	−	−	−
distributed	−	−	−	−	−	−	−	−	−	−	−	−	−	−	−	−	−	−	−	+	+	+
affricate	−	−	−	−	−	−	−	−	−	−	−	−	−	−	−	−	+	+	+	+	+	+
labial	+	+	+	+	−	−	−	−	−	−	−	−	−	−	−	−	−	−	−	−	−	−
round	−	−	−	−	−	−	−	−	−	−	−	−	−	−	−	−	−	−	−	−	−	−
coronal	−	−	−	−	+	+	+	+	+	−	−	−	−	−	−	−	+	+	+	+	+	+
anterior	+	+	+	+	+	+	+	+	+	−	−	−	−	−	−	−	+	+	+	+	+	+
high	−	−	−	−	−	−	−	−	−	+	+	+	+	+	+	+	+	+	+	−	−	−
back	−	−	−	−	−	−	−	−	−	+	+	+	+	+	+	+	−	−	−	−	−	−
low	−	−	−	−	−	−	−	−	−	−	−	−	−	−	−	−	−	−	−	−	−	−

	f	v	s	z	ṣ	ẓ	ɕ	x	ɣ	χ	ʁ	h	ɦ	r	hr	l	hl	w	j
syllabic	−	−	−	−	−	−	−	−	−	−	−	−	−	−	−	−	−	−	−
consonantal	+	+	+	+	+	+	+	+	+	+	+	−	−	−	+	+	−	−	−
sonorant	−	−	−	−	−	−	−	−	−	−	−	+	+	+	+	+	+	+	+
voiced	−	+	−	+	−	+	−	−	+	−	+	−	+	−	+	−	+	+	+
aspirated	−	−	−	−	−	−	−	−	−	−	−	−	−	−	−	−	−	−	−
continuant	+	+	+	+	+	+	+	+	+	+	+	+	+	+	+	+	+	+	+
nasal	−	−	−	−	−	−	−	−	−	−	−	−	−	−	−	−	−	−	−
strident	+	+	+	+	+	+	+	+	−	−	−	−	−	−	−	−	−	−	−
lateral	−	−	−	−	−	−	−	−	−	−	−	−	−	−	−	+	+	−	−

distributed	−	−	−	−	+	+	+	−	−	−	−	−	−	−	−
affricate	−	−	−	−	−	−	−	−	−	−	−	−	−	−	−
labial	+	+	−	−	−	−	−	−	−	−	−	−	−	+	−
round	−	−	−	−	−	−	−	−	−	+	+	−	−	+	−
coronal	−	−	+	+	+	+	+	−	−	+	+	+	−	−	−
anterior	+	+	+	+	−	−	−	−	−	+	+	+	−	−	−
high	−	−	−	+	+	+	+	+	+	−	−	−	−	+	+
back	−	−	−	−	−	+	+	+	−	−	−	−	−	+	−
low	−	−	−	−	−	−	−	−	+	+	+	+	−	−	−

図2.3　各音素の弁別的特徴

2.2.2　音節頭子音結合

　音節頭子音結合は25組あり、調音部位を同じくする鼻音が先行するタイプ（homorganic nasal preinitial）は、有声・無声両方の有気閉鎖音と有気破擦音に先行しうる。有声または無声の有気両唇閉鎖音は、歯摩擦またはそり舌摩擦の後続子音（spirant postinitial）とともに起こりうる。三子音の連結もいくつか起きる。ナムイ語ゾロ方言には以下の3種類の子音連結が存在する：

タイプⅠ：/mph, mb, ntsh, ndz, nth, nd, ntsh, ndz, ntɕ, ntɕh, ŋkh, ŋg, ŋqh, ŋɢ/

タイプⅡ：/ptɕh, phs, phʂ, bz, bẓ, mẓ/

タイプⅢ：/mphs, mphʂ, mbz, mbẓ/

　本言語では、頭位連結子音において有声唇震え音［B］を伴う歯音の同時調音が観察されることを指摘しておきたい。

| ᴿmbɛ | [mbɛʌ] | 'boil (n.), pus' |
| ᴿmbuli | [mbuliʌ] | 'search for' |

	ph	b	th	d	kh	g	qh	G	tsh	dz	tṣh	dẓ	tɕ	tɕh	dʑ	s	z	ʂ	ʐ
m	+	+	−	−	−	−	−	−	−	−	−	−	−	−	−	−	−	−	+
n	−	−	+	+	−	−	−	−	+	+	+	+	+	+	+	−	−	−	−
ŋ	−	−	−	−	+	+	+	+	−	−	−	−	−	−	−	−	−	−	−
p	−	−	−	−	−	−	−	−	−	−	−	−	+	−	−	−	−	−	−
ph	−	−	−	−	−	−	−	−	−	−	−	−	−	−	−	+	−	+	−
b	−	−	−	−	−	−	−	−	−	−	−	−	−	−	−	−	+	−	+

子音結合表

^{H}ndzu　　　　　[udzu˥]　　　　　　　'sit'
^{R}ntshɛ　　　　　[nts^{h}ɛ]　　　　　　'deer'
^{R}ntshu phu 'lungs'

2.3　音節構造

音節構造を以下に示す。

　　　　　　　　（Ci）（Cj）（V）V（V）（Cf）
　　　　　　　　　　　［glide］［glide］
　　　　　　　　6．ナムイ語の音節構造

　最小の音節の種類は、/a/（「間投詞」）を表す単語の一形態のような単一母音である。声門閉鎖音は子音なしで始まる音節のはじめに頻繁に現れるが、母音的頭子音と声門頭子音の間に音素的対立はない。

　ナムイ語の音節は以下の9種類である（F：下降調、R：上昇調、L：低調）。

　　　V　　　　　　^{F}a　　　　　　　　'already'

VC	ᶠan	'duck'
VV	ᴿai	'sentence particle'
C	ᴸm̩dzi̩	'barley'
CV	ᶠmo	'horse'
CVV	ᶠdia	'upward'
CCV	ᶠphs̩	'leaf'
CCCV	ᴸmbz̩	'cloth'
CVVV	ᶠdiau	'arise'

2.4 声調性

　ナムイ語は、意味を伝えるために、音節または音韻語に異なるピッチのバリエーションを有する声調言語である。表面声調対照が示される主要な特徴として機能する、ピッチの基本的な音響関連量はＦ０（基本周波数）である。ナムイ語の話者は、声のピッチ（総体的な高さ、または低さ）をコントロールしてＦ０にバリエーションをもたらし、語彙的に対立したな声調を生みだす。

2.4.1　ナムイ語の声調に関する先行研究

　これまでに、ナムイ語の声調に関する次の３つの研究が公表されており、いくつかの方言における音韻体系について初めて解説されている。それらは、孫宏開による木里（Muli）方言の解説、黄布凡、仁増旺姆による同方言の研究、および刘辉强による冕宁（Mianning）方言の紹介である。

2.4.1.1　孫宏開による研究（木里方言）（孫 1983：183）

　ナムイ語の声調の分析は孫教授が初めて行ったものである。同論文では、木里方言の声調に関して、ナムイ語には４声調体系があるという結論に達した。

第2章 音論

1. [55] high level   vu^{55} 'bear'   sɿ^{55} 'matter'   ni^{55} mi^{55} 'sun'
2. [53] high falling vu^{53} 'liquor'   sɿ^{53} 'pea'   ni^{53} 'two'
3. [33] mid level   vu^{33} 'intestine' sɿ^{33} 'amend'   ni^{33} 'to borrow'
4. [35] high rising   vu^{35} 'to burn'   sɿ^{35} 'firewood' ni^{35} 'to steam'

ここで、ある環境では、音調素[35]は[24]へと変化し、音調素[33]は低下降調の[31]へと変化ことがあることに留意されたい。音韻的条件については触れられていない。

2.4.1.2 黄布凡、仁増旺姆による研究（木里方言）（戴慶厦等1991：158）

黄布凡及び仁増旺姆の分析は孫のそれとは異なるが、両者とも同じ方言を扱っている。

1. [55] high level   qa^{55} qa^{55} 'to mount'   ʂu^{55} 'lice'
2. [53] high falling qa^{53} 'to peel'   ʂu^{53} 'steal'
3. [35] mid rising   qa^{35} 'a container' ʂu^{35} 'to feel depressed'
4. [31] mid falling   qa^{31} 'stove'   ʂu^{31} 'wheat'

声調素[55]と[53]は置き換え可能であり、声調素[35]と[31]は、音節の最後尾で[33]に変化する可能性がある、としている。

2.4.1.3 劉による研究（冕宁方言）（劉 1996：186）

最初にナムイ語の冕宁方言を調査したのは劉である。

1. [55] high level   mi^{55} 'female' bzu^{55} 'honey bee'   va^{55} 'to take'
2. [53] low falling   mi^{53} 'fire'   bzu^{53} 'sweet'   va^{53} 'Han Chinese'
3. [13] high falling mi^{13} 'ripen'   bzu^{13} 'to suspend'   va^{13} 'to crawl'
4. [31] low rising   mi^{31} 'monkey' bzu^{31} 'to overflow' va^{31} 'pig'

刘は、声調素［13］はすべての声調素のなかで最も低い周波数を示していると主張している。

2.4.1.4 筆者による解説（冕宁＝ゾロ方言）

1．high level mi^{55} 'female,
2．high falling mi^{53} 'fire'
3．low rising mi^{13} 'ripen'
4．low level mi^{11} 'monkey'

刘の分析にもとづけば、ナムイ語冕宁方言には高調（声調１）と高下降調（声調２）、低上昇調（声調３）、低調（声調４）という４つの対立的な音調素があるということだが、筆者が収集したゾロ方言の一次資料では、特に若年層の発話において声調素１および２は声調素２に融合し、その結果、三声調体系となっている者も存在していることを指摘しておきたい。

ナムイ語ゾロ方言の基礎語彙はほとんどすべて多音節であるため、単音節語を見つけるのはやや難しい。現在、筆者自身が収集している一次資料は、ナムイ語ゾロ方言の声調体系は木里方言のものとは基本的に異なるが、タマン語やグルン語のような、ネパールのチベット＝ビルマ語のそれには比較的近いことを示している。

尹（2016：8-9）は声調に関して黄（1992）と同様の解釈をしている。また、黄（2003：189）は孫（1991）の解釈となっている。

次節では、筆者がコンピュータソフトウェアベースの音響分析により行った、ナムイ語の声調体系に関する調査の手順と結果について発表する。

2.4.2 音響分析の手順

2.4.2.1 被験者

25歳から59歳の男性２名、女性２名により、本研究のための発話デー

タが生産された。被験者はすべて冕宁村で生まれ育ったネイティブスピーカーである。彼らは全員、録音時に通常の明瞭な発音と流暢さ、声、共鳴音を提示していると非公式に判断された。発話障害や聴覚障害を報告した者はいなかった。

2.4.2.2 発話材料と録音手順

録音は、被験者が音節とその個々に関連するナムイ語の単語の2セットを含む単語リストを読み上げて行われた。

録音は冕宁村連合郷政府で、AKG C451E マイクとパナソニックの SV 3700 DAT レコーダを44.1kHz samples/sec で用いて行われた。分析には Praat を用いた。

すべての被験者の音声は個別に録音された。彼らは通常の発話速度でテスト単語を読み上げるよう指示された。単語が適切なポジションで発音されるように、発話項目間で少なくとも3秒間の休止がとられ、これにより、リスト読み上げの影響を避けた。各被験者は、発話材料になじみ、適切な録音レベルが達成できるよう、十分な練習時間を与えられた。すべての録音において、マイクと話し手の口との距離は約30cmであった。これは録音中、信頼性のある強い発話信号入力ができるようにするためである。単語リストの読み上げが3回録音された。録音中、被験者は調査者によってモニターされた。筆者は正確な発音ができているか、話しぶりを判定し、満足できないときには繰り返しを求めた。被験者には通常の発話速度でテスト単語を読み上げるよう頼んだ。すべてのテスト音節が10回繰り返された。合計280個のトークンが選出されてピッチが追跡され、各トークンの基本的な周波数の輪郭が得られた。

2.4.2.3 分析

音響分析は KAY CSL 4300B (CSL：Computerised Speech Lab) を用いて行われた。CSL は16ビット入力のアナログ—デジタル・コンバータを提供し、録音物は10kHzの標本抽出率でデジタル化された。各トー

クンについて、持続時間と基本周波数が計測された。声調の持続時間の計測は音声波形によって行われた。これは慶應義塾大学大学文学部心理学専攻動物実験室で行われた。

　各テストトークンについて、基本周波数と持続時間が計測された。75ポイント広帯域フレームを用いて母音からＦ０値が取られ、フレームの長さは特定の話し手のＦ０幅により決定された。典型的なフレームの長さは25〜30msであった。ナムイ語の声調と相関して持続時間に差異があるため、４つのＦ０値を固定したパーセンテージ、すなわち０％、20％、40％、60％、80％、100％の地点で抽出することにより、Ｆ０輪郭が正規化された。これは、さまざまなＦ０輪郭間で直接比較ができるようにするためである。各テストトークンの持続時間が、圧縮された波形とフォルマント軌跡、そしてそれに対応する広域スペクトラムを同時に観察することで測定された。

2.4.2.4　正規化

　同じ言語形式であると知覚されるものについて、異なる話し手は異なる音響出力をする。話し手内または話し手間の差異を解決し、言語の不変の特徴を特定するために、音響学的研究では通常Ｆ０値を正規化する。個々の話し手のアウトプットを発音表記に変換するために、本研究ではz値の正規化が用いられた。

　z値の正規化手順はＦ０nom＝（Ｆ０i-x）/SDである。この公式において、Ｆ０がサンプリングポイント（周波数）で、xは全サンプリングポイントからの平均Ｆ０、そしてSDはこれらのポイントの平均値周辺の標準偏差である[3]。

2.4.2.5　テスト単語

　ここで用いたテスト単語は、次の４つのセットからなっている：単音

3　Rose（1996）を参照のこと。

節語、2音節語、3音節語、4音節語。本テストのために選ばれたこれらの語彙は、ナムイ語に実在する音節で、以下の如くである：

	単音節語	二音節語	三音節語	四音節語
T 1	mi	su-gu	ha-ta-ta	su-gu-su-gu
	'female'	'tomorrow'	'how'	'tomorrow（emphasis）'
T 2	mi	õ-dzo	na-mu-zɿ	na-mu-zɿ-χo
	'fire'	'Xichang（place）'	'Tibetan'	'Tibetans'
T 3	mi	buu-tsu	kʰa-bo-kʰa	kʰa-bo-kʰa-χo
	'ripen'	'cloth'	'border'	'borders'
T 4	mi	kʰo-bo	zu-bu-mi	zu-Bu-mi-χo
	'monkey'	'door'	'granddaughter'	'granddaughters'
				（χo：pl.）

表2.1　テスト語彙（名詞）

これらの語彙は自由形態素（たとえば、名詞、または指示詞と名詞の組み合わせ）であるので、筆者は2音節語と3音節語、4音節語のために、動詞または動詞的要素一式をもう一つ作成した。各セットは動詞＋完了形標識、および形容詞＋副詞化接辞（adverbialiser）で構成されている。

	二音節語	三音節語	四音節語
T 1	to-to	to-to-ny	zi-ga-ga-mu
	'to reach'	'reached'	'well'
T 2	tʰo-ko	tsʰo-ko-ny	a-za-za-mu
	'to cheat'	'cheated'	'slowly'
T 3	sɿ-ta	sɿ-ta-ny	qe-lele-mu
	'finish'	'finished'	'quietly'
T 4	ʂo-qo	ʂo-qo-ny	χo-χo-χo-mu
	'die'	'died'	'noisily'
			（also χo-χo-χo-m）

表2.2　テスト語彙（動詞）

2.4.3　結果

2.4.3.1　持続時間

以下のFigure 1では、ナムイ語ゾロ方言における語声調の平均持続

時間を示している。筆者は母音固有の持続時間も測定した。高母音と低母音の両方がＴ２をもつとき、高母音は低母音よりもCVからなる音節において持続時間が長いことがわかった。高母音と低母音はＴ３とＴ４をもつとき、CVからなる音節において持続時間が同じだった。

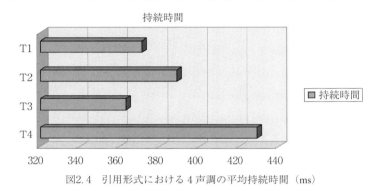

図2.4　引用形式における4声調の平均持続時間（ms）

2.4.3.2　オンセットとピーク

グルン声調のオンセットとピークを以下に示す。

	声調1		声調2		声調3		7. 声調4	
	O	P	O	P	O	P	O	P
	197.7	167.3	189.2	151.9	121.5	151.7	98.4	126.3

表2.3　ナムイ語ゾロ方言のOnsetとPeak（kHZ）

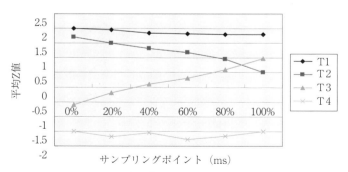

図2.5　平均Ｚ値で正規化されたＦ０軌跡

T1：F0軌跡は非常に安定した形を示している。下向き傾向の影響で、終点ではやや低めのF0値を示している。

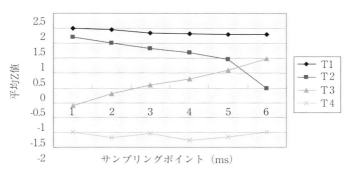

図2.6　平均Z値で正規化されたF0軌跡（2音節語）

T2：F0軌跡は母音ごとに異なっている。/a/の軌跡が直線的であるのに対し、/u/の軌跡は最も丸みがある。IF0（母音固有の基本周波数：intrinsic vowel fundamental frequency）は、この声調の経時的変化により、若年層よりも高齢者層において際立っている。しかし、話し手によるバリエーションも発見された。

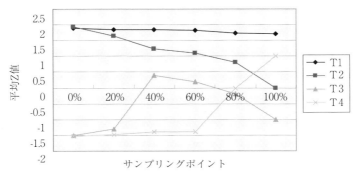

図2.7　平均Z値で正規化されたF0軌跡（3音節語）

T3：オンセットで、若年の話し手に高齢の話し手より広いF0幅とそれに伴うより広いF0分布が見られたが、これは読み方の違いを反映

していると想定される。

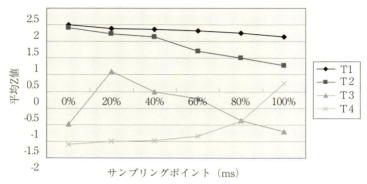

図2.8 平均Z値で正規化されたFO軌跡（4音節語）

T4：若年の話し手の（FO）幅は高齢の話し手のそれよりも広かった。オンセットと抑揚、ピークにおける話し手の測定値は非常に高い関連性があったが、ピーク（の測定値）だけが（FO）幅と有意に関連していた。オンセットと抑揚、ピークにおける話し手のFO値は互いに高い関連性があった。ここでも、ピークだけが（FO）幅と有意に関連していた。

2.4.3.3 声調値

本研究でのナムイ語ゾロ方言の各声調の声調値を特定する音響実験の結果は、以下のように要約できる：

10. 単音節語	多音節語の声調値		
声調値	語頭音節	語中音節	語末音節
55	55	55	55
54	55	33	22
24	11	55	22
11	11	11	33

表2.4 ナムイ語ゾロ方言の多音節語のピッチパターン

第 2 章 音論

　上に与えられた音韻データをもとに、ナムイ語の 4 声調の F0 軌跡について以下のように音韻的にまとめることができる。

	単音節語	二音節語	三音節語	四音節語
1.	HH	HH	HHH	HHHH
2.	HM	HM	HML	HMML
3.	LH	LH	MHL	MHLL
4.	LL	LM	LLM	LLLM

　上記のデータからわかるように、本言語のデフォルト声調は L である。ナムイ語では、複合において、複合語の 2 番目の構成要素は元の声調の特性を失う。つまり、ピッチのプロファイルは最初の構成要素の軌跡の特性によって決定されるか、または、ある一様な声調になる。接尾語による単語構成の領域において、接尾語は特有の声調素性をもつことができない。すなわち、そのピッチプロファイルはそれに先行する語幹のピッチ軌跡によって完全に決定されるか、または、すべての接尾語がある中立的で一様なピッチ軌跡をもつ。この意味において、ナムイ語ゾロ方言を語声調言語（word tone language）と呼ぶことができる。

　自律分節音韻論の枠組み内で声調を分析した結果として、以下の声調規則一式を提示したい。

a．デフォルト声調は L である
b．声調の消去・中立化
　　非語頭音韻から声調を消去する。
c．声調の関連づけ
　　声調を音節に 1 対 1 で、左から右に関連づける
d．声調の任意的な関連づけ
　　音節が声調の数より多い場合は、最後の声調を余分な音節に拡張する。

e．任意的な声調の関連づけ
　　声調が音節の数より多い場合は、余分な声調を最後の音節に関連づける。

2.4.3.4　声調の分布
　声調の分布は以下のとおりである。

声調1　　105シーケンス　　（4.0%）
声調2　　768シーケンス　　（26.6%）
声調3　　1507シーケンス　（52.8%）
声調4　　473シーケンス　　（16.6%）

　声調3は、この言語における習慣声調またはデフォルト声調というべきである[4]。

　また、アクセント論の観点から以下のように分析することも可能である：

　　　単音節語　二音節語　三音節語　四音節語　　声調

4　チベット＝ビルマ語の超分節現象の中でも最も良く知られているものの一つに、チベット語ラサ方言の複合語形成がある。チベット語ラサ方言には、ピッチについて以下の複合規則があるが、これはナムイ語ゾロのそれに類似したものである。チベット語ラサ方言の第2音節はつねに高いことは歴史言語学的観点からすると示唆的である。
　（1）高または高中＋高または低中−＞高高、（2）高または高中＋高中または低中低−＞高中、（3）低または低中低＋高または低中−＞低高、（4）低または低＋高中または低中低−＞低高中。換言すれば、チベット語ラサ方言における複合語のピッチパターンは、ピッチの最初の音節における最初の要素（高または低）と2番目の音節におけるピッチの最後の要素（下降する、または下降しない）により決定される。チベット語ラサ方言の複合語における声調特徴と声調特性は次のように要約できる：声調1［＋高］［−下降］、声調2［＋高］［＋下降］、声調3［−高］［＋下降］、声調4［−高］［−下降］。

1. /[○/   /[○○/   /[○○○/   /[○○○○/   High（H）
2. /○]/   /○]○/   /○]○○/   /○]○○○/   Falling（F）
3. /○/   /○○]/   /○○]○/   /○○]○○/   Rising（R）
4. /○/   /○○/   /○○○/   /○○○○/   Low（L）

2.5　ゾロ方言の強勢

　ナムイ語の多音節語において、音韻語の全般的な音素配列構造にかかわらず、わずかに強めの強勢はもっとも頻繁に語根の音節頭位に置かれる。したがって、たとえば、語根が単音節である二形態素の語においては、主な強勢は語根に置かれる。
　知覚的な話をすれば、ナムイ語のネイティブスピーカーは一番強い強勢のある音節の大半は概して最初の音節であることに同意する。筆者の音韻分析はこれを裏づけているが、さまざまな音節の強勢パターンには、全般的にきわめて顕著な差異はない。音節頭位は概してやや長めの母音持続時間を示し、最後から２番目や一番最後の音節よりも、母音が約３デシベルほど、ごくわずかに大きめの振幅を示す。
　筆者は、母音の持続時間と振幅の差異により、語尾強勢の音韻的証拠をもつ一定数の単語に気付いた。これらの単語は２番目の音節にある母音の継続時間が比較的長く、２番目の音節にある母音は、音節頭位の母音（語頭母音）よりも５から７デシベル大きい振幅を示す。これらの単語における語尾強勢パターンは、単独で発音される際と及び発話中の両方のコンテクスト、および同じ単語のさまざまな繰り返しにおいて起きる。ここでは、強勢のトピックについてはこれらの観察に留めておく。

2.5.1　イントネーションのパターン

　イントネーションはナムイ語の音韻学の重要な部分ではない。ナムイ語は声調言語であるため、興奮して話すときでも、ピッチには非常にわずかのバリエーションしかない。ときどき、非常に高い下降ピッチが強

調するのに用いられる。しかし、これは高い声調の単語にのみあてはまる。イントネーションが単語に影響を及ぼす方法は、それが主要な単語クラスのものであるかどうかによる。グルン方言の音韻学におけるもっとも大きな変化は、テンポの変化に訪れた。ゆっくりとした慎重なペースが、かつては規範であった。

2.5.2 叙述文

ナムイ語には叙述文と同時に、明白な動詞をもたない同等のパターンがある。筆者の観察によれば、叙述文にはSOV語順と同様、OVSパターンも見られる。しかし、SOVパターンでは、OVSパターンよりも動詞がより基本的なものに見える。これらの叙述文タイプにおける通常のピッチメロディーは、低音または中音で始まり、まんなかで上昇し、最後に低音へ下降する。強勢はまず、比較的高いピッチで、次に音量の増加により、表現される。

2.5.3 疑問文

極性疑問文と情報疑問文の両方における普通の強勢パターンは、中音または低音で始まり、高音で終わる。「はい」か「いいえ」で答える質問を作るために、疑問標識/-a/がときどき文末の単語に付けられる。それはつねにイントネーションが高く、そのことは通常、単語全体に影響を及ぼす。この文は最後で（音程が）下降せず、通常のパターンを壊している。低音で始まり、中音で終わる。最後の単語が2つの音節を持っている場合、通常は再度下降するが、音節が1つしかない場合は、音節あたり1つのピッチレベルしかありえないので、中音にとどまるしかない。

疑問視疑問文は、もしその文が叙述文であったら、求められた情報が入るだろうところに疑問詞を当てはめて形成される。それは、ときどきは文の最後だが、多くの場合そうではない。疑問詞はそれが置かれている文のパートにふさわしいイントネーションがつく。それにはイント

第 2 章 音論

ネーション一式はない。むしろ、イントネーションパターンは文レベルの現象である。

2.6 借用語音韻論

本章の最後で、漢語からの借入語の音韻論について少々触れておく。ここに挙げるのは漢語からの借用語にのみ見られる音形である。

2.6.1 語頭子音

漢語四川方言と、ナムイ語における漢語からの借入語とのあいだにみられる語頭子音の対応については以下のようにまとめられる：

語頭子音		例	
漢語四川方言	ナムイ語	漢語四川方言	ナムイ語
p	p	巴 pa 1	pa55
ph	ph	怕 pha 4	pha13
m	m	马 ma 3	ma53
f	f	烦 fan 2	fan31
t	t	但 tan 4	tan13
th	th	头 thəu 2	thəu31
ts	ts	再 tsai 4	tsai13
tsh	tsh	床 tshua 2	tshuaŋ31
s	s	术 su 4	su13
z	z	日 zɿ 2	zu31
tɕ	tɕ	脚 tɕyo 2	tɕyõ31
tɕh	tɕh	气 tɕhi 4	tɕhi13
n	n	路 nu 4	nu13
ɕ	ɕ	心 ɕin 1	ɕin55
k	k	国 kue 2	kuə31

63

kh	kh	开 khai 1	khai55
ŋ	ŋ	安 ŋan 1	ŋan55
x	h	花 xua 1	hua55
ɕ (i)	j	义 i 4	ji13
ɕ (y)	y	雨 y 3	y53
ɕ (w)	w	晚 uan 3	uan53

2.6.2 韻尾

漢語四川方言と、ナムイ語における漢語からの借入語とのあいだにみられる韻尾の対応については以下のようにまとめられる：

韻尾		例	
漢語四川方言	ナムイ語	漢語四川方言	ナムイ語
ɿ	ɯ	资 tsɿ 1	tsɯ55
i	i	比 pi 3	pi53
u	u	佛 fu 2（〜教）	fu31
y	y	鼠 ɕy 3	ɕy53
ɚ	ɚ	儿 ɚ 2	ɚ31
a	a	巴 pa 1（pha 2 俗）	pa55
ia	ia	加 tɕia 1	tɕia55
ua	ua	耍 sua 2	sua31
e	e	得 te 2	te31
ie	ie	灭 mie 2	mie31
ue	uə	国 kue 2	kue31
ye	ye〜ie	月 ye 2	ye31
o	o	乐 no 2（快〜）	no31
yo	ỹõ	略 nyo 2	nỹõ31
ai	ai	街 kai 1	kai55

iɛi	jai	孩 ɕiɛi 2	ɕjai31
uai	wai	坏 xuai 4	xwai13
ei	ai	贝 pei 4	pai13
uei	wai	屡 nuei 3	nwai53
au	au	包 pau 1	pau55
iau	iau	刁 tiau 1	tiau55
əu	au	头 thəu 2	thau31
iəu	iu	丢 tiəu 1	tiu55
an	an	班 pan 1	pan55
iɛn	iæn	边 piɛn 1	piæn55
Uan	uan	决 tuan 4 (决〜)	tuan13
yɛn	y̆õn	员 yɛn 1	y̆õn55
ən	ən	门 mən 2	mən31
In	in	林 nin 2	nin31
uən	uən	纯 suən 2	suən31
yn	yn	运 yn 4	yn13
aŋ	aŋ	党 taŋ	taŋ
iaŋ	iaŋ	阳 iaŋ	iaŋ
uaŋ	uaŋ	床 tshuaŋ	tshuaŋ
oŋ	oŋ	贸 moŋ	moŋ
yoŋ	yoŋ	容 yoŋ	yoŋ

2.6.3 声調

漢語四川方言と、ナムイ語における漢語からの借入語とのあいだにみられる声調の対応については以下のようにまとめられる：

声調		例	
漢語四川方言	ナムイ語	漢語四川方言	ナムイ語
阴平 35	第一調 55	西（〜方）	ɕi55
阳平 33	第四調 31	文（〜章）	wən31
上声 53	第二調 53	勇（〜敢）	joŋ53
去声 213	第三調 13	信（〜用）	ɕin13

第3章　語及び名詞形態論

本章ではナムイ語ゾロ方言における語及び名詞形態論について扱う。

ナムイ語ゾロ方言で「語」に相当する形態素は 'ᴴsa'' であるが、この形式は「発話におけるひとつのかたまり」を意味し、一語であったり、いくつかの要素で構成されていたり、あるいは完全な句乃至は節であったりする場合もある。しかしながら、音韻と形態、意味特性、統語機能の観点から、節と語を区別できるものと考える。

ここでは、語は母語話者の認識する意味上のかたまりによる分節によって認定されるものとし、音声面のみで区切ることのできないものとして扱う。

3.1　ナムイ語における「語」

ナムイ語のゾロ方言の語は、「通常の発話ではあいだに休止符を含む新しい要素を挿入することができない最小の自由形態素」と定義し得る。語は少なくとも1つ（またはそれ以上）の音節で構成される。たとえば、'ᴸchi'（「1」）や 'ᶠvu'（「酒」）、'ᴸg'ə'（「雌牛」）は、それぞれ一音節に対応する1語である。また、1つ以上の音節に対応する語も、'ᴿhimi'（「太陽」）、'ᴿqhadri'（「椀」）、'ᴴshugu'（「明日」）、などがあるが、これらは二音節で構成されている。二音節の語では、最初の音節は通常、2番目の音節よりも弱めに強勢をつける。三音節の語では、最初の音節は通常、2番目の音節よりも弱めに強勢をつけ、2番目の音節は通常、3番目の音節よりも弱めに強勢をつける。多音節語の最後の音節の強勢が失われると、その強勢は最初の音節に移るため、多音節語においては、

1　羌語の 'sa' と同源形式であると考えられる。

強勢は最後の音節または最初の音節に置かれる。しかしながら、これらのストレスは言わば慣習的なものであり本方言では強勢は弁別的ではない。

語とは別に、ナムイ語ゾロ方言には接頭辞があり、これは後続する形態素と共に現れる。接頭辞には方向接頭辞、否定接頭辞がある。

語は意味的、形態統語的な性質にもとづいて分類可能である。名詞、動詞、形容動詞（状態動詞の一部と見做す）は開いた類（open class）である。その他の、副詞、代名詞、数詞、数量詞、類別詞、間投詞、語尾不変化詞などは閉じた類（closed class）である。本章では、各語類の形式と統語的役割について論じる。

3.2 名詞

ナムイ語のゾロ方言の名詞は、数標識や定／不定標識、助数詞句が後続しうる自由形態素と定義することができる。名詞は繋辞（繋辞（コピュラ））を使用しなくては述語にはなれない。また、名詞のなかには性標識や指小辞標識がつくものがある。名詞は、意味的・統語的な特性の観点から、さらに細かく、普通名詞、固有名詞、人名詞、場所名詞、時間名詞に区分することができる。派生名詞には4種類ある。次節では、その形態と機能について論じる。

3.2.1 普通名詞

一般的な概念を表す普通名詞には、性標識、数標識、指小辞標識、定／不定標識、格標識、比較標識、話題標識が付きうる。意味論的には、これらの名詞は中核項や斜格項として使われる。統語的には、名詞句の主部として生起したり、修飾語として使用されたりする。

3.2.2 固有名詞

固有名詞は2つの下位分類、すなわち、地名を表す名詞と人名を表す

第3章 語及び名詞形態論

名詞に分類される。地名を表す名詞は単独でも用いられるが、処格標識、奪格標識、比較標識、話題標識が付けられ、通常、斜格項として使用される。固有名詞は (3.1) と (3.2) にあるように、名詞を直接修飾できる。

(3.1)　ᶠno　　　　　ᶠnamuzi　　　　-a
　　　 2 sg　　　　 Tibetan　　　　 Q
　　　'Are you Tibetan?'

(3.2)　ᴴnga　　　　ᴴondzo-mu　　　ᴿdzu
　　　 1 sg　　　　 Xichang-ABL　　come
　　　'I am from Xíchāng.'

人名は全ての種類の格標識や話題標識、比較標識にも付けられるが、他の標識は付けられない。意味論的かつ／または統語的に、人名は普通名詞のように、中核項または斜格項や、名詞句の主部として用いられたり、名詞の修飾語になったりできる。

(3.3)、(3.4) に挙げるのは、ナムイ＝チベット族の主要な姓及び名である。以下は、例えばナムイ語で「ᶠag'u」姓であった者は漢語では一律「韓」姓を名乗っている事を意味する。

(3.3)　漢語姓　　ナムイ語姓
　　　 李　　　　ᴿlontʙu, ᴸnjaka, ᴿnjaku, ᴿagu, ᴸhapa, ᴸnja la, ᴸmərli[2]
　　　 張　　　　ᴿzridja, ᴸg'adzɨ
　　　 蘭　　　　ᴿlakhʉ, ᴸjapa, ᶠshu nga

2　ᴿlontʙu, ᴸnjaka, ᴿnjaku, ᴿagu, ᴸhapa, ᴸnja la の間での通婚は可能である。また、ᴸnjaka, ᴿnjaku, ᴸmərli 間の通婚は可能である。

楊	ᴸyadzɨ, ᴸpami
韓	ᶠag'u
伍	ᴿjɛ ntʙʉ
趙	ᴸmbər ngngər
吉	ᶠpaci
冉	ᴿzrar ngər
饒	ᴸdrophi
高	ᴸkoliga
甘	ᴿchato
書	ᶠkushu
唐	ᴴha mbʉ
穆	ᴸtakɛr
布	ᴸaphʉ, ᴸmuji
単	ᴸsha ntʙʉ

(3.4) ナムイ語の名（頻度順）

ᴿshatimi　女性

ᴸvatshʉmi　女性

ᴸshongoji　男性

ᴿjothimi　女性

ᴸnandrɨmi　女性

ᴿandomi　女性

ᴸuchimi　女性

ᴸXodjuphi　男性

ᴸnodraji　男性

ᴿphotshoji　男性

ᶠdradraji　男性

ᶠjoshiji　男性

ᴸshiapjiji　男性

第 3 章　語及び名詞形態論

ᶠshazraji　男性
ᶠjozoji　男性
ᶠybʉji　男性
ᴿlombuji　男性
ᶠtshubʉji　男性
ᴿdrapərji　男性
ᶠjodzo　男性
ᴸqodraji　男性
ᴿjɛsami　女性
ᶠnjagumi　女性
ᴸdjumami　女性
ᴿjondomi　女性
ᴿjomu　女性
ᴸthʉkhimi　女性

　本書の研究調査地である連合郷の行政区画のナムイ語名は以下に掲げる通りである：

核桃 2 組　　ᴸvandʙʉfʉ
核桃 4 組　　ᴿyamantʉ
木耳 4 組　　ᴸjazontʉ
木耳 4 組　　ᶠpacintʉ
木耳 1 組　　ᶠgʻahʉntʉ
庄子 3 組　　ᴸanndʙʉzriva
庄子 2 組　　ᴸgʻajizɩva
大川亳村　　ᴿlakhʉntʉ
蘭河郷　　　ᴿlasantʉ
脂窩 1 組　　ᴸlawontʉ
脂窩 3 組　　ᴸhaqantʉ

3.2.3 場所名詞

場所名詞は概して空間的定位を示す語である。ゾロ方言の場所名詞は、4方向の区別を表す。各場所語は、近接（proximal）、遠位（distal）、遠隔（remote）、超遠隔（far remote）の形態をとる。ナムイ語ゾロ方言の場所名詞を以下に示す。

	近接	遠位	遠隔	超遠隔
straight up	^{H}tashi	^{H}chichi	^{H}chichichi	^{H}lotashi
straight down	^{H}thashi	^{H}chichiko	^{H}chichichiko	^{H}lothashi
upstream	^{H}yor	^{H}chiyor	^{H}chichiyor	^{H}loyor
downstream	^{H}shor	^{H}chishor	^{H}chichishor	^{H}loshor
inside	^{H}ku	^{H}chiku	^{H}chichiku	^{H}loku
outside	^{H}zra	^{H}chizra	^{H}chichizra	^{H}lozra
front	^{H}tadia	^{H}chidiako	^{H}chichidiako	^{H}lotadia
back	^{H}srə	^{H}chisrə	^{H}chichisrə	^{H}losrə

図3.1 方向を表す語彙

場所を表す語彙形式は、固有名詞とは異なり処格標識は付かないが、(3.5) にあるように奪格標識を付加ことができる。

(3.5) ^{H}no ^{H}tashi-mu ^{L}lu-nɨ
　　　2 sg　　　above-ABL　　　look. at-PERF
　　　'You looked at (it) from above.'

(3.6) ^{H}no ^{H}thashi-mu ^{L}lu-nɨ
　　　2 sg　　　down-ABL　　　look. at-PERF
　　　'You looked at (it) from downside.'

3.2.4 時間名詞

時間名詞はさまざまな時間の区切りや、現在からみた時点に言及するものである。以下は時間名詞の例である。

天	day	ᴿhata
今天	today	ᴿtani
明天	tomorrow	ᴸshugu
後天	day atrer tomorrow	ᶠnosho
大後天	day after day after tomorrow	ᶠnoniisho
昨天	yesterday	ᶠzɯnii
前天	day before yesterday	ᴸshinii
大前天	day before day before yesterday	ᴿshicinii
今天早上	this morning	ᴿdasho
明天早上	tomorrow morning	ᴿshugunadje
今天晚上	this evening	ᴸtahũ
明天晚上	tomorrow evening	ᶠsohũ
後天晚上	day after tomorrow evening	ᶠnosohũgu
昨天晚上	yesterday evening	ᶠyuhũ
前天晚上	day before yesterday evening	ᴿshihũ
白天	daytime	ᶠhiminigu
夜間	nighttime	ᴸhũkhu
整天	whole day	ᴸdjinimu
天亮、黎明	dawn	ᶠmyando
日出	sunrise	ᶠhimidjudju
早晨	morning	ᴸniadzɨ
上午	before noon	ᴿnikhu
中午	noon	ᴿnikhu
下午	afternoon	ᴸhũ

| 傍晩 | sunset | ᴸhŭkhu |
| 晩上 | evening | ᴸhŭngu |

時間名詞には処格標識、比較標識、または話題標識が付き、動詞複合体を修飾できるが、文節レベルを修飾する副詞としてよく使用される。これらは以下にあるように、話題標識をとることのできるトピック＝コメント構文の話題の位置にくることがある。

(3.7) ᴸiniashi   ᴴtsho-ci-lu......
     before-TOP   man-one-CL......
     'Once upon a time, there was a man who......'

(3.8) ᴿtani   ᶠso   ᴿpe-nɨ
     today-TOP   thre   become-CSM
     'Today is the third'

(3.9) ᴿtani   ᴿmima   ᶠphiomu
     today-TOP   sun   good
     'Today is a good day.'

時間名詞はまた名詞句の主部を修飾することもできる。時間名詞が名詞を修飾するときは、以下にあるように、その名詞に先行する。

(3.10) ᴸnga   ᴿtani-ko   ᴸmu ᴸdzu-shica-nɨ
      1 sg   today-GEN   thing do-finish-become
      'I finished that day's work.'

(3.11) ᴸchi   ᴸchinɨɨ-ko   ᴸmu ᴸdzu-shica-nɨ
      3 sg   that day-GEN   thing do-finish-become

'S/he finished that day's work.'

繋辞（コピュラ）節においては、時間名詞は次の例のように、繋辞（コピュラ）節の話題として機能することがある。

(3.12)　^{R}tani-di　　　^{L}kushi　　　　^{R}dzji
　　　　Today-TOP　　new year　　　COP
　　　　'Today is the Spring Festival.'

(3.13)　^{L}shugu　　　　^{R}sihngciyi　　　^{R}dzji
　　　　tomorrow　　　Monday　　　　COP
　　　　'Tomorrow is Monday.'

3.2.5　派生名詞（名詞化）

ゾロ方言では、動作主名詞を形成するために名詞化標識 '-su' が付け加えられた動詞または名動詞句で、これは動詞によって表現された活動を行っている人物に言及する。以下は、動作主の名詞化の例である。

(3.14)
^{H}lu　　　'to learn'　　　　＋　　　-su　^{H}lusu　　　　　'apprentice'
^{R}bu　　　'to run'　　　　　＋　　　-su　^{R}busu　　　　　'waiter'
^{F}g'odjə　'hair' + kər 'to cut' ＋　-su　^{F}g'odjəkərsu　　'barber'

以下では、様々なタイプの派生名詞の意味と用法を見ていく。

3.2.5.1　他動詞

筆者の観察によれば、他動詞からの派生名詞は agentive な読みと instrumental な読みの2通りの解釈を許容する。解釈は文脈で判断可能であるとのことである。

(3.15)　　　　　　　agentive reading　　instrumental reading
　ᴿche tɨ ꟳkai su　　car-driver　　　　instrumental for driving
　ꟳmi tci su　　　　 fire-maker　　　　 something for making a fire
　ꟳmi qa su　　　　 fire-fighter　　　　 fire-extinguisher
　ꟳzɨ ga su　　　　 fisherman　　　　 a tool for fishing
　ᴸngɨ tcʰi su　　　 cowherd　　　　　 something for herding cattle
　ᴸdra ᴸdzidzi su　　cook　　　　　　　cooking utensil
　ᴸgo ru su　　　　 doctor　　　　　　 pain killer

3.2.5.2　能格動詞

能格動詞とは、自動詞・他動詞いずれにも用いられる動詞のうち、自動詞として用いた場合の主語と、他動詞として用いた場合の目的語との意味役割が同じであるようなものを指す。能格動詞からの派生名詞は以下の如くである。この場合 event 的な読みと non-event 的な読みの2通りの解釈を許容する。解釈は文脈で判断可能であるとのことである。

(3.16)　　　　　　　event reading　　　　　　　　　　　　non-event reading
　ᴿmərmər su　　　 someone who is screaming　　　　　 screamer
　ᴸlopər su　　　　 someone/something that is jumping　 jumper
　ᴸkana tchi su　　 someone/something that is running　 runner
　ꟳmbər su　　　　someone who is walking　　　　　　 walker
　ᴸdzindri su　　　 someone who is laughing　　　　　　 ―
　ᴸngũndju su　　　someone who is crying　　　　　　　 ―

3.2.5.3　非対格動詞

非対格動詞とは、主語になるものが内項つまり意味上の主語になるものを指す。つまり、自動詞のうち非対格動詞はテーマのような主語を持っているものである。

(3.17) ᶠyoqo   ᴿvər   ᴿdji-gu   ᴿndju
       home   arrive   one-CL   guest
       'A guest arrived at (someone's) house.'

(3.18) ᴿfukər   (qolo)   ᴸtsho   ᴸlamo   ᴿci-gu   ᴿsho ko-nɨ
       village LOC   man   old   one-CL   die-PERF
       'An old man died in the village.'

(3.19) ᴿko bo   ᶠbər   ᶠche zi   ᴿci-bʉ   ᴿntcita
       door   mouth   car   one-CL   park
       'A car is parked at the door.'

(3.20) ᶠjɨ va   ᴿdiomu   ᴸvie   ᴿci-chɨ   ᴿdja
       ground surface snow   one-CL   exist
       'The ground is covered with a coat of fallen snow.'

(3.21) ᴸhanzɨ   ᴿdiomu   ᴿngu   ᴿci-la   ᴿqololuta   ᴿzahu
       sea   surface ship   one-CL   downward   sink
       'A ship sank at the sea.'

(3.22) ᴸshiqa   ᴿci-sha   ᴿzoko
       foot   one-CL   puncture
       'He had a cut on his foot.'

(3.23) ᴸdiɛnshii   ᴿdiomu   qo   ᴿkapi   ᶠfu-nɨ
       (ᴸdiɛnshii< Chi. diànshì［電視］'TV')
       television surface   on   dust   blow-PERF
       'The television is covered with a coat of blown dust.'

(3.24) ᴿbutsʰɨ   ᴿdiomu   ᴿcii-pia   ᴿkarpar-nɨ
       cloth   surface one-CL   break-PERF
       'The cloth is torn with a hole in it.'

(3.25) ᴿtabi   ᴿdiomu   ᶠluku   ᴿtcii-lu   ᴿkər-nɨ
       hill   surface hole   one-CL   dig-PERF
       'There is a cave dug on the hill.'

非対格動詞から派生した名詞は以下のような event 的な読みの解釈のみ許容する。

(3.26)   event reading   non-event reading
   ᴿdju su (ᴿvar)   a arrived guest   ―
   ᴸdji ta su (ᶠche zi)   a parked jeep   ―
   ᴸzahu su (ᴿⁿgu)   a sunken boat   ―
   ᴸcoqu su (ᴸtsholu mo)   a deceased old man   ―
   ᴸkaʲpəʲ-nɨ su (ᴿciipia)   a punctured hole   ―
   ᴸkaʲpəʲ-nɨ su (ᴸqaji)   a broken thermos bottle ―
   ᶠfu su (ᴿkapi)   a blown dust   ―
   ᴸdzidzi-nɨ su (ᶠloku)   a torn opening   ―
   ᴿka-nɨ su (ᶠluku)   a dug-hole   ―

3.2.5.4 他動詞の内項

以下の動詞は event 的な読みと non-event 的な読みの 2 通りの解釈を許容する。解釈は文脈で判断可能であるとのことである。

(3.27)   event reading   non-event reading
   ᴸkhukhu-nɨ su (ᴸdrikaza)   polished shoes   shoes to polish
   ᴿlu su (ᴿⁿdzigi)   books read   books to read

ᴿⁿgʉ su (ᴿbʉ tsʰʉ)	clothes worn	cloth to wear
ᴿdja su (ᴸdjashi)	stewed chicken	chicken to stew
ᴸdri su (ᴸⁿdzi gi mi dju)	hand-copied poems	poems to copy
ᴿⁿdi su (ᴸtsʰʉ gʉ)	medicine taken	edicine for oral intake
ᴿkhʉdraku su (ᴿba ⁿdji bi gji)	a picked-up wallet	*a wallet to pick up

最後の例 ᴿkhʉdraku su (ᴿba ⁿdji bi gji) は「盗まれる財布」ではなく「盗まれた財布」の解釈しか容認されない。

(3.28) a. ᶠchi   pər   ᴿndisu-nɨ   su   ᴸtsʰʉ gʉ   ᴿri pi   ᴿshicia
          3 sg AGT   eat   NOM   medicine   throw   finish
          'He vomited all the medicine he has taken.'

   b. ᶠti tsʰa ᴸtsʰʉgʉ ᴸⁿdĩ ⁿdi su,   ᶠciitsʰa ᴸtsʰʉ gʉ ᴿja su
      this   medicine eat   NOM that   medicine oil   NOM
      'This drug is for oral intake; that drug is an ointment.'

(3.29) a. ᶠchi   ᴸgu   su   ᴿbʉtsʰʉ   ᴸpʰuⁿdjo   ᶠgəjəʲ   ᴿci-la
          3 sg wear NOM cloth   expensive   very   one-CL
          'What he wore was a very expensive suit'

   b. ᶠchi ko   ᴸngbʉ ᴸhɛr   lɛ   ᶠchi ko   ᴿdju
      3 sg GEN wife   buy   and   3 sg BENE exist
      'His wife bought him something to wear.'

(3.30) ᶠtĩ   ᴿndjigi   ᴿlu   ᴿvu   ᴿdjo   ᴸgərdjər
       this   book   read   interest   exist very
       'This book reads very well.'

(3.31) ᶠpʰio ᴸtshʉ gʉ ᶠndʉ di ᴸqa ᴸgəˈdjəˈ
good   drug   take then bitter very
'A good medicine tastes bitter.'

3.2.6　代名詞

特定物の概念を表すのではなく現実の場面において指示の役目を果たす機能をもつ指示代名詞は人称代名詞、再帰代名詞、指示代名詞、疑問代名詞、及び不定代名詞に下位分類される。

3.2.6.1　人称代名詞

ナムイ語ゾロ方言では、人称代名詞で3つの人称と3つの数が標示される。一人称非単数形には排他的か包含的かの区別は存在しない。また、下の図で示したように、代名詞の双数形もあり、日常会話では多用される。

	単数	双数	複数
1人称	ᴴnga	ᶠnganyiku	ᶠngaXo
2人称	ᶠno	ᶠnonyiku	ᶠnoXo
3人称	ᶠchi	ᶠchiinyiku	ᶠchiXo

表2　ナムイ語ゾロ方言の人称代名詞

代名詞は動作主・経験者・授受の起点、属格、被動作者で以下のように格変化をする。これは周辺諸言語には見られないナムイ語に特有な現象である。

	S/A	GEN	P
1 sg	ᴴnga	ᶠniɛ	ᶠnga
2 sg	ᶠno	ᶠnɛ	ᶠna
3 sg	ᶠchi	ᶠchɛ	ᴴcha

表3　人称代名詞の格変化

人称代名詞は句・節のすべての位置に生起する可能性がある。三人称代名詞は、先に述べた指示対象に言及するために前方照応的に使用されることがある。

(3.32) ^Fchi   ^Fnga   ^Lmbo
    3 sg   1sg   beat
    'S/he beats me.'

3.2.6.2 再帰代名詞

再帰代名詞は、単数形は正規の代名詞をベースとし、同一音節を3度繰り返して表す。複数形は複数標識を3度繰り返して表す。なお双数形の再帰代名詞は確認できなかった。

	単数	複数
1	^Fnganganga	^FngaXoXoXo
2	^Fnonono	^FnoXoXoXoXo
3	^Fchichichi	^FchiXoXoXoXo

再帰代名詞を用いると、同じ再帰代名詞が他動詞節の行為者と受動者の両方を表現するために用いられ、行為者を表す項は動作主標示をとる。

(3.33) ^Fnganganga-pər   ^Fnga   ^Llu
    1 sg：REFL-AGT   1sg：REFL   look. at
    'I myself am looking at myself.'

(3.34) ^Fchichichi-pər   ^Hcha   ^Lmbo
    3 sg：REFL-AGT   3 sg：REFL   beat
    'S/he is beating herself himself.'

(3.35) ^FchiXoXoXoXo-pər   ^FchiXo   ^Fkotshɨ

```
3 pl-REFL-AGT          3 pl          ask
```
'They ask themselves.'

3.2.6.3 指示詞

指示詞は近方と遠方（それぞれ '^Hta' と '^Hchi'）の観点で二項対立を示している。近方（proximate）は指示対象が話し手に近いときに使われる。遠方（distal）は言及された対象が遠くにあるか目に見えないときに使われる。指示詞の分類を以下の図に示す。

近方	遠方	意味
^Hta-tsho	^Hchi-tsho	人間の指示対象（「この人」「あの人」）
^Hta-Xa	^Hchi-Xa	量（「これだけ」「あれだけ」）
^Hta-lu	^Hchi-lu	もの（「これ」「あれ」）
^Hta-dia	^Hchi-dia	場所（「ここ」「あそこ」）
^Hta-dri	^Hchi-dri	場所（「こっち側」「あっち側」）
^Hta-chu	^Hchi-chu	場所（「ここ」「あそこ」）
^Hta-hata	^Hchi-hata	時間（「このとき」「あのとき」）
^Hta-adjimɛ	^Hchi-adjimɛ	種類／手段（「こんなふうに」「あんなふうに」）

表9 指示代名詞

近方を表す '^Hta' と遠方を表す '^Hchi' は指示詞の基本的形式のように思われる。人間の指示対象に言及する指示代名詞 '^Hta-tsho, ^Hchi-tsho' は、指示代名詞 '^Hta/^Hchi' + 人 '-tsho' で形成される。量に言及する指示代名詞 '^Hta-Xa'（「これら」）／'^Hchi-Xa'（「あれら」）は、量を表す標識 '-Xa' と '^Hta/^Hchi' から成る。物に言及にする指示代名詞 '^Hta-lu/^Hchi-lu' は指示代名詞 't ^Hta/^Hchi' と類別詞 '-lu' の組み合わせである。意味的または構文的に、場所を表す '^Hta-dia'（「ここ」）／'^Hchi-dia'（「あそこ」）と '^Hta-chu'（「ここ」）／'^Hchi-chu'（「あそこ」）のあいだに差異はない。方法に言及する指示代名詞 '^Hta-adjimɛ'（「こんなふうに」）／'^Hchi-adjimɛ'（「あんなふうに」）は指示代名詞 '^Hta/^Hchi

＋類別詞 'adjimɛ'（「種類」）で構成されている。

　指示代名詞は自由代名詞と指示形容詞、両方の用法で同じ形態をもつ。指示代名詞は自由代名詞として用いられると、NPの主部として機能することがある。指示代名詞が形容詞であれば、NPの主部を修飾することができる。

(3.36)　ᴴchi dia-di......
　　　　there-TOP......
　　　　'As for that place, ...'

(3.37)　ᴴta-lu　　　　ᶠniɛ　　　　　　　ᴸdzi
　　　　this-CL　　　1sg：GEN　　　　COP
　　　　'This（thing）is mine.'

3.2.6.4　疑問代名詞
　疑問代名詞は内容に関する質問を尋ねるのに使用される。主な疑問代名詞は以下のとおりである。

ᶠhadji	'who'	ᶠtihū	'what'
ᶠhabuta	'how many/how much'	ᶠasho	'where'
ᶠashi	'which'	ᶠtishi	'what'
ᶠhatadzithu	'when'	ᶠhatata	'why'
ᶠhabuta	'how long'	ᴴhatamu	'how'

3.2.6.5　不定代名詞
　不定代名詞 '-yabe' は、NPの主部として用いられることがあり、またNPの主部の修飾語として使用されることもある。

(3.38) ᴸtsho-yabe
man-some
'someone'

(3.39) ᴸqadji-yabe
thing-some
'something'

(3.40) -ᴸtsho-hũyabe
man-some
'some people'

(3.41) ᴸqadji-hũyabe
thing-some
'other things'

3.3 数詞と数量詞

ほとんどの場合、数詞と数量詞はNPの主部を修飾するために用いられる。名詞を修飾するときはつねに、修飾する名詞のあとに続く。

3.3.1 数詞

ナムイ語ゾロ方言では、数詞体系は純粋な十進法である。

ᴸtsi	1	ᴸhĩXotsi	11
ᴸni	2	ᴸhĩXoni	12
ᴸso	3	ᴸhĩXoso	13
ᴸzi	4	ᴸhĩXozi	14
ᴸnga	5	ᴸhĩXonga	15

ᴸqhu	6	ᴸhĩXoqhu	16
ᴸsi	7	ᴸhĩXosi	17
ᴸhĩ	8	ᴸhĩXohĩ	18
ᴸnggu	9	ᴸhĩXonggu	19
ᴸhĩXo	10	ᴸnihĩXo	20
ᴸsohĩXo	30	ᴸzihĩXo	40
ᴸngahĩXo	50	ᴸnganghĩXo	50
ᴸqhuhĩXo	60	ᴸsihĩXo	70
ᴸhĩhĩXo	80	ᴸngguhĩXo	90
ᴴhĩ	100	ᴸtu	1,000
ᴸmɛ	1,0000	ᴴdzra	100,000

ナムイ語ゾロ方言の序数詞体系は以下の通りである。

ᴸciG'ua	'first'	ᴸhĩXotsiG'ua	'eleventh'
ᴸniG'ua	'second'	ᴸhĩXoniG'ua	'twelfth'
ᴸsoG'ua	'third'	ᴸhĩXosoG'ua	'thirteenth'
ᴸziG'ua	'fourth'	ᴸhĩXoziG'ua	'fourteenth'
ᴸngaG'ua	'fifth'	ᴸhĩXongaG'ua	'fifteenth'
ᴸqhuG'ua	'sixth'	ᴸhĩXoqhuG'ua	'sixteenth'
ᴸsiG'ua	'seventh'	ᴸhĩXosiG'ua	'seventeethn'
ᴸhĩG'ua	'eighth'	ᴸhĩXohĩG'ua	'eighteenth'
ᴸngguG'ua	'nineth'	ᴸhĩXongguG'ua	'nineteenth'
ᴸhĩXoG'ua	'tenth'	ᴸnihĩXoG'ua	'twentieth'

3.3.2 数に関する表現

数に関する表現としては以下の形式がある。

(3.42)

^{F}ta 'several'、^{F}tau 'approximately'、^{R}tzrɨzrɨ 'many'、^{H}matu 'few'

3.3.3 類別詞（classifier）

類別詞はつねに、数字または指示代名詞とともに、後者が名詞句の主部を修飾するときに生起する。以下は、個別の従前全く記述がなされてこなかったナムイ語の類別詞の一覧である（数詞 'ci'（「1」）を付けて記述した）。

^{t}ci-khʉ	used for meat
^{t}ci-lo	used for meat
^{t}ci-ka	used for rice (ten litter)
^{t}ci-shi	used for rice (one 升)
^{t}ci-bʉ	used for rice (one 合)
^{t}ci-mu	used for ricefield
^{t}ci-psʉ	used for textile
^{t}ci-cu	used for textile (one 尺)
^{t}ci-dzrɨ	used for textile (one 寸)
^{t}ci-phi	used for cock, ox
^{t}ci-luka	used for bird
^{t}ci-dju	used for pair (eg. Shoes)
^{t}ci-bʉ	used for stone
^{t}ci-bʉ	used for turf
^{t}ci-gər	used for leather
^{t}ci-chə	used for leather
^{t}ci-bʉ	used for wine
^{t}ci-kha	used for wine
^{t}ci-pu	used for wine
^{t}ci-pia	used for paper

第3章 語及び名詞形態論

ᵗci-pu	used for sheet, book, chair
ᵗci-djɨ	used for hand, leg
ᵗci-ka	used for cigar
ᵗci-kha	used for fruit
ᵗci-mər	used for money
ᵗci-lu	used for sentence
ᵗci-kala	used for tree
ᵗci-la	used for pen, bone, , tooth, knife
ᵗci-lu	used for house
ᵗci-hlɛ	used for month
ᵗci-dzja	used for meal
ᵗci-ndjo	used for rope
ᵗci-sha	used for raindrop
ᵗci-lu	used for character
ᵗci-la	used for finger
ᵗci-bu	used for fart, shit
ᵗci-pi	used for drink
ᵗci-pia	used for spit
ᵗci-la	used for dish
ᵗci-lu	used for hat, cap
ᵗci-tsa	used for kind
ᵗci-gu	used for man
ᵗci-ku	used for story
ᵗci-ti	used for road
ᵗci-psɨ	used for leaf
ᵗci-tsha	used for thing
ᵗci-dzi	used for thing

3.4 名詞句の形態

本節では、名詞句の形態について論じる。性標識、指小辞標識、関係接頭辞、定／不定標識、数標識、格標識、及び比較標識をそれぞれ扱う。

3.4.1 性標識

ナムイ語ゾロ方言では、動物を含む有生物（animate）を表すものは、その性を標示される。さまざまな接尾辞が、男性または女性の性をコード化するために、名詞に付け加えられる。性標識は動物と花に付加されるが、金属や器具の質の良し悪しを表す際に文法的に標示されることもある。接尾辞 '-ko' は「男性性」を標示し、'-mi' は「女性性」を標示する。以下はその例である。

(3.43) ^Fdra-ko（phu³）
cock-MAS
'cock'

(3.44) ^Fdra-mi
hen-FEM
'hen'

(3.45) ^Lmolojijo-ko
ox-MAS
'ox'

(3.46) ^Rgɯmi

---

3 この例の場合は^Fdra-phu の方が優勢であるとのことである。

ox-FEM
'cow'

(3.47) ᴿva-ko
pig-MAS
'pig'

(3.48) ᴿva-mi
pig-FEM
'sow'

(3.49) ᶠmo-ko
horse-MAS
'horse'

(3.50) ᴸmo-mi
horse-FEM
'mare'

(3.51) ᶠchi-ko
dog-MAS
'dog'

(3.52) ᶠchi-mi
dog-FEM
'bitch'

3.4.2　指小辞標示

ナムイ語ゾロ方言の指小辞標識 'atsutsu' は '-atsɯtsɯ'（「小さい」）に関連しているかもしれないが、以下の例にあるように、名詞のあとに生起して指小辞を標示する。

(3.53) ^{L}dzadzaku-atsutsu
　　　　pot-DIM
　　　　'small pot'

なお、逆の大きい意味を表す標識は 'bzi' である[4]。

(3.54) ^{H}yoko-bzi
　　　　house big
　　　　'big house'

3.4.3　親族名称

兄弟姉妹を表す名称は以下の如くである。

	男性		女性	
	同性	異性	同性	異性
年上	^{F}apo	^{R}ŋim	^{L}ajamo	^{R}mudzɿm
年下	^{L}ɡudz	^{L}nimomo	^{L}ɡudzɿmo	^{R}mudzɿmoatsutsu

表3　兄弟姉妹を表す語彙

ナムイ語では、親族名称の「兄」と「姉」は、もともと家族の構成員を呼ぶために用いられていた。しかし、親族用語は家族ではない者を呼ぶときにも用いられる。以下は親族名称（呼びかけ語）の例である。例

4　この形式の来現は目下不明である。

90

えば、最初の例では年上男性が年下男性に呼びかける場合 ᴿGᴜdzɪ が用いられる。

(3.55)

年上	男性	→	年下	男性	ᴿGᴜdzɪ
年上	男性	→	年下	女性	ᴿimomo
年上	男性	→	年上	女性	ᴿnyimi
年下	男性	→	年上	男性	ᴸapo
年下	男性	→	年上	女性	ᴿnyimi
年下	男性	→	年下	女性	ᴿnimomo
年上	女性	→	年上	男性	ᴿmundzɨmo
年上	女性	→	年下	男性	ᴿmundzɨmoatsᵾtsᵾ
年上	女性	→	年下	女性	ᴿGᴜdzɨmo
年下	女性	→	年上	女性	ᴸajamo
年下	女性	→	年上	男性	ᴿmundzɨmo
年下	女性	→	年下	男性	ᴿmundzɨmo-atsᵾtsᵾ

3.4.4 定／不定

ナムイ語ゾロ方言では、定と不定の区別がある。接尾辞'-ci'は、指示対象が特定できないとき、不定名詞句を標示する。これは動物にも無生物にも用いられる。不定標示'-lu'は類別詞'lu'と一緒に用いられることが多く、たとえば'ꟳtsho-ci-lu'は「一人の人間」または「一つの物体」を指す。定性を表すには'-thu'を用いる。

(3.56) ᴿahi-lu   ꟳpacilu   ᴸdja
        earth-LOC   stone-INDEF   exist
        'There is a stone on the ground.'

(3.57) ᴴyoko   ᴴtsho-cilu   ᴸdja

   home   people-INDEF   exist
   'There is a person at home.'

(3.58) ^Ftĩgo-thu   ^Lthu phu ma-dʒo
   walking. stick-this：CL value-INDEF NEG-exist
   'This walking stick is not valuable.'

3.4.5　数標示

　名詞の数を標示する文法形式（語尾変化）はないが、名詞句のなかの数の意味を示す接尾辞はいくつかある。ナムイ語ゾロ方言では、概して、'-Xo'（複数の数詞類別詞）はたいてい、以下の例のように名詞と指示代名詞と共起し、複数の数をコード化し、また、'-ci'（「１」）のあとに付いて 'ci-Xo'（「いくつかの」）を形成する。以下はその例である。

(3.59) ^Rrabi-diomu ^Hko-ci-po ^Lyahamu Lndashit-shia
   hill-top tree-（one）-PL all fell-CSM
   'All of the trees on the hill have been cut down.'

(3.60) ^Lhabutachi ^Lchi   ^Lshi-shia
   many   dog   die-CSM
   'Many dogs were killed.'

3.5　名詞句関係形態素（格標示）

　本節では格標示（後置詞）の形式と機能について論じる。これは動詞と項、または項同士の関係を標示するものである。文の主項の意味論的、語用論的な役割は、主に文の構成要素の順序と以下の後置詞により表現される。ナムイ語ゾロ方言には以下の格標識があることがわかっている。

1. ø　　　　主語（agantive）・対格（accusative）・所有者（possessive）・
　　　　　　　着点（goal）・場所（locative）・時点（temporal）
2. ko　　　　属格（genitive）
3. pər　　　 行為者（agentive）
4. dia　　　 与格（dative）
5. mi　　　　受益者（benefactive）
6. mu　　　　具格（instrumental）
7. ʉ　　　　 具格（instrumental）
8. khəsrɨ　　具格（instrumental）
9. mu　　　　奪格（ablative）、変格（translative）
10. tahi　　　到格（terminative）
11. toto　　　到格（terminative）
12. suni　　　通格（perlative）
13. qolo　　　処格（内）（locative）
14. diamo　　 処格（上）（locative）
15. pər　　　 処格（場所）（locative）
16. tani　　　向格（allative, location）
17. luta　　　向格（allative, direction）
18. na　　　　共格（comitative）
19. chomu　　 共格（comitative）
20. maza　　　比格（comparative）

　これらの標識は一般に独立して用いられるが、処格標識と奪格標識、2つの処格標識、または意味標識と話題標識が一緒に用いられることもある。他動詞の文と二重目的語の文においては、行為者が話題である場合、行為者を表している NP は、動作主標識をとる必要はない。一般に、標識の付いた構成要素の順序があるときや、行為者の動作主性を強調する必要があるときのみ、(5) のように、動作主標識/-pər/が行為者を表す NP のあとに用いられる。

形式	意味
ø	A、S、P（無標）、所有者の項（2.1）
ko	所有者の名詞修飾句（4.2）
pər	知覚感覚の主体、原因（2.2）
dia	P（2.1）、受領者（4.3）
mi	受益者（4.3）
mu	道具（4.5）
ʉ	
khəsrɨ	
mu	起点（3.3）
	変化の結果（3.2）
tahi	まで（3.2）
toto	
suni	経路（3.4）
qolo	位置（中）（3.1）
diamo	位置（上）（3.1）
pər	位置（のところ）（3.1）
tani	着点（4.4）
luta	着点（4.4）
na	随伴者（4.1）
chomu	
diomu	比較の対象（優勢）（4.6）
mazɨ	比較の対象（劣勢）（4.6）

表3.1　ナムイ語ゾロ方言の格表示形式

3.6 S/A/P を標示する形式

3.6.1 S/P を標示する形式

S/P はゼロで現れる。S は基本的に行為者であるか有生性の有無に関わらずゼロで現れる。

(3.61) ^{F}hin ^{R}dru
  rain (n.) rain (v.)
  'It rains.'

(3.62) ^{F}ngaXo ^{R}mbɛr
  1PL go
  'We go.'

P は有生性に関係なくゼロで現れることが多い。P を明示する場合、または強調する場合は〈-dia〉で表わされる。

(3.63) ^{H}nga ^{F}titsa (-dia) ^{L}zriga
  1sg this like
  'I like this.'

(3.64) ^{H}nga ^{F}na ^{L}zriga
  1sg you.OBJ like
  'I like you.'

(3.65) ^{H}nga ^{L}ja (-dia) ^{R}shishi
  1sg food cook

'I cook meal.'

(3.66) ᶠno   ᶠnamuji   ᶠci-gu   ᴿji
        2 sg   Tibetan   one-CL   COP
        'I am Tibetan.'

(3.67) ᶠchi   ᴸbaji   ᴿjikɨ
        3 sg   money   have
        'He has money.'

(3.68) ᶠno   ᴿlakhɨ   ᴸa-jo
        2 sg   child   NEG-have
        'you don't have children.'

3.6.2 A を標示する形式

行為主体を明示もしくは強調するときは〈-pər〉が現れる。基本的にAとPは語順によって表わされる。即ち、ナムイ語では特に指定がない限りAPVの語順で要素が並べられる。

(3.69) ᴴnga-pər   ᶠchi   ᴿmbo-nʉ
        1 sg-AGT   3 sg   beat-PRF
        'I hit him.'

(3.70) ᶠchi-pər   ᶠja   ᴸmər-nʉ
        3 sg-AGT   chicken   grasp-PRF
        'He caught a chicken.'

(3.71) ᴿxala-pər   ᴿxatsitsi-ci-lu   ᴴGɛ-hɛr
        cat-AGT   mouse-one-CL   hold in one's mouth-leave

'A cat held a mouse in her mouth.'

また〈-pər〉は有意志性別（Volitionality）とも関係なく現れる。

(3.72) ^Fchi-pər   ^Lhinhinmu   ^Fnukha   ^Lkaerper-nʉ
3 sg-AGT   intentionally   bowl   break-PRF
'He broke the bowl purposefully.'

(3.73) ^Fchi-pər   ^Rmakalihumu   ^Fnukha   ^Lkaerper-nʉ
3 sg-AGT   unintentionally   bowl   break-PRF
'He broke the bowl unpurposefully.'

知覚感覚の主体を明示する際は〈-pər〉が義務的に現れる。

(3.74) ^Fchi-ko   ^Rmi   ^Fnga-pər   ^Rnjopərhin-nʉ
3 sg-GEN   name   1 sg-AGT   forget-PRF
'He forgot my name.'

(3.75) ^Lucimi-pər   ^Fnga-ko   ^Rgopa-nʉ
Ucimi-AGT   1 sg-GEN   loset-PRF
'Ucimi lost mine.'

(3.76) ^Lucimi   ^Fnga (-pər)   ^Lndoher-nʉ
Ucimi   1 sg-AGT   see-PRF
'Ucimi saw me.'

自然現象が主体である場合も〈-pər〉が義務的に現れる。

(3.77) ^Fmusu-pər   ^Rshipo   ^Ffu-le   ^Ljapu-nʉ

```
         wind-AGT    tree         blow-and    fall-PRF
         'window fell trees.'
```

(3.78) ᶠmuvomərmər-pər ᴿchala   ᶠci-pha   ᴸshi-lE   ᴸshoko-nɨ
       thunder-AGT   tiger   one-CL   kill-and   die-PRF
       'Thunder killed a tiger.'

3.6.3 LOCAL な意味役割を標示する形式

3.6.3.1 存在・出来事生起の位置を標示する形式

存在及び出来事の生起の位置を表すためには、⟨-qolo⟩「〜の中で」、⟨-diamo⟩「〜の上で」、⟨-pər⟩「〜の所で」が用いられる。

⟨-qolo⟩「〜の中で」は2次元及び3次元的広がりのある場所の内部での存在・出来事の生起を表示するのに用いられる。

(3.79) ᴸnzu-qolo   ᴿzi   ᴿjo
       river-LOC   fish   exist
       'There are fish in the river.'

(3.80) ᶠluqa-qolo   ᶠdzɨ   ᴸzɨ
       bowl-LOC   water   exist
       'Water is in the bowl.'

(3.81) ᴿshueshao-qolo ᴸzrigi   ᴴso
       school-LOC   letter   learn
       'study at school.'

⟨-diamo⟩「〜の上で」は物理的に上または表面である場合に用いられる。

第3章　語及び名詞形態論

(3.82)　^{F}chi　　　　　^{F}kr-diamo　　　　^{R}yka-dzidzimu
　　　　3 sg　　　　 bed-LOC　　　　　sleep-PROG
　　　　'He is sleeping on the bed.'

(3.83)　^{F}chi　　　　　^{F}kr-diamo　　　　^{R}yka-dzidzimu
　　　　3 sg　　　　 bed-LOC　　　　　sleep-PROG
　　　　「彼はベッドの上で寝ている」

(3.84)　^{L}mashi-diamo　　^{L}gocy　　　^{R}ci-la　^{L}dra
　　　　desk-LOC　　　　neeldle　　 one-CL　EXIST
　　　　'There is a needle on the desk.'

〈-pər〉「～の所で」は通常「～の家で」の意味を表わし、フランス語の chez と同じ用法である。

(3.85)　^{H}nga-pər　　　^{L}badzɨ　　^{F}tshɨ-su　　^{F}chi-tsho-chi-gu-su
　　　　1 sg-LOC　　　money　　lend-SU　　def-man-one-CL-SU
　　　　'the person who lent money at my place.'

3.6.3.2　移動の着点を標示する形式

移動の着点を表す形式としては、〈-tahi〉「～まで」がある。到格（terminative）の用法である。

(3.86)　^{H}nga　　^{F}hatamu　　^{F}dzolo-mu　　^{R}chengdu-tahi　^{R}mbɛr
　　　　1 sg　　　how　　　Mianning-ABL　Chengdu-TRM　　go
　　　　'How can I get to chéngdū from Dzolo'?

(3.87)　^{R}diamu-mu　　^{R}ahin-tahi
　　　　lower-ABL　　 upper-TRM

99

'from the top to the bottom.'

なお時間的な着点は〈-toto〉で表わされる。

(3.88) ᴴnga   ᴿju-su   ᶠjithu-toto
       1 sg   come-SU   time-TRM
       'untill I come.'

変化の着点、即ち変格 (translative) は〈-mu〉「～に、～へと」で表わされる。

(3.89) ᴸzɨpzɨ-nji-ya-su-di   ᴿgedzi-nji-ya-mu   ᴸshija-nɨ
       young beast-two-cl-Su-TOP   bird-two-cl-TRNS   change-PRF
       'The two beasts kids changed in to little birds.'

(3.90) ᴸtalisutsho-di   ᴸtsholu-mu   ᴸshishita........
       others-TOP   beast-TRNS   turn
       'The others turned into beasts........'

3.6.3.3 移動・時間的区間の起点を標示する形式

移動・時間的区間の起点は共に〈-mu〉「～から」で表わされる。

(3.91) ᶠno   ᶠausro-mu   ᴿju?
       2 sg   where-ABL   come
       'Where are you from?'

(3.92) ᴴnga   ᴿyamatu-mu   ᴿju?
       1 sg   Yamatu-ABL   come
       'I am from yamatu.'

(3.93) ᶠngoXo   ᶠno-mi   ᶠonjo-mu   ᴸzaju-su
     1 pl   2 sg-BENE   Xichang-ABL   come-EMP
     'We come from Xichang for you.'

(3.94) ᴸsrichini-mu   ᶠnga   ᶠnamuji-sha   ᴴso
     year before last-ABL   1 sg   Tibetan-language   learn
     'I have been learning Namuyi since the year before last.'

3.6.3.4 移動の通過点を標示する形式

移動の通過点を表すには〈-suni〉「～を通って、～経由で」が用いられる。

(3.95) ᴴnga   ᶠhatamu   ᶠdzolo-suni   ᶠnima-tahi   ᴿmbɛr
     1 sg   how   Dzolo-PERL   Tibet-TRM   go
     ''How can I get to Tibet by way of Dzolo?'

3.7 その他の標示形式

3.7.1 共格を標示する形式

〈-na〉、〈-chomu〉「～と」は随伴者の表示に用いられる。並列された名詞句を繋ぐ場合や同等比較でも用いられる。

(3.96) ᶠchi   ᶠnga-na   ᴿchikɛr   ᶠhɛr-nʉ
     3 sg   1 sg-COM   salt   buy-PRF
     'I bought salt with him.'

(3.97) ᶠchi-na   ᶠnga   ᴿchikɛr   ᶠhɛr-nʉ
     3 sg-COM   1 sg   salt   buy-PRF

「私は彼と塩を買った」

(3.98)　ᶠchi　　　　ᶠnga-chomu　　　ᴿchikɛr　　　　ᶠhɛr-nʉ
　　　　3 sg　　　1 sg-COM　　　　salt　　　　　buy-PRF
　　　「私は彼と塩を買った」

(3.99)　ᶠno-na　　　ᶠchi　　　　ᴿdidi　　　　　ᴸta
　　　　2 sg　　　　COM　　　　3 sg　　　　　same　tall
　　　「あなたと彼は同じくらい背が高い」

(3.100)　ᶠnga-no-na-chi　　　　ᴿjomu　　　ᶠnamuji-sha　　ᴴso
　　　　1 sg- 2 sg-COM- 3 sg　together　　Tibetan　　　learn
　　　「私とあなたと彼は一緒にナムイ語を勉強する」

3.7.2　属格を標示する形式

　〈-ko〉の基本的な機能は属格表示であり、名詞句に付加されて及び名詞節に付加されて後続名詞の修飾部を形成する際に用いられる。

(3.101)　ᴴnga-ko　　　ᴿdzigi
　　　　 1 sg-GEN　　book
　　　　'my book.'

(3.102)　ᶠnyE-adia　　　　　　ᶠGumi　　　ᴿhɛ
　　　　1 sg. GEN-father　　　body　　　good
　　　　'My father is fine.'

(3.103)　ᶠno-ko　　　ᴿbitshɨ　　ᴸandindɨ　　ᶠlaha
　　　　2 sg-GEN　　cloth　　　short　　　　very
　　　　'your cloth is too small.'

第 3 章 語及び名詞形態論

ナムイ語には譲渡可能／譲渡不可能の区別があり、身体の一部等譲渡不可能を表す際には〈-ko〉は現れない。

(3.104) a. ᴴnga-ko   ᴸtholo   b. ᴴnga   ᴸlaka
　　　　　 1 sg-GEN   hat   1 sg   hand
　　　　　 'my hat.'   'my hand.'

　　　　c. ᶠno-ko   ᴿlatho   d. ᴸchi   ᴸmɛrbo
　　　　　 2 sg-GEN   watch   dog   tail
　　　　　 'my watch.'   'dog's tail.'

　　　　e. ᶠchi-ko   ᶠkhuzu   f. ᴸva   kha
　　　　　 3 sg-GEN   tub   pig   mouth
　　　　　 'his tub.'   'mouth of pig.'

3.7.3 与格を標示する形式

ナムイ語では三項動詞の場合、所謂直接目的語が無標となり間接目的語は〈-dia〉を伴って表わされる。

(3.105) ᴴnga   ᶠchi-dia   ᴸsho-nʉ
　　　　 1 sg   3 sg-DAT   say-PRF
　　　　 'I said to him.'

(3.106) ᴸsaerbu   ᴸbiho-dia   ᴸdrigi   ᴸso
　　　　 teacher   student-DAT book   teach
　　　　 'Teachers shows students him to read.'

(3.107) ᶠchiXo   ᶠG'oatha   ᶠnga-dia   ᶠkongo
　　　　 3 pl   before   1 sg-DAT   hate

'They disliked me preriously.'

(3.108) ᶠshushu-pər　　ᶠnga-dia　　　ᴿpingo　　ᴸchi-lu　　ᴸko
　　　　3 sg-AGT　　1 sg-DAT　　apple　　one-CL　　give
　　　　'My uncle gare me an apple.'

(3.109) ᴴnga　　　　ᶠchi-dia　　　ᴸbaji　　ᴸko-nʉ
　　　　1 sg　　　　3 sg-DAT　　money　　give-PRF
　　　　'I gave him money.'

受益者（benefactive）は〈-mi〉で表わされる。

(3.110) ᶠshushu-pər　ᴿpingo　　ᴸchi-lu　　ᶠnga-mi　　ᴸko-nʉ
　　　　3 sg-AGT　　apple　　one-CL　　1 sg-BEN　　give-PRF
　　　　'My uncle gave me an apple.'

(3.111) ᴴnga　　　ᴸbaji　　　ᶠchi-mi　　　ᴸko-nʉ
　　　　1 sg　　　money　　3 sg-BEN　　give-PRF
　　　　'I gave him money.'

3.7.4 向格を標示する形式

〈-tani〉及び〈-luta〉「〜に向かって」は向格（allative）を表す。

(3.112) ᶠchi　　　　ᴿrabi-tani　　　　ᴿmbɛr-su
　　　　3 sg　　　mountain-ALL　　walk-EMPH
　　　　'He will walk towards the mountain.'

(3.113) ᶠchi　　ᶠnga (-pər) -luta　　　ᴿndzu
　　　　3 sg　　1 sg (-LOC) -ALL　　sit

'He sits at me.'

3.7.5 具格を標示する形式

〈-mu〉、〈-ʉ〉、〈-khəsrɨ〉は具格（instrumental）を表す。

(3.114) ᶠchi-pər　　　ᴸjata-mu　　　　　ᴸka-nʉ
　　　　3 sg-AGT　　scissor-INST　　　cut-PRF
　　　　'He cut with a scissor.'

(3.115) ᴴnga　　　　ᴿbi-mu　　　　ᴸdrɨgi　　ᴿzrə
　　　　1 sg　　　　pen-INST　　　letter　　write
　　　　'I write with a pen.'

(3.116) ᶠchi　　　　ᴿgə-ʉ　　　　　ᴿbɨtshɨ　　ᴿtrɨ
　　　　3 sg　　　　dresser-INST　　clothe　　pack
　　　　'He puts clothes in the dresser.'

(3.117) ᴴnga　　　　ᴿpinzɨ-khəsrɨ　　ᴴvu　　　ᴿtrɨ
　　　　1 sg　　　　bottle-INST　　　wine　　pack
　　　　'I pour liguor into a bottle.'

3.7.6 比較を標示する形式

比較（comparative）を表す形式としては、〈-diomu〉「より〜だ（優勢比較）」及び〈-mazɨ〉「より〜だ（劣勢比較）」がある。

(3.118) ᶠno　　　　ᶠchi-diomu　　ᴿnga-khuru　　ᶠdiatrɨ
　　　　2 sg　　　　3 sg-COMP　　five-age　　　big
　　　　'You are five years older than him.'

(3.119) ᶠno   ᶠchi-diomu   ᶠnyichu-zɨ   ᶠdiodzɨ
       2 sg   3 sg-COMP   two inches   big
       'you are two cm taller than him.'

(3.120) ᶠti-po   ᶠchi-po-mazɨ   ᴴta
       this-tree   that-tree-COMP. NEG   tall
       'This tree is not as tall as that one.'

第4章　動詞形態論

　本章ではナムイ語の動詞にかかわる諸形式について扱う。
　まず触れておきたいことは、主語と述部との間に呼応の関係はない点である。また、ナムイ語ゾロ方言にはテンス（時制）・アスペクト（体）・ムード（相）は明示的に表示されるものではなく、文脈依存となっている。テンス（時制）通常時間を表す副詞や名詞によって表される相対的時制である。
　はじめに動詞複合形式を提示しておく。

　　　（否定辞）-本動詞-（助動詞）-（TAM 接辞）―（疑問接辞）

否定辞：'ma-', 'ta-' etc.
助動詞：= 'g'udzə', 'kərndzi' etc.
TAM 接辞：'dio', 'i', 'chi' etc.
疑問接辞：'-ya', '-madzi' etc.

4.1　動詞の分類

　ゾロ方言の動詞は、動詞がとりうる項の数に照らして、自動詞、他動詞、二重目的動詞、自他動詞に分類できる。自動・他動両方の用法で同じ形態をとり、行為者に関する違いのみが文中で起きる動詞もある。他動詞は使役構文を用いることにより、自動詞から形成することができる。他動詞は使役標示を付け加えることで、二重目的動詞にすることができる。
　さまざまな動詞の種類について論じるにあたり、ここでは自動詞の単一直接項［single direct argument］に［S］、他動詞の行為者に［A］、他

動詞の受動者に［P］を用いることにする。

4.1.1　自動詞

　自動詞は一つの中核項をとる。すなわち、主語を取るが直接目的語を取らない動詞である。ナムイ語ゾロ方言ではつねに、意味論的に、または統語論的に一つの項がある。

(4.1)　 ^{R}himi　　　　^{L}djudju
　　　　sun［S］　　　rise
　　　　'The sun rises.'

(4.2)　 ^{F}chi　　　　 ^{F}mja-lɨ　　　　　　^{F}goshishɨ
　　　　3 sg　　　　　eys［S］-LOC　　　 ache
　　　　'He has a pain in his eyes.'（lit. 'His eyes are aching'）

(4.3)　 ^{R}laku　　　　^{F}ũɨ dju
　　　　kid［S］　　　cry
　　　　'The kid cries.'

(4.4)　 ^{F}chi pər　　 ^{F}hi-nɨ
　　　　2 sg ERG　　 escape-PERF
　　　　'You escaped.'

(4.5)　 ^{R}shipo　　　^{F}diadji　　　　　 ^{R}chi-po
　　　　tree　　　　　big　　　　　　　　one-CL
　　　　'The tree is big.'

(4.6)　 ^{R}shipo　　　^{Fn}djulɛ　　　　　^{F}diadji-nɨ
　　　　tree　　　　　long　　　　　　　 big-PERF

'The tree became big.'

(4.7) ᴿbutsʰᵾ   ᴸsuta-nɨ
      cloth   tight-PERF
      'These clothes become tight.'

(4.8) ᴿnzu   ᴸatsᵾtsᵾ-nɨ
      river   small-PERF
      'A (The) river becomes small.'

(4.9) a. ᶠnga   ᶠlamo   (4.9) b. ᶠnga   ᶠlamo-ni
         1sg   old   1sg   old-PERF
         'I am old.'   'I grew up.'

畳語形式（reduplicated adjectives）は状態動詞を表し、名詞化標識 '-su' と共起する。

(4.10) ᶠno   ᴸjɛnjɛn   ᴿsu   ᴿhu   ja   ᴸpjapja   ᴿsu   ᴿhu
       2sg   round   NOM   need or   flat   NOM   need
       'Do you need the roundest one or the flattest one?'

(4.11) ᶠchi   ᴿjotsʰajotsha   ᶠsu   ᶠjɛhɛr
       3sg   light   NOM   carry on one's back
       'He carries the light one on his back......'

4.1.2 他動詞

他動詞は2つの項を取る。典型的な他動詞は意味的に行為の主体となる行為者と被行為者を必要とし、統語的には主語や目的語の意味役割に関して少なくとも2つの明示的な名詞項を要求するものである。

(4.12) a. ᶠnga   pər   ᶠchi¹   ᶠbo-nɨ
　　　　1 sg [A]　ERG　3 sg　beat-PERF
　　　　'I beat him.'

(4.12) b. ᶠtchi   pər   ᶠnga²   ᶠbo-nɨ
　　　　3 sg [A]　ERG　1 sg　beat-PERF
　　　　'He beats me.'

(4.13) ᶠchi   ᴿdjigi   ᶠchi-bu   ᶠso-nɨ
　　　3 sg [A]　book [P]　one-CL　read-PERF
　　　'S/He reads a book.'

ある特定の文脈では、文脈で判断できる場合他動詞の2項のうちの1項は明示的に標示されないこともある。

(4.14) a. ᶠnga   ᴿdja   (ᶠci dja)   ᶠdji-dj ɨ dj ɨ mu
　　　　1 sg [A]　food [P]　one-CL　eat-PROG
　　　　'I am eating a meal.'

(4.14) b. ᶠnga   (ᴿdja)   ᶠdji-dj ɨ dj ɨ mu
　　　　1 sg　food [P/φ]　eat-PROG
　　　　'I am eating.'

(4.15) ᴿci kər   ᶠhẽ-nɨ
　　　salt [P]　buy-PERF

1　この例文ではᶠchĩも現れた。
2　この例文ではᶠngāも現れた。

'Salt has been bought.'

(4.16)　ᴿikha　　　ᴸtu-nɨ
　　　　tea [P]　　pour
　　　'Tea has been made.'

(4.17) a.　(ꟳnga)　　　　ᴿci kɛr　　　ꟳhẽ-nɨ
　　　　　1 sg [A]　　　salt [P]　　buy-PERF
　　　　'I bought salt.'

(4.17) b.　ᴿchi kær　　　(ꟳnga)　　　ꟳhẽ-nɨ
　　　　　salt [TOP]　　1 sg [A]　　buy-PERF
　　　　'Salt, I bought.'

(4.18) a.　(ꟳnga)　　　　ᴿikʰa　　　ᴸtu-nɨ
　　　　　1 sg [A]　　　tea [P]　　pour-`ERF
　　　　'I have been made tea.'

(4.18) b.　ᴿikha　　　　(ꟳnga)　　　ᴸtu-nɨ
　　　　　tea [TOP]　　1 sg [A]　　pour-PERF
　　　　'Tea, I have been made.'

4.1.3　存在動詞

　存在構文及び所有構文は以下のように 6 種類の存在動詞のうち一つが節の末尾に現れる。

(4.19)　ꟳama　　　　ꟳyoko　　　ᴿndjo　　　(animate)
　　　　mother　　　home　　　exist
　　　'Mother is at home.'

(4.20) ᶠnga-ko   ᶠasha   ᴸdja?   (general)
       1 sg-GEN   where   exist
       'Where is my hat?'

(4.21) ᴴchi   ᴿmoga   ᴿdjɨkʉ   (inanimate)
       3 sg   power   exist
       'S/he has power.'

(4.22) ᴴluqha-qolo ᴿdrɨ   ᴸdjɨ   (liquid)
       bawl-LOC   water   exist
       'Water in the ball.'

(4.23) ᴴnga   ᴸgudji   ᴸci-ja   ᴸdjo   (possession)
       1 sg   younger.brother one-CL   exist
       'I have a younger brother.'

(4.24) ᴿrabi   ᴸdiamu   ᴿshipo   ᶠdiobʉ   ᴸndzje (plant)
       Mountain top.LOC   tree   many   exist
       'On the top of this hill there are a lot of trees.'

4.1.4 二重他動詞

二重他動詞は項を3つ取る動詞を指す。ナムイ語ゾロ方言にいては、二重他動詞の間接項はつねに与格や処格標示が付加される。

(4.25) a. ᶠnga   ᴸdjigi   ᴿci-pu   ᶠchi-mi   ᴸko-nɨ   [unmarked]
          1 sg   book   one-CL   3 sg-DAT give-PERF
          'I gave him a book.'

(4.26) b. ᶠchi   ᶠnga-pər   ᴸdjigi   ᴿci-pu   ᴸko-nɨ
           3 sg   1 sg-ERG   book   one-CL   give-PERF
           'I gave him a book.'

(4.27) c. ᴸdjigi   ᴿtʃi-pu ja   ᶠchi-mi   ᶠnga-pər   ᶠchi-mi ᴸko-nɨ
           book   one-CL TOP   3 sg-DAT   1 sg-ERG   give-PERF
           'I gave him a book.'

4.1.5 自他同形動詞

ナムイ語ゾロ方言では、いくつかの動詞は自動詞・他動詞で全く同じ形式で現れる。

(4.28) a. ᴸkær pər-nɨ
          break-PERF
          'It has broken.'

(4.29) b. ᶠnga   pər   ᶠchi   ᴸkær pər-nɨ
          1 sg   ERG   it   break-PERF
          'I broke (it).'

(4.30) a. ᴿbʉtsʰʉ   ᴸGafu-nɨ
          cloth   dry
          'The clothing is dry.'

(4.30) b. ᴿchi-pər   ᴿbʉtsʰʉ   ᴸGafu-nɨ
          3 sg-ERG   cloth   dry
          'He brought the clothing dry.'

4.2 結合価

4.2.1 結合価を増加させるデバイス

(4.31) a. ^Fnga　　^Rci kær　^Fhɛ̃-nɨ　　　　　[transitive-two argument]
　　　　　 1 sg　　salt　　　buy-PERF
　　　　　 'I bought salt.'

(4.31) b. ^Rci kær　^Fnga-dia　　^Fhɛ̃-ji　　[causativized transitives]
　　　　　 salt [P]　1 sg-OBJ [A]　buy-CAUS
　　　　　 'I was cause to buy salt.'

(4.32) a. ^Fnga　^Rbɨtsʰɨ　^Rci-la　　^Rbulɛ　^Fchi　ko　　[ditransitive]
　　　　　 1 sg　 cloth　　one-CL　　send　　3 sg　give
　　　　　 'I will send him a piece of clothing'

(4.32) b. ^Fchi　^Fnga-dia　^Rbɨtsʰɨ　^Rci-la　　^Rbulɛ　^Fno ko-ji
　　　　　　　　　　　　　　　　　　　　　　　　　　　　　 [causativized transitives]
　　　　　 3 sg　1 sg-OBJ　clothing　one-CL　　send　　2 sg give-CAUS
　　　　　 'He let me send you a piece of clothing'

4.2.2 結合価を減少させるデバイス

(4.33) a. ^Fnga　　　　^Fchi　　　^Lzriga
　　　　　 1 sg [A]　　3 sg [P]　love
　　　　　 'I love her.'

(4.33) b. ^Fnga-χo　　　^Ldridri ga
　　　　　 1 sg-pl. [S]　love

'We love each other.'

(4.34) a.　 ^{F}chi　　 ^{F}diadji　su　　　　 ^{Fchi} ^{L}atsɯtsɯ　su　　　　 ^{L}thie
　　　　　 DEF　big　　NOM[A]　　DEF　small　　NOM[P]　　bite
　　　　 'The big one bites the small one.'

(4.34) b.　 ^{F}chi-niku　　　　 ^{L}thiethie-djo
　　　　　 3sg-DUAL[S]　bite-EXIST
　　　　 'The two dogs bite each other.'

4.3　形容詞（状態叙述自動詞）

　形容詞は動詞の一種である。なぜならば、コピュラを用いなくても、それらは述語になれるからである。また、形容詞が述語として用いられるとき、それらは非状態動詞と同じ動詞形態をとるからである。

(4.35)　 ^{H}pho　　　　 ^{R}bzi
　　　　 tree[S]　　big
　　　　 '(The) tree is big.'

(4.36)　 ^{H}pho　　　　bzi-nɨ
　　　　 tree[S]　　big-CSM
　　　　 'The trees became big.'

　形容詞は述語として機能するとき、(4.37)と(4.38)にあるように、他動詞と同じ人称標示形態をとることができる。

(4.37) a.　 ^{H}nga　　 ^{R}bzi　　　　　b.　 ^{H}nga　　 ^{R}bzi-nɨ
　　　　　 1sg　　　big　　　　　　　　　　 1sg　　　big-CSM

115

     'I am old.'   'I grew up.'

(4.38) a. ᴴno   ᴿbzi   b. ᴴno   ᴿbzi-nɨ
     2 g   big   2 sg   big-CSM
     'You are old.'   'You grew up.'

 形容詞は、述語として使用されるのに加えて、名詞の主部のあとに付いて、その名詞を修飾する。形容詞が名詞の述語または修飾語であるとき、それらは程度の副詞をとることができる。以下は、形容詞を修飾する程度の副詞とともに、述語または修飾語として用いられている形容詞の例である。

(4.39) a. ᴴpho   ᴿbzi   ci-lu   (modifier)
      tree   big   one-CL
      '(a) big tree'

    b. ᴴpho   (ti-pho)   ᴿbzi   (predicate)
      tree   this-CL   big
      '(This) tree is big.'

(4.40) a. ᴿmetho   ᴴsem   (ci-lu)   (modifier)
      flower   red   one-CL
      '(a) red flower'

    b. ᴿmetho   (ti-lu)   ᴴsem   (predicate)
      flower   this-CL   red
      '(This) flower is red.'

4.4 繋辞（コピュラ）

ナムイ語ゾロ方言には 'ᴿndji' という形式の繋辞（コピュラ）が存在する。繋辞（コピュラ）'ᴿndji' は同定構文、等位構文、限定構文、疑似分裂構文に使われる。また、名詞化動詞のあとにもくることも可能である。多くの場合、連結詞補文または疑似分裂構文のなかの節が不定標識 '-ci' をもつとき、繋辞（コピュラ）は省略される。

(4.41) ᴴti-lu　　　ᴿbʉtsʉ　　Fɲɛ　　　ᴿndji
　　　 this-CL　　 clothing　 1sg：GEN　COP
　　　 'This item of clothing is mine.'

(4.42) ꟳchi-Xo　　　ᴿshathi　　ᴸna-piepie-ci　（ᴿndji）
　　　 that-PL　　　table　　　black-REDUP-INDEF　COP
　　　 'Those tables are very black ones.'

(4.43) ᴴnga　［ᴸmo　 ᴴtsɛ-ni　 ᴿlo-ni-ci］　　　（ᴿndji）
　　　 1sg　 horse　 ride-ADV　come-CSM-INDEF　COP
　　　 'It is on horse that I came here.'

しかしながら、以下の (4.62) のように名詞化標識を用いるとコピュラの使用が義務的となる。

(4.44) ᴴnga　［ᴸmo　 ᴴtsɛ-ni　 ᴿlo-ni-ci］　　　　　　su　　　ᴿndji
　　　 1sg　 horse　 ride-ADV　come-CSM：1-INDEF　 NOM　　COP
　　　 'It is on horse that I came here.'

ナムイ語ゾロ方言には多くの種類の動詞複合体の形態がある。たとえ

ば、人称標識、方向／方位標識、相標識、否定標識、禁止標識、許可標識、証拠標識、使役標識、相互標識、法標識がある。

多くのチベット‐ビルマ語派の言語同様、動詞に再帰動詞の標識はない。また、再帰的な意味を本来備えている動詞はない。再帰代名詞は再帰／強調の意味を表現するために用いられ、項として機能する。態の区別はない。

4.5 人称標示

ナムイ語ゾロ方言には人称標示は存在しない。

(4.45)　 ᴸnga　　　　　ᴴchu　　　　　　ᴿdzɨ
　　　　 1sg　　　　　 meal　　　　　　eat
　　　　 'I am eating.'

(4.46)　 ᴸngaXo　　　　ᴴchu　　　　　　ᴿdzɨ
　　　　 1pl　　　　　 meal　　　　　　eat
　　　　 'We two are eating.'

(4.47)　 ᴴno　　　　　 tshu　　　　　　 ᴿdzɨ
　　　　 2 sg　　　　　meal　　　　　　 eat-2
　　　　 'You are eating.'

(4.48)　 ᴸnga　　　　　ᴸmu　　　　　　 ᴸdjumu
　　　　 1 sg　　　　　thing　　　　　　do
　　　　 'I will work.'

(4.49)　 ᴴno　　　　　 ᴸmu　　　　　　 ᴸdju-ma　　　ya?
　　　　 2 sg　　　　　thing　　　　　　do-NEG　　　 Q

'Will you work?'

(4.50) ᴸchi　　　ᴸmu　　　ᴸdjumu　　　ᶠgu-djə
　　　 3sg　　　thing　　 do　　　　　need
　　　 'S/he will work.'

(4.51) ᴸnga　　　ᴸmu　　　ᴸdju-nɨ
　　　 1sg　　　work　　　do-PERF
　　　 'I worked.'

(4.52) ᴸchi　　　ᴿdziko-nɨ
　　　 3sg　　　eat-PERF
　　　 'S/he has eaten.'

4.6　方位／方向標示

　ゾロ方言では、話し手からみた動作の方向を標示する3つの接頭辞がある。接頭辞 'luo-' は「上向きの方向へ」、'mi-' は「下向きの方向へ」、'khyi-' は「前向きの方向へ」をそれぞれ意味する。

　以下は動詞に付加される方向接辞の例である。

方向接辞	例	意味
luo	luo-bu	上方へ行く
mi	mi-bu	下方へ行く
khyi	khyi-bu	前方へ行く

方向接辞	例	意味
luo	luo-dju	上方へ来る
mi	mi-dju	下方へ来る

| khyi | khyi-dju | 前方へ来る |

　方向性を本来備えていない動詞は通常、方向接頭辞をとらない。老年層話者の発話では以上の形態をとるが、大部分の話者では以上の方向接辞は失われてしまっている。形容詞や感情動詞、情緒動詞、思考動詞、発話動詞、感覚動詞などの動詞は一つだけ接頭辞をとったと推定されるが、現代ナムイ語では用いられない。

(4.53)　^{H}kɛ-diomu　　^{R}njo
　　　　bed-on　　　　sleep
　　　　'to get into bed'

方向接辞をとる動詞の他の例としては以下のものがある。

(4.54)　a．ze-^{F}chɨ
　　　　　DIR-return
　　　　　'to return (money), pay back'

(4.54)　b．xe-nju
　　　　　DIR-forget
　　　　　'to forget'

4.7　アスペクト標示

　アスペクト標示には9つの異なる種類がある。これらのうち、完了相、状態変化相、継続相は接尾辞を伴う接頭辞によって標示される。一方、前望相、起動相、状態変化相、繰り返し相は接尾辞によって標示され、反復相は動詞の畳語化により標示される。これらの接頭辞の一つを単純に用いる以外に、特定の意味を持たせるために、これらのさまざまな種

類の標示を興味深く組み合わせることもある。

4.7.1 前望相（prospective aspect）

ナムイ語ゾロ方言では、前望相は、一人称、二人称の行為者の場合は、人称標識と組み合わせて前望標識 'ᴴkumu'（「～をするところである／まさに～しかかっている」）により表現される。母型動詞 'da-vaze'（「開始する」）はまた、(287) および (288) のように、任意で前望相の前に付け加えられる。

(4.55) ᴸŋa ᴴkumu ᴸdja ᴸshishi gədjə
　　　 1 sg PROS　　meal　　do　　need
　　　 'I am about to cook.'

(4.56) ᴸchi ᴴkumu ᴸdja ᴸshishi gədjə
　　　 3 sg PROS　　meal　　do　　need
　　　 'S/he is about to cook.'

(4.57) 及び (4.58) のように、前望標識 'ᴴkumu' を状態変化標識 '-ni' とともに用いて、前望相を標示することも可能である。

(4.57) ᴴkumu ᶠshulu ᴿzrabu-nɨ
　　　 PROS　 wheat　 harvest-CSM
　　　 'The wheat should be about to be harvested.'

(4.58) tʰsi ᴴkumu ᴿdja ᴿdzɨ-nɨ
　　　 3 sg PROS　 meal　 eat-CSM
　　　 'S/he is about to eat.'

4.7.2 起動相 (inchoative aspect)

起動相は行為または出来事がまさに始まったことを標示する。ナムイ語ゾロ方言では通常、(4.59)～(4.60)のように、起動相は、動詞に'-dio'(「開始する」)が後続して標示される。

(4.59) ᴴhĩ   ᴿdʒu-dio
       rain   fall-start
       'It has begun to rain.'

(4.60) ᴴŋa   ᴸdjigi   ᴴso-dio
       1sg   book   read-start
       'I have begun to read.'

(4.61) ᴴŋa   ᴸdʲashishi   ᴿdju-dio
       lse:TP   cook   do-start
       'I have started to cook.'

4.7.3 状態変化相 (CSM of state)

状態変化相は最近の状態や状況の変化を表現する。この相は以下の例のように、動詞に状態変化標識'-i'を付加して標示される。

(4.62) ᴿchoXo   ᴴnga-mako   ᴿhanini   ᶠndzugu   ma-ndzi-i
       3pl   1sg-DAT   few days   food   NEG-eat-CSM
       'They made me not eat for a few days.'

(4.63) ᴸtani-dia   ᶠashacini-i
       today-TOP   which day-CSM
       'What day is it today?'

(4.64) ᶠtidzrɨka   bɯtshɯ   ᴸchi-lasu   ᴸkɛrpəy-ɨ
      leather   wear   one-CL   break-CSM
      'The leather became worn out.'

(4.65) ᴴmu   ᴴhi   ᴸndzu-ɨ
      sky   rain   fall-CSM
      'It has started to rain.'

(4.66) ᴿlakɯ   ᶠgundju-ɨ
      child   cry-CSM
      'The child cried.'

4.7.4 継続相（continuative aspect）

　継続相は、過去または現在または未来の時間枠で進行中に行為に言及する。ゾロ方言では、文末助詞'-sei'がこの意味に用いられる。以下の例を確認したところ、その行為は中断を伴わないという含意があるようである。

(4.67) ᴴnga   ᴿdjigi   ᴸci-bu   ᴸso-sei
      1 sg   book   one-CL   read-CONT
      'We are reading a book"

(4.68) ᴴchi   ᴴdzu-sei
      3 sg   eat-CONT
      'S/he is still eating.'

　文末助詞'-sei'は未来の時間枠で用いられる場合、継続的に進行しているか、または、中断したかもしれないが、あとでもう一度継続する予定の行為に言及する。以下はこの意味を表す例である。

(4.69) ᴴchiXo   ᴴdzu-cu-sei
      3 pl   eat-want-CONT
      'They will still want to eat.'

(4.70) ᴴchiXo   ᴸso-cu-sei
      3 pl   read-want-CONT
      'They will still want to read a book.'

(4.71) ᴿcithuci,   ᴴdzu-cu-sei
      one time   eat-want-CONT
      'For a while, s/he will still eat

母語話者によると継続標識 '-sei' と関係があるというは '-e' は '動詞-e-動詞' の形式で、「同時に何かをしている」場合に、同時に起きている行為を表現するために用いることが可能である。

(4.72) ᴴchi   ᴸⁿdzɨ-e-ⁿdzɨ,   ᴸso-e-so
      3 sg   eat-CONT-eat,   read-CONT-read
      'S/he eats while reading a book.'

(4.73) ᴴchi   ᴸlu-e-lu,   ᴸzrɨ-e-zrɨ
      3 sg   look-CONT-look,   smile-CONT-smile
      'S/he smiled while reading (it).'

継続標識は追加の意味を表現するために、助数詞句とともに現れることがある。

(4.74) ᴴnika   ᴸzrɨ
      a-little   eat

'Eat some more!'

4.7.5 完了相 (perfective aspect)

完了は動詞 'shica'（「完成する」）を本動詞として、または、この動詞のあとに状態変化接尾辞 'nɨ' と共起させて表現される。

(4.75) ᴸchi　　　ᴸchinɨi-ko　　ᴸmu　　　ᴸdzu-shica-nɨ
　　　 3 sg　　 that day-GEN　　thing do-finish-become
　　　 'S/he finished that day's work.'

(4.76) ᴴngoXo-ko　　ᴸndzuu　　 ᶠndzɨ-shica-nɨ
　　　 1 pl-GEN　　 food　　　 eat-finish-become
　　　 '(We) have run out of food.'

(4.77) ᴴnga　　　 ᶠtitʰusɨni　　ᶠndzɨ-nɨ
　　　 1sg　　　 just　　　　 eat-become
　　　 'I have just eaten.'

ナムイ語ゾロ方言では接尾辞 '-chi' を伴うことによって経験の意味を表現することもできる。

(4.78) ᴴno　　　 ᴿcəngtu　　 ᴸto-chi
　　　 2 sg　　　Chengdu　　go-CSM
　　　 'You have been to Chengdu.'

(4.79) ᴴci　　　 ᶠmu-shi　　 ᴸdzɨ-chi
　　　 3 sg　　 horse-meat　 eat-CSM
　　　 'S/he has eaten horse meat.'

(4.80) ᴴno　　　ᶠtcoŋko　　ᴸto-a-chi
　　　 2 sg　　 China　　　go-Q-CSM
　　　 'Have you ever been to China?'

ナムイ語ゾロ方言における完了相は、以下のように、本動詞 'ᴸshoko³'
(「完了する」) により標識されることもある。動詞 'ᴸshoko' はまた本
動詞としても用いられる。

(4.81) ᴸchi　　　ᴸchinɨi-ko　ᴸmu　　　ᴸdzu-shoko-nɨ
　　　 3 sg　　　that-day　　thing　　 do-finish-become
　　　 'S/he finished that day's work.'

(4.82) ᴴngoXo-ko　　ᴸndzuu　　　ᶠndzɨ-shoko-nɨ
　　　 1 pl-GEN　　 food　　　　eat-finish-become
　　　 '(We) have run out of food.'

(4.83) ᴴnga　　　　ᶠtitʰusɨni　　ᶠndzɨ-shoko-nɨ
　　　 1sg　　　　just　　　　　eat-finish-become
　　　 'I have just eaten.'

4.7.6　繰り返し (repetition)

繰り返しはある行為を「ふたたび」することを意味する。この形式は、
文末接辞 '-səu' によって表現される。これは状態変化標識とともに用
いることができる。

(4.84) ᴴhĩ　　　　ᴿdju-səu
　　　 rain　　　 fall-again

3　南西部標準漢語である西南官話からの借用語であると思われる。

'It is raining again.'

(4.85) ᴸvie   ᴿdʒu-səu
       snow   fall-again
       'It is snowing again.'

(4.86) ᴴnga   ᴿdʒigi   ᴸlu-səu-ɨ
       1sg   book   look-again
       'I have begun to read again.'

(4.87) ᴴno   ᴿcəngtu   ᴸbərsəu-ya
       2 pl   Chengdu   go-again-Q
       'Did you go to Chengdu again?'

4.7.7　未完了相（imperfective）

　非標示の相形式は、進行中の動作、また、習慣的な動作を含め、未完了動作を表す用法は、「しばしば／たいてい／いつ何かをする」、または「何かをすることに慣れている」という意味をコード化する。ゾロ方言では文末に'-to'を付加して習慣的な意味を表現する。

(4.88) ᴴnga   ᴿdʒigi   ᴸlu-to
       1sg   book   look-usually
       'I usually read books.'

(4.89) ᴸchi   ᴴGoa   ᴸvu   ᴸdzi-to
       3 sg   before   wine   drink-usually
       'S/he used to drink wine（but now s/he does not drink much/doesn't drink anɨ more).'

(4.90) ᶠapo   ᴿguji   ᴸmbo-to
      elder. brother younger. brother   hit
      'The elder brother often hits the younger brother.'

4.7.8 反復相（iterative）

　反復相は相互行為よりもむしろ、行為の反復をもともと含む行為を表現する。ナムイ語ゾロ方言では、この相は畳語動詞＋'so'と'pər'により表現される。以下はその例である。

(4.91) ᴸkoto-lotsʰɯ-pəˈ
      hide-seek-REDUP-do
      'to play hide and seek'

(4.92) ᴸshishi-so
      wash-REDUP-do
      'to be glooming'

(4.93) dzɪdzɪ-so 'to train'
      train-REDUP-do
      'to train'

4.8　否定標示

　否定標示は句内のいずれかの動詞が否定されているかにより、動詞の前に、またはのように本動詞の前に付け加えられて、否定句を形成する。否定接辞は直後に後続する動詞のみに影響を及ぼす。

(4.94) ᴴama   ᴸyɛgaga,   ᴸloci-ma-ku
      mother   asleep   get. up-NEG-can

'(My) mother is asleep and won't get up.'

否定の接頭辞 'ma-' は未完了節と完了節の両方に用いられる。未完了形は「動詞＋ma+ya 'する'」、完了形は「ma＋動詞」の形式で表される。

(4.95) ᴴnga   ᴸndzɨ-ma-ya
       1 sg   eat-NEG-do
       'I do not eat.'

(4.96) ᴴnga   ma-ᴸndzɨ
       1 sg   NEG-do
       'I did not eat.'/'I have not eaten.'

(4.97) ᴴno   ᴸbandzɨ   ᴴnga   ᴸko   ma-ya
       2 sg   money   1 sg   give   NEG-do
       'You do not give me money.'

(4.98) ᴴno   ᴸbandzɨ   ᴴnga   ma-ko
       2 sg   money   1 sg   NEG-give
       'You did not give me money.'

否定接頭辞 'ma' とは別に、禁止（否定命令接頭辞）'ta' もまた、否定の意味を表す。

4.9 モダリティ

モダリティは節の義務的または認識的なものがある。義務的モダリティには、義務（〜をすべきである、〜する義務がある、〜をしなくて

はならない)、能力 (〜できる)、必要性 (〜をする必要がある)、許容 (〜してよい) が含まれる。認識的モダリティには確率と可能性が含まれる。ナムイ語ゾロ方言には、本動詞 (英語と漢語においては法的助動詞と並列) や副詞、助詞の使用により獲得される数多くのモダリティ的意味と用法がある。

4.9.1 義務的モダリティ

4.9.1.1 義務

接尾辞 '-g'udzə' 義務を表すモダリティ要素である。

(4.99)　^{H}nga　　　^{R}tani　　　^{H}nzrɨ　　　^{L}Ga-g'udzə
　　　　1 sg　　　today　　　fish　　　grasp-must
　　　'I must catch a fish today.'

(4.100)　^{L}chi　　　^{R}tani　　　^{R}bu-g'udzə
　　　　3 sg　　　today　　　go-must
　　　'Today s/he must go.'

(4.101)　^{H}no　　　^{F}ti-djoga-ci　　　^{H}ca-g'udzə
　　　　2 sg　　　this-thing-CL　　　finish-must
　　　'You must finish this thing.'

二重否定の形式をとり強い義務を表すこともできる。

(4.102)　^{R}tani　　　　^{R}ɨ-ma-ca-ma-Xa
　　　　today　　　　house-NEG-clean-NEG-do
　　　'Today I have to cleanup the house.'

動詞 'kərndzi' (「〜すべきである」) は比較的弱い義務を標示する。

(4.103) ᴸchi   ᴿtani   ᴴngolu   ᴿbu-kərndzɨ
       3 sg   today   clinic   go-should
       'S/he should go to see a doctor.'

(4.104) ᴴno-yoyo   ᴸgudjɨ--kərndzɨ
        2 sg-self   take care-should
        'You should take care of yourself.'

(4.105) ᴴno   ᴸnimiatsumu   ᴸti-kərndzɨ
        2 sg   carefully   do-should
        'You should do the thing carefully.'

 '-gədzə' は英語の 'need' のような義務的モダリティを表現することがある。

(4.106) ᴿchoXo-kolo   ᴸso-ku   ᴿbu-gədzə
        3 pl-LOC   three-CL   go-need
        'Among them three persons need to go.'

4.9.1.2　許可

'na'（「〜してもよい、〜できる」）は、何かをする許可を表現するために用いられる。疑問文では 'a-ha' という形式が用いられる。

(4.107) ᴴnga   ᴸti-lu   ᴸdzɨ-aha
        1 sg   this-CL   eat-may （Q）
        'May I eat this?'

(4.108) ᶠnoXo   ᴿbu-na
        2 pl   go-may

'You are allowed to go.'/'You may go.'

4.9.1.3 能力

能力は、自然の(身体的な)能力または習得された能力を表現する'mba'(「できる(may, can)」)、または習得された能力を示す'ku'(「できる」)によって表現される。

(4.109) ^Fti-mu-ci-pha ^Lkanaci ^Hku-mba
 this-horse-CL-CL fast run-can
 'This horse can run fast.'

(4.110) ^Hno ^Rndjigi ^Ldzrɨ a-ku
 2 sg letter write Q-can
 'Can you write?'

(4.111) ^RcoXo ^Rndjigi ^Ldzrɨ-ku
 3 pl letter write-can
 'They can write.'

4.9.2 認識論的モダリティ

認識論的モダリティには確率と可能性が含まれる。ナムイ語ゾロ方言には可能性のモダリティがある。この形式はどのような相接尾辞と人称標示にも後続する助詞 'kər' によって表現される。

(4.112) ^Hno ^Fva-ndjigi ^Ldzrɨ-kər
 2 sg Han letter wrie-probably
 'You probably write Chinese characters.'

(4.113) ^Hci ^Fva-ndjigi ^Ldzrɨ-ku-kər

第4章　動詞形態論

```
         3 sg       Han letter      write-can-probably
         'S/he probably write Chinese characters well.'
```

(4.14)　ᴿcəngtu o　　ᴿbu-kər
　　　　 Chengdu　　go-probably
　　　　 'They probably went to Chengdu.'

4.10　結合価変化の手段（valency changing devices）

　ナムイ語ゾロ方言の動詞は概して、自動詞か他動詞かがはっきりしているが、両方の働きをする動詞もいくつかある。動詞の結合価を変える手段は2つしかない。一つは使役接尾辞の使用による結合価の増加、もう一つは相互行為を標示するために他動詞を重複させて結合価を減らすことである。動詞の結合価を減らすための受動態構文または再帰態／中間態はない。また、受動者項を付け加える機能を有する適用構文も存在しない。

4.10.1　結合価の増加

　'-ndo' は自動詞と他動詞の前に付け加えられて使役形を形成する。それにより、これらの結合価が変化して、それぞれ他動詞と二重目的語動詞になる。

Intransitive :

(4.115)　ᴿbɯtsɯ　　　ᴿgafu
　　　　 clothes　　　 dry
　　　　 'The clothes have dried.'

Causativized intransitive :

(4.116)　ᴴci-pər　　　ᴿbɯtsɯ　　　ᴿgafu-ni

  3 sg-AGT clothes dry-become

  'S/he caused the clothes to dry.'

(4. 117) ^FngachoXo-pər ndo-bu

    1sg : TP   CAUS-go

    '(They) will have me go.'

Transitive :

(4. 118) ^Hnga ^Lchi ^Lhɛ-nɨ

    1 sg salt buy-PERF

    'I bought salt.'

Causativized transitive :

(4. 119) ^Lchi ndo-^Lbaho-nɨ

    salt CAUS-buy-PERF

    'Salt was bought.'/'Someone had salt bought.'

(4. 120) ^Hnga-pər ^Lchi ndo-^Lbaho-nɨ

    1 sg-AGT CAUS-buy-PERF

    'I caused salt to be bought.'

4.10.2　結合価の減少

 自動詞は、動詞を重複させて相互語を作ることにより形成される。これにより、動詞の項の数が減る。以下はその例である。

Transitive Intransitive

^Lnɨa 'lick' > nene 'lick each other'

^Lbo 'beat' > ^Lbobo 'beat each other'

^Fdzə 'connect' > ^Fdzə dzə 'mutually connect'

(4.155)　ᶠapo　　　　　　ᴿnimomo　　　　　ᴿitʰa　(transitive)
　　　　 elder. brother　 younger. sister　scold
　　　　 'The elder brother is scolding the younger sister.'

(4.156)　ᶠapo　　　　　　ᴿnimomo　　　　　ᴿitʰa-itʰa　(intransitive)
　　　　 elder. brother　 younger. sister　scold-REDUP
　　　　 'The elder brother and the younger sister are quarreling.'

　ナムイ語ゾロ方言では、相互構文において畳語動詞を用いない場合は、副詞 'ᴸnonga' とともに生起し、「何かを相互的なことをすること」を標識する。

(4.157)　ᶠchini-ku　　　ᴸnonga　　ᴸdziga
　　　　 3 pl　　　　　 mutually　love
　　　　 'They two love each other.'

(4.158)　ᶠchini-ku　　　ᴸdziga-dziga
　　　　 3 pl　　　　　 love-REDUP
　　　　 'They two love each other.'

(4.159)　ᶠchi-niku　　　ᴸnonga　　ᶠŋamu
　　　　 3 sg-two　　　 mutually　help
　　　　 'Both of them help each other.'

　このようにして、相互語は標示され、他動詞は自動詞に変化する。また、(4.81) のように、もともと相互的な意味を有する動詞もいくつかある。

(4.160)　ᶠchiXo　　　　ᴸmbondjo

          3 dl   fight each other
          'They two are fighting.'

4.11 法（ムード）

　法は発話により叙述された物事の状態に対する話し手の主観的態度を表現する文法的カテゴリーである。ナムイ語ゾロ方言には、平叙、命令、禁止、疑問、感嘆、勧奨、許可、願望の法の標示がある。

4.11.1 平叙（直説）法

　ナムイ語ゾロ方言において平述（直説）法は無標の形式で現れる。用

(4.161) ᴴŋa   namuzɿ
        1 sg   Nàmùyì
        'I am a Nàmùyì.'

(4.162) ᶠapu   ᴸcinimuta   ᴸudzrimbo
        elder. brother   often   beat：3
        'The elder brother often beats (the younger brother).'

4.11.2 命令法

　動詞の命令形は文末助詞 'dia, -go' を付加するとにより形成される。この形式は聞き手が行為を行うよう命令されるときに用いられる。その話題はつねに二人称であるが、あからさまに表現されないことがある。

(4.163) ᴸndzudia
        eat-IMP
        'You eat!' (Polite)

(4.164) ᴸndzu-go
eat-IMP
'You eat!'（Polite）

(4.165) ᴸndzu
eat
'You eat!'（Impolite）

(4.166) ᴴno   ᴸndzu
2 sg   eat
'You eat!'（Impolite）

4.11.3 疑問法

　二人称の行為者または話題があり、動詞が未完了相をとる場合、助詞 'a-' が二人称標識のあとに付いて、極性疑問文を作る。

(4.167) ᴴno   ᴸndzɨgi   a-lu-sei
2 sg   book   Q-look-still
'Are you still reading?'

(4.168) FcoXo   ᴸndzɨgi   ᴸlu   a-chi
3 pl   book   look   Q-do
'Have they read the book?'

(4.169) ᴴno   a-ndzu
2 sg   Q-eat
'Have you eaten?'

　疑問疑問文では、答えの構成要素がどこに生起しようとも、その疑問

代名詞は元の位置に生起する。所謂 in-situ 型の言語である。

(4.170) ᴴti　　　ᴸndzigi　　ᴸci-busu　　ᶠashadja
　　　　this　　book　　　one-CL　　 where
　　　　'Where is the book?'

(4.171) ᴿchiXo　　ᶠhatabu　　　ᴸi
　　　　3 pl　　　what-time　　go
　　　　'When are they going to go?'

4.11.4 禁止法

　禁止（否定命令）は接頭辞 'ta-' を動詞の前に付け加えることで形成される。禁止は、話し手が聞き手にある行為をしないように要求することを表現する。

(4.172) ᶠtha-ndzu
　　　　PROH-eat
　　　　'Don't eat!'

(4.173) ᶠtha-gũndju!
　　　　PROH-cry
　　　　'Don't cry!'

(4.174) ᶠtha-mər
　　　　PROH-chase
　　　　'Don't chase (them)!'

(4.174) ᶠtha-gʉ
　　　　PROH-wear

'Don't wear (it)!'

(4.175) ᶠtha-hũ!
   PROH-go
   'Don't go!'

(4.176) ᶠtha-mərmər
   PROH-make. noise
   'Don't make noise!'

(4.177)のような2人称主語に二重否定が来るときは強い禁止の意を表す。

(4.177) ᴴno ma-dia-ma-ha!
   2 sg NEG-come-NEG-OK
   'Don't not come!'((You) must come!)

4.11.5 感嘆法 (exclamative)

ナムイ語ゾロ方言の感嘆文は、感嘆詞を(4.101)および(4.102)のように、文頭または文末で用いることにより形成される。

(4.178) ᴴndza-gəndzrə
   good-EXC
   'How pretty!'

(4.179) ᴸGoa-gəndzrə
   pity-EXC
   'Oh, so pitiful!'

4.11.6 勧奨法（hortative）

勧奨は行為が起こるべきであると願う、または提案するのに用いられる。この形式は以下のように、文末に 'shɨ' を動詞に付け加えることにより表現される。

(4.180) ^RngoXo　　^Lmindzu-shɨ
　　　　 lpl　　　　　sit. down-CSM
　　　　 'Let's sit down.'

(4.181) ^RngoXo　　^Lcomu　　^Lndzɨgi ^Llu-shɨ
　　　　 book　　　　together　look. at-CSM
　　　　 'Let's read a book.'

4.11.7 許可法（permissive）

この形式は、被使役者が一人称代名詞のとき、上記の勧奨法同様、文末に 'shɨ' を動詞に付け加えることにより表現される。

(4.182) ^Hno-ko　　^Rbi　　^RngoXo-mako　　djishɨ
　　　　 2 sg-GEN　pen　　1 pl-DAT　　　　use-CSM
　　　　 'Let us use your pen.'

(4.183) ^Hnga-mako　^Hno-ko　　^Lndzɨgi　^Llu-shɨ
　　　　 1 sg-DAT　　2 sg-GEN　book　　　look-CSM
　　　　 'Let me read your book.'

4.11.8 願望法（optative）

助動詞 '-shɨdzrɨ' は特定の行為を行う意志を表現する。

(4.184) ᴴnga　　ᴴi-ci-lu　　　ᴸshuhũ-shɨdzrɨ
　　　　1 sg　　house-one-CL　build-want
　　　　'I want to build a house.'

(4.185) ᴿngoXo　ᴸdzabi-diomu　ᴸbu-shɨdzrɨ
　　　　1 pl　　mountain-top　climb-want
　　　　'We want to go up the mountain.'

以下のようなフレーズを文頭において、希望を表現することも可能である。

(4.186) ᴸnimishɨdzrɨ-ushie,　ᴸshugu　　ᴴhimi　　ᴿdjudju
　　　　hope-case　　　　　tomorrow　sun　　　appear
　　　　'Hopefully, it will be sunnɨ tomorrow.'

第5章　その他の構造

本章では、前章までで扱ってこなかったその他の文構造について触れる。具体的には、構成素順序、疑問文、否定文、存在構文および所有構文、トピック＝コメント構文などである。

5.1　構成素順序

本節では、まず、名詞句の構造について論じ、その後、動詞複合体の構造について説明する。また、節の構成素順序についても論じる。

5.1.1　名詞句構文

ナムイ語ゾロ方言の名詞句の最小構文は単独の名詞である。名詞は1つ以上の修飾語をとることができる。普通名詞は常に固有名詞に先行し、特定名詞は総称名詞の前に生起し、代名詞の属格形は通常、それが修飾する名詞の前にくる。形容詞はそれだけで名詞を修飾するときはその名詞に続くが、形容詞＋その他の修飾語が名詞を修飾するときは、形容詞は通常、名詞に先行する。指示詞＋類別詞（DEM-CL）がそれだけで名詞を修飾するときは、その名詞に後続するか先行する。指示詞は通常、他の修飾語も同じ名詞を修飾するときは、その名詞に後続する。数詞は類別詞（NUM-CL）があとに来なくてはならず、それが修飾する名詞に続く。関係節は名詞句の主要部に先行または後続することが合は、数量類別詞を伴う指示詞はその名詞に後続しなくてはならない。

名詞句の主要部としての名詞の機能は別として、特定の文脈においては、指示類別句、助数詞句と、（不）定標識により名詞化された特定の動詞は、名詞句の主要部として用いることができる。ナムイ語ゾロ方言の名詞句の最大構造を図6に示した。

（属格）＋（Rel）＋（Adj）＋NOUN＋（DEM＋（NUM_CL）＋（IN)DEF）
図6　名詞句の構造

以下は、個々の要素の組み合わせとなりうるものの例である。

普通名詞は（5.1）のように、常に固有名詞に先行する。

(5.1)　普通名詞　　　固有名詞
^{L}apo　　　　　^{R}nonbu
elder. brother　Norbu（a person name）

固有名詞はまた、(5.2)のように、総称名詞の前に生起する。

(5.2)　特定名詞　　　総称名詞
^{L}dzolo　　　　^{L}tshue
Dzolo　　　　　village
'Dzolo'（villa 属格 ame）

属格は（5.3）のように、つねに名詞の前に現れる。

(5.3)　属格　　　　　名詞
^{F}nyε　　　　　^{L}butsʉ
1 sg：属格　　　clothing
'my clothing,

指示代名詞はつねに類別詞または助数詞をとり、それが名詞を修飾するときは、主に名詞のあとに生起する。しかし、名詞の前に他の修飾語がない場合は、指示類別句はまた（5.5）のように、それが修飾する名詞の前に生起することがある。

(5.4) 指示詞―類別詞　　名詞
　　　 ᴴti-lu　　　　　　 ᴸbutsʉ
　　　 this-CL　　　　　 clothing
　　　 'this clothing'

(5.5) 名詞　　　指示詞―類別詞
　　　 ᴸbutsʉ　　 ᴴti-lu
　　　 clothing　 this-CL
　　　 'this clothing'

形容詞は通常、単独で名詞を修飾するときは、名詞のあとに現れる。

(5.6) 名詞　　　形容詞
　　　 ᴴhadzɨ　　ᴴdiasɛdiasɛ
　　　 river　　 long-REDUP
　　　 'long river'

助数詞句はつねに、(5.7)のように、名詞句の主要部のあとに現れる。

(5.7) 名詞　　　数量詞―類別詞
　　　 ᴸbutsʉ　　ᴸso-la
　　　 clothes　 three-CL
　　　 'three pieces of clothing'

名詞が属格相当句と指示詞＋類別詞句（助数詞句）により修飾された場合、その属格相当句は名詞に先行し、一方、もう一つの修飾語句は名詞に後続する。

(5.8) 属格　　　　　N　　　　　DEM-CL

	ᴴnga	ᴸbutsʉ	ᴸso-la
	1sg：属格	clothing	that-CL

'that clothing of mine'

(5.9)

	属格	N	DEM	NUM-CL
	ᴴnga	ᴸbutsʉ	ᴴti	ᴸso-la
	1sg：属格	clothing	that	three-CL

'those three pieces of my clothing'

　名詞が指示詞＋助数詞句と関係節、形容詞により修飾された場合、形容詞と関係節は名詞の前に現れるが、指示詞＋助数詞句は名詞のあとに現れる。

(5.10) Rel＋Adj＋N＋DEM＋NUM－CL

ᴸnha	ᶠzɪni	ᴸhɛr su	ᶠhiju	ᴸbutsʉ	ᴴti	ᴸso-la
1sg：TP	yesterday	buy NOM	blue	clothing	that	three-CL

'those three pieces of blue clothing that I bought yesterday'

5.1.2　動詞複合体構文

　最小の動詞複合体は無標の動詞である。動詞は最高4つまで接頭辞―禁止接頭辞、方向接頭辞、否定接頭辞、継続接頭辞―をとることができる。禁止接頭辞があれば、それはつねに方向接頭辞および／または否定接頭辞の前に現れる。方向接頭辞があるときは、継続接頭辞と否定接頭辞がともに動詞に先行し、否定接頭辞は方向接頭辞に後続し、継続接頭辞は否定接頭辞に後続する。助動詞および「来る」／「行く」のような方向動詞はつねに本動詞に後続する。前望標示が節にあるときは、助動詞の有無にかかわらず、それは本動詞に生起する。証拠標識があるとき、それは動詞複合体の最後の要素に生起する。

　使役接尾辞と繰り返し接尾辞、状態変化接尾辞、証拠接尾辞が一緒に

動詞に後続するとき、使役接尾辞は動詞の直後に続き、繰り返し接尾辞は使役接尾辞に続き、また状態変化接尾辞に先行する。

以下は個々の要素でできる組み合わせの例である。以下に、ナムイ語ゾロ方言に現れる動詞文の様々な例を見ていく。

(5.11)　^Hchi　　　^Lhashɨ　　　^Fma-lodju.
　　　　3 sg　　　 still　　　　NEG-come in
　　　　'S/he still has not come in.'

証拠性（evidentiality）のような以下の構文も散見される。ナムイ語ゾロ方言では証拠性は義務的標示ではない。

(5.12)　^Hno　^Lthso　^Lmako　^Hvu　^Lndzishɨ　^Lcu（Hearsay）
　　　　2 sg　 man　 some　 wine　 drink　　　HEARS
　　　　'You are going to have (someone) drink.' (I heard)

(5.13)　^Hno　^Lthso　^Lmako　^Hvu　^Lndzishɨ　^Lwo
　　　　2 sg　 man　 some　 wine　 drink　　　HEARS
　　　　'You are going to have (someone) drink again.' (I heard)

(5.14)　^Hno　^Lthso　^Lmako　^Hvu　^Lndzishɨ　^Lya
　　　　2 sg　 man　 some　 wine　 drink　　　HEARS
　　　　'You had (someone) drink.' (I heard)

(5.15)　^Hno　^Lthso　^Lmako　^Hvu　^Lndzishɨ　^Lyɛ
　　　　2 sg　 man　 some　 wine　 drink　　　HEARS
　　　　'You had (someone) drink.' (I heard)

(5.16)　^Hno　^Lthso　^Lmako　^Hvu　^Lndzishɨ　φ

| | 2 sg | man | some | wine | drink | guess |

'You had (someone) drink.' (I guess)

(5.17) ᴴno ᴸthso ᴸmako ᴴvu ᴸndzɨshɨ ᴸndohɛ
2 sg man some wine drink VISUAL
'You had (someone) drink.' (I saw)

(5.18) ᴴno ᴸthso ᴸmako ᴴvu ᴸndzɨshɨ ᶠsuya
2 sg man some wine drink again
'You had (someone) drink again.' (I heard)

5.1.3 節の構成素順序

上記で名詞句と動詞複合体の構造を示した。我々は、ナムイ語ゾロ方言の節の構成要素の順序を、名詞句構造と動詞複合体構造の観点から見ることができる。ナムイ語ゾロ方言における節の構成素の標準的な順序は Figure 8 にあるとおりである。

(ⅰ) Noun phrase + Verb complex　　　　　　　　(Intransitive clause)
(ⅱ) Noun phrase 1 + Noun phrase 2 + Verb complex　(Transitive clause)
Figure 8. The canonical constituent order of the clause

自動詞節は名詞句＋動詞複合体で構成されているが、他動詞節は2つの名詞句＋動詞複合体から成る。これは基本的な節の構造で、他の要素もまた可能である。

5.2 疑問文

ナムイ語ゾロ方言には3種類の疑問文がある。たとえば、極性疑問文、代替疑問文、疑問詞疑問文である。極性疑問文については7.2.1で、代

第5章　その他の構造

替疑問文は7.2.2、疑問詞疑問文については7.2.3で論じている。

5.2.1　極性疑問文

極性疑問文とは、情報を懇願したり、ものや行為を要求したりし、それに対する返事が「イエス」か「ノー」である疑問節をいう。ナムイ語ゾロ方言は、文の終助詞'-ya'を使って上昇声調で、または、助詞'-madzi'を使って下降声調で、この種の疑問をコード化する

(5.19) ᴴno　　ᴿndzigi　　alu　　sei　　（Y）ŋalusei（N）malu
　　　 2 sg　book　　　look　 still
　　　 'Are you still reading?'

(5.20) ᴴno　　　　ᴸto-a-chi
　　　 2 sg　　　 go-QUES-EXPERIENCE
　　　 'Have you been there?'

　　　（Y）ᴿtochi　　（N）ᴿto-machi
　　　 'Yes, I have.' 'No, I haven't.'

(5.21) ᴴchi　　　ᴴno-a-sʉ
　　　 3 sg　　 2 sg-QUES-know
　　　 'Does s/he know you?'

　　　 ᴸma-dzi
　　　 NEG-COP
　　　 'No, she doesn't.'

(5.22) ᴸgədʒə　　su　　　ᴸma-dzi
　　　 true　　　NOM　　NEG-COP

'It isn't true, I guess?'（disbelief）

5.2.2　選択疑問文

疑問標識 'mɛ' は 'V-mɛ-否定-V' 構文において、2つの動詞のあいだに生起して、代替疑問文を形成することがある。

(5.23)　^Cchi　　　^Ryoko　　^Ldjo　　　mɛ-a-djo?
　　　　3 sg　　　home　　exist　　　QUES-NEG-exist
　　　　'Is s/he at home or not?'

(5.24)　^Hno　　　^Fgobo　　zoko mɛ-a-zoko
　　　　2 sg　　　cold　　　feel QUES-NEG-feel
　　　　'Are you cold or not?'

(5.25)　^Hno ^Hchi　　^Hhũ mɛ-a- hũ?
　　　　2 sg this　　　want-QUES-NEG-want
　　　　'You will want it, right?'

5.2.3　疑問詞疑問文

疑問詞疑問は節を疑問として標示し、どのような情報が要求されているのかを示すものである。ナムイ語ゾロ方言の疑問詞疑問文は、疑問詞を英語のように文頭の位置に動かすのではなく、標準漢語同様、陳述文で疑問に対応する名詞が置かれるのと同じ統語的位置に、疑問文で置く。

(5.26)　^Hno　　^Lhadju ?　　　　　（human）
　　　　2 sg　　who
　　　　'Who are you?'

(5.27)　^Hti　　^Lhadju-ko　　^Lqadzi ?　（possessive）

　　　　　this　　　who-gen　　　thing
　　　　　'Whose thing is this?'

(5.28)　　^{H}no　　　^{L}hũ　　　^{L}djiga ?　　　（inanimate）
　　　　　2 sg　　　what　　　like-2
　　　　　'What do you like?'

(5.29)　　^{H}ti　　　^{F}hũtsa ?　　　　　（inanimate）
　　　　　this　　　what
　　　　　'What is this?'

(5.30)　　^{F}hũtsa　　　　^{H}mu-kərndri ?　　　（inanimate）
　　　　　what-CL　　　do-CSM
　　　　　'What should done?'

(5.31)　　^{F}ashadja　　　　　　　（location）
　　　　　where
　　　　　'Where is (it) ?'

5.3　否定文

　ナムイ語ゾロ方言では、否定は否定接頭辞 'ma-' または禁止接頭辞 'ta-' を動詞の前に付け加えることにより形成される

(5.32)　　^{H}nga　　　^{R}bərdzi　　ma-drikʉ
　　　　　Lsg　　　money　　NEG-exist
　　　　　'I have no money.'

(5.33)　　^{H}chi　　^{L}dioma　　sho　　mana　　　^{L}su　　madzɪ

  3 sg speech talk NEG. very NOM NEG-COP

  'S/he is not extraordinarily talkative.'

(5.34) ^Hno ta-bu

    2 sg PROH-go

    'You do not go.'

5.3.1　否定のスコープ

　ナムイ語ゾロ方言では、否定を表す語の位置がスコープに影響することがある。否定標識は、動詞複合体に含まれる一つの特定の構成素にスコープを持つ。

(5.35) -ga   ma-djiga

    -TOP   NEG-like

    'As for ……, I do not like them.'

(5.36) ^Hchi ^Ldjudju ^Ldia ma-ha

    3 sg out   come NEG-can

    'S/he cannot come out.'

(5.37) ^Hchi ^Ldia ma-mbana

    3 sg come NEG-may

    'Her/his not coming is allowed.'（S/he is allowed to not come.）

(5.38) ^Hchi ma-dia ma-mbana

    3 sg NEG-come NEG-may

    'Her/his not coming is not allowed.'（S/he must come.）

5.3.2 二重否定

ナムイ語ゾロ方言において、二重否定は２つの動詞、または本動詞と助動詞あるいは本動詞と存在動詞を否定に用いる。

(5.39)　ᴴchi　　　ma-bu　　　ma-ha
　　　　3 sg　　　NEG-go　　　NEG-exist
　　　　'S/he must go.'（lit.: S/he doesn't not go.）

5.4　存在構文と所有構文

存在構文及び所有構文は以下のように６種類の存在動詞のうち一つが節の末尾に現れる。

(5.40)　ᶠama　　　ᶠyoko　　　ᴿndjo　　　（animate）
　　　　mother　　home　　　exist
　　　　'Mother is at home.'

(5.41)　ᶠnga-ko　　ᶠasha　　　ᴸdja?　　　（属格 eral）
　　　　1 sg-属格　where　　　exist
　　　　'Where is my hat?'

(5.42)　ᴴchi　　　ᴿmoga　　　ᴿdjɨkɨ　　　（inanimate）
　　　　3 sg　　　power　　　exist
　　　　'S/he has power.'

(5.43)　ᴴluqha-qolo　ᴿdrɨ　　　ᴸdji　　　（liquid）
　　　　bawl-LOC　　water　　　exist
　　　　'Water in the ball.'

(5.44) ᴴnga   ᴸgudji   ᴸci-ja   ᴸdjo   (possession)
       1 sg   younger. brother   one-CL   exist
       'I have a younger brother.'

(5.45) ᴿrabi   ᴸdiamu   ᴿshipo   ꟳdiobɨ   ᴸndzje (plant)
       Mountain top. LOC tree   many   exist
       'On the top of this hill there are a lot of trees.'

5.5 トピック＝コメント構文

本節では、ゾロ方言のトピック＝コメント構文と話題化について説明する。7.6.1. 非標示のトピック＝コメント構文

ナムイ語ゾロ方言の無標のトピック＝コメント構文を図11に示す。

NP 1 [TOPIC] + [(NP 2) + verb complex] [COMMENT]
図11　トピック＝コメント構文の基本構造

文頭に現れる名詞句は話題として機能するが、その他の項＋動詞複合体はトピックとして機能する。

(5.46) ᴴchi   ꟳkobo   ꟳdjukhunyo   ᴸcikuku   ma-shatsɨ   ᴿzuti
       3 sg   door   behind   noise   NEG-make   sit
       'S/he is sitting quietly behind the door.'

(5.47) ᴴchi-pər   ᴸmashi   ᴿtrhitrhi   ᴸkərpər-ni
       3 sg-AGT   table   leg   break-CSM
       'S/he broke the legs of the table.'

(5.48) ᴿrabi   ᴸdiamu   ᴿshipo   ᶠdiobʉ   ᴸndzje
     Mountain top. LOC   tree   many   exist
     'On the top of this hill there are a lot of trees.'

(5.49) ᴸzruphia   ᴸdiamu   ᴸtshʉ   ᶠdiobʉ   ᴸciphi   ᴿndjo
     grassland-LOC LOC   sheep   many   a herd   exist
     'There are a crowd of sheep on the grassland.'

5.6 漢語からの文法借用

以下、単文・複文の順に文法借用について見てゆく。

5.6.1 単文

基本的な構成素の順序は、ナムイ語が［SOV］であるのに対し漢語は［SVO］である。

(5.50) ᶠŋa   ᴿdo ga   ᴸdzɯ
     私   昼食   食べる   '私は昼食をとる'

若年層（特に十代の話者）の発話に以下のような構造を持つものが見られた。頻度としてはそれぞれ（2a）・（3a）の方がはるかに高い。

(5.51) ᶠŋa   ᴸdʒigi   ᴸhũ   =＞ （2b） ᶠŋa   ᴸhũ   ᴸdʒigi
     私   本   要る   私   要る   本
     '私は本が要ります'

(5.52) ᶠŋa   ᴸdʒigi   ᶠma   hũ   =＞ （3b） ᶠŋa   ᶠma   hũ   ᴸdʒigi
     私   本   否定   要る   私   否定 要る   本
     '私は本は要りません'

5.6.2 複文

複文に関しては、補文が主節動詞に後置される構造をとるものが見られるがこれもやはり若年層に顕著である。老年層は SOV 構造が優勢である。なお、年齢層を問わず、「言う」は VO 型が優勢であるが、「思う」は OV 型が優勢である。

(5.53) ᶠŋa ᴿmu [ᶠma sɯ ᴸdi ᶠma sɯ o]
　　　 私　 言う 否定　 知る 助詞 否定 知る SFP
　　　 '知らないって言ったら知らない'

(5.54) ᶠtɕhi [ᴿtɕhoχo ᴸbɯ ᴿkə˩] ᶠʂɯ ẓi
　　　 彼　 彼ら　 行く 可能　 思う
　　　 '彼は、彼らは行けると思っているらしい'

助動詞は S の直後に立つのが一般的である。

(5.55) ᶠŋa ᴸtɕu ᴸtɕi lu ᶠtan dʒo
　　　 私　～たい ちょっと 望む　'ちょっと見てみたい'

知覚動詞（見る・聞く・分かる等）も VO 型が出やすい。

(5.56) ᶠŋa ᴿndohæ˩ ᶠsu tɕhi ᶠdyo ndy ᴸgə dʒə ᴸtɕhi gu
　　　 私　 見る　 犬　　 大きい　 非常に 一　 量詞
　　　 '私には大きな犬が見える'

5.6.3 数量詞

5.6.3.1 名量詞

ナムイ語本来の［名詞＋数詞＋量詞］の順序が、漢語型の［数詞＋量

第5章　その他の構造

詞＋名詞］になるものが見られる。

(5.57)　^{R}tso　^{R}so　ku　＝＞　^{R}so　ku　^{R}tso
　　　　人　　三　　个　　　　三　　个　　人

(5.58)　^{R}betshu　^{F}nænqhæ˧˥　^{F}nila⁵　＝＞　^{F}nila　^{F}nænqhæ˨˩　^{R}betshu
　　　　衣服　　　黒　　　　　両件　　　　　両件　　黒　　　　　衣服

　ナムイ語の［名詞＋指示詞＋数詞＋量詞］の順序が、漢語型の［指示詞＋数詞＋量詞＋名詞］になるものも見られる。

(5.59)　^{R}so dzi̥　^{F}tɕhi　^{R}so　ja　＝＞　^{F}tɕhi　^{R}so　ja　^{R}so dzi̥
　　　　学生　　　那　　　三　　个　　　　那　　　三　　个　　学生

5.6.3.2　動量詞

　ナムイ語の［数詞＋量詞＋動詞］の順序が、漢語型の［動詞＋数詞＋量詞］になるものもわずかながら見られるが、多くは以下のようになる。

(5.60a)　^{L}tɕi　dzə˩　^{F}o pu　(5.60b)　^{F}so　dzə˩　^{R}dia
　　　　一　　回　　会う　　　　　　　　三　　回　　来る
　　　‘一度会う’　　　　　　　　　　　‘三度来る’

5.6.3.3　形容詞

　形容詞は、ナムイ語は［名詞＋形容詞］の順である。

(5.61)　^{F}ŋa　^{F}ʂu gu　^{R}bu tshu　^{F}ʂi tsa　^{L}ɣə
　　　　私　　明日　　　衣服　　　　新しい　　着る
　　　‘私は明日新しい服を着ます’

157

量詞を含む場合、ナムイ語の［名詞＋数詞＋量詞＋形容詞］の順序が、漢語型の［数詞＋量詞＋形容詞＋名詞］となる場合もある。

(5.62) ^{F}ŋa ^{F}ʂu gu ^{R}bu tshɯ ^{L}tɕi lu ^{F}ʂi tsa ^{L}γə
　　　　私　明日　　衣服　　　一件　　新しい　着る
　　　　'私は明日新しい服を着ます'

5.6.3.4 疑問詞の繰り返しによる前後呼応形式（Cross Clause Correlation）[1]
　ナムイ語における疑問詞の繰り返しによる前後呼応形式は漢語からの借用である。

(5.63) ^{F}hu tsa ^{L}so ^{F}hutsa ^{L}ku
　　　　何　　　学ぶ　何　　　　出来る　'学びたいことは何でも学べる'

5.6.3.5 副詞
　いくつかの副詞が漢語から借用され、漢語同様の語順で用いられている。

(5.64) ^{F}ŋa ^{F}je ^{F}ʂu ʑi ma to
　　　　私　也　思う　　否定　到る　'私も思い至らない'（＝想不到）

以下の例では、若年層は（16.b）を用いることが多い。

(5.65) ^{L}tɕi ^{L}dzə' lo ^{F}ɕo sɯ
　　　　一　　回　　　言う　もう一度　'もう一度言って下さい'

---

1 この構文に関する（特にチベット＝ビルマ諸語の）包括的な議論は、Huziwara, Keisuke. 2005. Correlative construction in Cak. Paper presented at the 11th Himalayan Languae Symposium held at Chlalongkorn Univeristy, 7 Dec, 2005. を参照。また、チノ語の例については、林（2004）を参照。

(5.66) ᴸtɕi dzəˡ lo ᴿtsæi ɕo
　　　 一　 回　　再　　言う　'もう一度言って下さい'

5.6.3.6 側置詞（Adposition）

　側置詞は、ナムイの後置詞が一貫して用いられ、漢語の前置詞的要素は借用されていないようである。

(5.67) ᴸinia̠ʂi ᴿnoχo ko ᴸaphuavu di ᶠnima ᶠɬasa mu ᴸzadu su
　　　 昔々　 我々　の　祖先　　は　チベット　ラサ　から　来る　SFP
　　　 '昔々、我々の祖先はチベットのラサから来ました'

5.6.3.7 接続詞

　以下のような接続詞がそのまま借用されている。

(5.68) …… ᶠtan ʂɯ, ᶠtɕhi ma ᶠvəˡtshi se
　　　　　 但是　　彼　　否定　結婚　まだ
　　　 'でも、彼は未婚です'

(5.69) ᶠŋa mu ᶠma sɯ tɕu ᶠma sɯ o
　　　 私　言う　否定　知る　就　否定　知る　SFP
　　　 '知らないって言ったら知らない'

5.6.3.8 語気助詞（sentence-final particle）

　以下のような西南官話に見られる語気助詞が借用されている。

(5.70) ᶠma dʐi a

　　　　　否定　COP　SFP　'違うんだ！'　阿［a］感嘆

(5.71) ᶠma　dʐ　i　o
　　　　　否定　COP　SFP　'違うんだよ！'　呵［o］強調・注意を喚起

(5.72) ᶠno ai
　　　　　あなた SFP　'あなたは？'　噯［ai］特指疑問

(5.73) ᶠma　dʐ　i　ba?
　　　　　否定　COP　SFP　'違うでしょう？'　吧［ba］推量

　以上ナムイ語における漢語からの借用と思われる現象について見てきた。この他にも彝語からの影響も考慮に入れねばならぬが、今後はバイリンガル研究・ダイグロッシア研究にも貢献できるようなコード＝スウィッチング・コード＝ミキシングの現象を含めた厳密な、深い分析を伴う、精度の高いナムイ語の記述的研究を目指してゆく所存である。

第5章 その他の構造

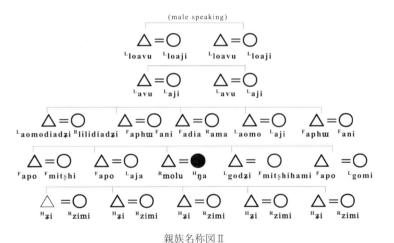

親族名称図Ⅰ
Paternal Relatives and Male Siblings' Offspring
(male speaking)

親族名称図Ⅱ
Maternal Relatives and Female Siblings' Offspring
(male speaking)

ナムイ語テキスト

(1) ᴸiniashɨ di ᴿshamⁿdo ᴿtsholu ᴸtsho ᴸⁿdrɨ
 ancient CONNECTOR miserable beast man eat
 昔々、人を食べるある哀れな獣がいました。

(2) ᴿmuzrɨmo ᶠso=ku ᴸdzro di ᴸtɛ ʰitɛie=ho
 elder brother three=CL EXIST CONNECTOR hunt=go
 あるところに３人の兄妹がいて彼らは狩りに出かけました。

(3) ᴸna ᴸhun ᴸdia ᴸdi ᴿtsholu ᴸtsho ᴸndrɨ ᴸdzu
 dark sky become CONNECTOR beast man eat come
 夜も更けて、獣は男を食べに来ました。

(4) ᴸmudrɨmo ᴸnyimomo ᴸdia ᴸhungu di ᴸkʰobo ᴸtikuta
 elder brother younger sister DAT sky dark CONNECTOR gate closed
 兄妹は夜も更けたので家の門に鍵を掛けました。

 mazɨdi ᴿtsholu ᴸtsho ᴸndrɨ ᴿdia
 otherwise beast man eat come
 さもないと獣が食べに来てしまうからです。

(5) ᴿtsholu ᴸnyimomo ᴸtshoqa lɛ ᴴnga ᴴno=ko ᴿama
 beast younger sister cheat CONNECTOR 1 sg 2 sg=GEN mother

 ᴴno ᶠlaka ᴸkhidzrɨkhɨ ᶠkɨmɨ ᴿlondrɨ
 2 sg hand window inside extend

獣は「お前のお母さんだよ。お前の手を窓に出しておくれ」と言って妹を騙したけど

(6) ^{H}nga=ko ^{R}ami ^{R}drijamadzrɨsu ^{H}nga su ^{R}tsholu=ko ^{F}laka
1sg=GEN mother whether it is or not 1sg know beast=GEN hand
妹は「本当に私の知ってる母かしら。」と思っていると

(7) ^{R}ndzrɨlo ^{R}padʒu diɛ ^{L}hun ^{L}ndie ^{R}laco ma ^{L}ndre
extend enter hair exist bracelet NEG bring
獣の手が髪にまで伸びてきたけど、その腕にはブレスレットがありませんでした。

(8) ^{L}nyimomo ^{R}tsholu dia ^{H}nga ^{H}no=ko ^{R}ama di ^{H}lakahũ ma ndzie
younger sister beast DAT 1sg=GEN 2sg=GEN mother hand hair NEG exist
妹は獣にこう言いました「私の母の手には毛なんか生えてないわよ。

(9) ^{L}laco ^{L}ndzriɛ ^{R}tsholu ^{H}cigu su ^{R}ikhʉ ^{H}dzrə ^{R}djita ^{L}laka=ko ^{R}hun
bracelet wear beast one-CL NOM outside toward exist hand=GEN hair
ブレスレットをつけてるのよ。」

^{H}kərpu ny ^{L}suni ^{H}laco ^{L}ndjie ^{H}padju
pull out PFT so bracelet wear come
そこで獣は、手の毛を毟りながらあわててブレスレットをつけに行きました。

164

(10) ᴸnimomo ᴸcigusu ᴴtrədi jo = ko ᴸama ᴴdzɨ ᴸŋulɛ
younger sister this think 3 sgREFL = GEN mother really
この妹はこう考えました。「実は母は本当に戸を開けて獣はうちに入って来ちゃったんだ。

ᴸkhobo pho ᴴlo-padja = ny ᴸmərdi ᴴama ma dji ᴸmulɛ
door open enter-come = PFT after mother NEG exist but
戸を開けて獣が家に入ってから、母がいなくなっちゃんたんだ。」と。

(11) ᴸtsholu ᴴhunkhuciti diɛ ᴸnimomo ᴴcigu ci pər ᴸdziko = ny
beast midnight younger sister this 3 sg AGT eat = PFT
真夜中に、妹は獣を食べてしまおうとしました。

(12) ᴸcigu pər di ᴿbərhin = ny ᶠmərcinidiɛ ᴴnimomo ᴴcigusu pər
this AGT escape = PFT the second day younger sister this AGT
獣は逃げて、あくる日妹は

(13) ⁿdzɯkɯ pər ᴴɕolo = po diomu ᴸndzutidi ᴴci = ko ᴴGodjɨmo = ko
well pear tree = CL on sit 3 sg = GEN sister = GEN
獣が梨の木の下に座っているのを見つけると、獣の妹が

(14) ᴸtitʃilalɛ ᴿⁿdzɯkɯ qolo ʂa-dʒu
intestines 3 sg bring CONNECTOR well inside wash-come
臓物を持ってきて、井戸で洗っているのがわかりました。

(15) ᴸajamo ᴴɕipo diomu ᴿndzri ta ᴴGundju = ny di mjabu ci = drər
elder sister tree on exist CONNECTOR cry = PFT tear one = CL
獣の妹は木の所にいて驚いて、

(16) ᴴgopa lɛ ⁿdzukukolo ᴴzadju ᴸtsholu ᴿcignsu diɛ ᴴhomolɛ tani
     shed well inside fall come beast this why today
     井戸の中に落ちてしまいました。獣は「どうして今日は

(17) mudi pʰio ᴸgədʒər suni ᴿhin dju ᴴdiomu lo ᴴludie
     whether good very but rain fall upwards look
     天気がこんなにも良いけど雨が降り出しそうな気がする」と言いました。

(18) ᴸajamo ᴴchipər ᴿndohɛr=ny ᶠmərdi ajamo ᴿtchi pər ᴴlodia
     elder sister 3 sg AGT see=PRF after elder sister 3 sg AGT come
     人間の姉が来たのを見て

(19) kutsɯlɛ ᶠtsʰolu dia ᴿiki tʃɪ=pia ᶠlapa-dia lɛ ᴴɕipo ᴸndrindrɨ=nydio
     worry beast say oil one=CL bring-come and tree touch=PFT
     CONNECTOR
     驚いて獣にこう言いました「油を手に取って木に触ったら

(20) ᴸno lodia ᶠɛba tsholu ᴴdzɨlɛ ikiɛ ᴴlapadʒu lɛ ᴴɕipo
     2 sg climb can beast oil bring come then tree
     お前は木に登れるようになるから、油を持ってきさえすれば

(21) ᴸndzrindrɨ=nymərdi ᴿɕipo shɛlɛ ᶠlobu ma-ɛba ᶠajamo ᴴci
     touch=PFT tree slip climb NEG-can elder sister 3 sg
     木から滑り落ちることはなくなる」と。

(22) ᴴtshɯoka sʉ ᶠtsholudia ᴿnolihunlɛ ᴴjoko ⁿdo ᶠcinla ᶠla-padia
     cheat again beast 2 sg go back house arrow one=CL bring come
     人間の姉はもう一度獣を騙して「お前は家に矢を取りに行って来

い」と言いました。

(23) ᴴnga ᶠsholo ᴴzalɛ ᶠnodiaci ᴿtsholu dji ᴴi lɛ ᴿlapadjunimərdiɛ
    1 sg pear 2 sg eat beast really believe then bring
    果たして獣は本当に信じこんで矢を持ってきました。

(24) ᴿajamo ᶠpər ɕolo ᶠpadjulɛ ⁿdo diomu ᶠzatashisuni
    elder sister pear bring arrow on
    人間の姉は矢を手に取りました。

(25) ᴸtshludia ᴿkhotsho ᶠxatala ᶠnga ᶠɕolo ᶠnoci ᴿtsholu ᶠdji lɛ
    beast mouth open 1 sg pear 2 sg eat beast really believe
    獣に口を開けさせて「私の梨をお前にあげるわ」。獣は本当に信じ
    てしまって

(26) ᶠkhotshoxatala ᶠajamo pər ᶠtʃoɢo ᴸɢoacilu ᶠci=mi ᶠcidiɛ
    mouth open elder sister AGT the first one=CL 3 sg=BENE eat
    口を開けたところ、人間の姉は一口目は梨を食べさせました。

(27) ᶠtsholu ᶠjo ᴸɕilicisoso ᶠkhalikhasoso
    beast say onomatope onomatope [extremely delicious]
    獣は「実にうまい実にうまい」と口にしました。

(28) ᴸmərkocidzərdi ᴿajamo pər ⁿdo ᴿdjilasu ʰoqotsho ᶠluta
    the second time elder sister AGT arrow use mouth towards
    二口目はは獣の口に向かって

(29) ᴸmitsotso ᶠnyipadi ᴿtsholuteipər ᴸtsotsolɛ ᶠɕoko=ny
    arrow shoot after that eventually die=PFT

矢を射ったころ、獣は死んでしまったとさ。(終)

ナムイ語語彙集

　本語彙集の配列及び番号付けは『方言詞彙調査手冊』(CHILIN Project, Princeton University, 1972) に見える類語枠組みに基づいている。なお、『方言詞彙調査手冊』にある任意の項目についてナムイ語のデータが存在しない場合は、その項目番号が欠番となっており、結果として番号は不連続となっていることに留意されたい。

項目番号	漢語	英語	ナムイ語
0100000	自然、自然現象	nature, natural phenomena	
0101001	天空	sky	^{F}mnakha
0101002	天亮了	the day breaks	^{F}myando
0101003	天黑了	night falls	^{H}nahũ
0101004	天邊	horizon	^{F}mnakhazrime
0101005	太陽	sun	^{R}hĩmĩ
0101006	出太陽	the sun rises	^{R}himi^{R}dzruzru
0101007	日落	the sun sets	^{R}himi^{L}qhɛ
0101008	晒	to sun	^{R}himi^{R}g'a
0101009	照	to shine	^{R}zo
0101011	月亮	moon	^{R}dawa
0101015	月光	moonlight	^{R}dawa^{H}zo
0101016	星	star	^{R}dri
0101020	光	light	^{R}zo
0101021	閃鑠	to twinkle	^{F}tsipha
0101022	亮	bright	^{R}dohɛji
0101024	暗	obscure, dark	^{R}nahu
0101025	黒	pitch dark	^{L}nakhi
0101026	影	shadow	^{R}nahũ
0101027	風	wind	^{F}musu
0101028	（風）吹	(wind) to blow	^{H}fu
0101029	刮風	the wind blows	^{F}musudadji
0101030	（風）停	the wind stops	^{R}mafu
0101036	雨	rain	^{R}hĩ
0101037	下雨	it rains	^{F}hĩdru
0101038	淋雨	to get drenched by the rain	^{F}hĩdru
0101039	晴雨	the rain ceases	^{L}liqho
0101040	大雨	heavy rain	^{H}hĩdia^{F}dzumudru
0101041	小雨	drizzle	^{H}hĩLatsʉtsʉ

0101042	驟雨	shower	ꟳkhumdju
0101044	雨點	raindrop	ꟳhīlulu
0101045	滴	to drip	ꟳndrə
0101046	虹	rainbow	ᴿgan
0101047	雲彩	cloud	ᴿdruva
0101048	雲散	the clouds disperse	ᴸyokoyomu
0101049	晚霞	rosy clouds, rosy sunset	ᴿdruvaluta
0101050	霧	fog, mist	ᴿgɛra
0101056	霜	frost	ᴿmuphə
0101057	雪	snow	ꟳvie
0101058	化雪	the snow melts	ᴿviehua
0101059	溶解	to melt	ᴴdzuduzhua
0101060	冰雹	hail	ꟳndro
0101061	下雹子	the hail falls	ᴿndrodju
0101062	閃電	lightning	ꟳmuərzupa
0101064	雷	thunder	ꟳmuvo
0101065	打雷	it thunders	ꟳmuvomərmər
0101066	雷劈	to be struck by a thunderbolt	ꟳmuvoukhi
0101067	天氣	weather	ꟳmutsaliqo
0101068	晴天	fine day, nice day	ᴸhimichi
0101069	陰天	cloudy day	ꟳmatsa
0101070	下雨天	rainy day	ꟳhidru
0101071	天旱	drought	ꟳndzrivakapa
0101072	水土	climate	ꟳndrudzuva
0102000	地理、火	earth, fire	ꟳdzuva, ꟳmi
0102001	地	the earth	ꟳdzuva
0102003	地上	ground	ꟳdzuvaphu
0102004	地震	earthquake	ꟳdzuvuliɛ
0102005	裂	to crack	ꟳkərpər
0102006	濕地、沼澤	swamp	ꟳnzushubi
0102007	土（乾的）	soil, earth	ᴸdri
0102008	泥（濕的）	mud	ᴿyaki
0102010	石頭	stone	ᴸlupu
0102011	大石頭	rock	ᴸlupuꟳdiaposu
0102013	沙	sand	ᴸdjevivi
0102014	山	hill	ᴿdzəbi
0102015	山頂	peak	ᴴgakuBu
0102016	山半腰	halfway up a mountain	ᴴgakudjiti
0102017	山脚	foot of a hill	ᴴgakudjamər
0102018	山坡	slope of a hill	ᴸdrivapopo
0102019	山崩	landslide	ᴸdravibyo
0102020	小山	mound	ᴸgakuatsutsu
0102021	童山	hill without vegetation	ᴿzrandi
0102022	山巖	cliff	ᴿzraku

0102025	山谷	valley	ᴿrakhər
0102026	山坑	ravine, pit	ᴸzraku
0102027	山澗	gorge	ᴸzraluku
0102028	山洞	cave	ᶠluku
0102029	窟窿	hole	ᶠluku
0102031	縫	crack	ᴸzrakərkər
0102032	水	water	ᴸndzru
0102033	水面	surface of water	ᴸndzrudimu
0102034	水底	bottom of water	ᴸndzrukolo
0102035	結冰、凍	to freeze	ᴸndzrugota
0102036	冰	ice	ᴸndzrundzru
0102037	（水）流	to flow	ᶠzuzaqo
0102038	（水）沖	(water) to wash	ᶠzuzri
0102039	大水	flood	ᶠzudiadju
0102041	泛濫	to flood	ᶠzudzudjamo
0102042	浮	to float	ᴸbzu
0102043	沈	to sink	ᶠzukuozako
0102046	瀑布	waterfall	ᶠzuvudje
0102051	波浪	wave	ᶠzuvulie
0102060	沙灘	sandy beach	ᴸdjevivie
0102063	湖	lake	ᴿbotho
0102064	河	river	ᴿhanji
0102065	河岸	river bank	ᴸchibu
0102066	渡口	ford	ᶠzug'odza
0102067	池塘	pond	ᴿchithang
0102068	溪	stream	ᴿkaboatsʉtsʉ
0102070	泉	spring	ᴿranzɨ
0102071	冒泡	to foam	ᶠdzudzuva
0102072	金子	gold	ᶠhɛ
0102073	銀子	silver	ᶠngu
0102074	銅	copper	ᴴki
0102075	銅綠	verdigris	ᶠhɛdru
0102092	霉	mildew, mold	ᴿphohoto
0102093	灰塵	dust	ᴸdzrikavi
0102095	粉	powder	ᴿdrove
0102096	末子	dust	ᴿdjapər
0102097	泡沫	foam, froth	ᴸzriba
0102098	火	fire	ᶠmi
0102099	燒	to burn	ᶠmimaka
0102100	着火	on fire, to catch fire	ᶠmimakalihʉ
0102106	烟	smoke	ᶠmikhu
0102107	燻	to smoke	ᶠmikhulaha
0102108	火焰	flame	ᶠmindje
0102109	水蒸氣	vapor, steam	ᴿsa

0102110	上流	upper course of a river	ᶠndrungu
0102111	下流	lower course of a river	ᶠndrumər
0102112	河床	river-bed	ᴿkapo
0102114	凝固	to congeal	ᴸfudrikalanya
0102115	淹	to inundate	ᴿngku
0103002	順風	to go with the wind	ᶠmizufu
0103003	頂風	against the wind	ᶠmuzukata
0103004	爬山	to climb a hill	ᴿrabibər
0103005	上山	to mount a hill	ᴿrabibər
0103006	下山	to descend from a hill	ᴸzalidia
0103009	順水	with the current	ᶠndruqaqanbər
0103010	逆水	against the current	ᶠndrudzər
0103011	溺	to drown	ᶠndruhota
0103012	潛水	to dive	ᶠndruahyomuchi
0103013	截水	to stop the flow of water	ᴿkhərta
0103014	疏通水流	to dredge a river	ᴿkhərzahusi
0103015	水閘	water gate	ᶠndrukobo
0103016	水〈土霸〉	embankment	ᶠndrutogo
0103017	堤防	dike	ᴸndupadri
0103018	航海	to navigate	ᴸnguchi
0103021	乘涼	to enjoy coolness	ᴴshushubuyu
0103022	世界	world	ᶠnanakayaku
0103023	溝渠	ditch	ᴿkabodre
0103024	丟在水裡	to submerge	ᶠndruvudjumici
0200000	動物	animals	ᴸkozra
0200001	（動物）產子	(animals) to give birth to the young	ᴸzupzudja
0200004	尾巴	tail	ᴿmərpo
0200005	搖尾	to wag the tail	ᴸmakudzabudzru
0200006	爪子	claw	ᴸtritri
0200007	抓	to claw	ᴴg'ər
0200008	蹄子	hoof	ᴸkalu
0200009	角	horn	ᶠkukɛr
0200010	茸	soft core of the young antler of the deer	ᴸchiekuqa
0200011	反芻	to chew the cud	ᶠdruliga
0200012	龍	dragon	ᶠlodre
0200013	群	herd	ᴿdziphi
0201000	走獸	beasts	ᶠbikodra
0201001	禽獸	beast	ᶠbikodra
0201002	老虎	tiger	ᴿla
0201003	獅子	lion	ᴿtrhala
0201004	豹子	leopard	ᴸdje
0201005	狼	wolf	ᴸdjie

0201006	狐狸	fox	^{R}dya
0201008	野猫	fox, wildcat	^{L}ndu
0201010	象	elephant	^{H}linbuchu
0201012	鹿	deer	^{L}che
0201013	馴鹿	roedeer	^{L}lo
0201014	野猪	wild boar	^{R}banyo
0201015	熊	bear	^{H}vu
0201016	猴子	monkey	^{L}mi
0201018	貉	badger	^{R}vaphu
0201019	刺蝟	porcupine	^{R}phu
0201021	兔子	rabbit	^{R}toli
0201022	老鼠	mouse	^{R}ha
0201026	吼	to roar (as lion)	^{L}ndo
0202000	飛禽	fowl	^{R}bi
0202001	鳥	bird	^{L}gidjibi
0202003	翅膀	wing	^{L}duka
0202004	羽毛	feather	^{L}gidjihũ
0202007	啄	to peck	^{R}bupa
0202010	蛋	egg	^{R}rangu
0202011	尾椎	fleshy part of bird's tail	^{L}madrio
0202012	老鷹	hawk	^{R}ga
0202014	燕子	swallow	^{R}bibaba
0202015	烏鴉	crow	^{F}laqo
0202016	喜鵲	magpie	^{R}chacha
0202017	麻雀	sparrow	^{L}landridri
0202018	鴿子	pigeon	^{R}thoyie
0202020	斑鳩	turtledove	^{R}thoyie
0202022	黃鶯	finch, oriole	^{R}alayu
0202025	啄木鳥	woodpecker	^{R}zumie
0202026	孔雀	peacock	^{R}suphie
0202027	雁	wild goose	^{H}ku
0202030	雉、野鶏	pheasant	^{R}he
0202032	鷺鶏	heron	^{L}anya
0202033	蝙蝠	bat	^{R}hadru
0203000	家畜	domestic animals	^{L}kodjer
0203001	牲口	livestock	^{F}mo
0203002	公牛	ox	^{R}ligu
0203003	母牛	cow	^{R}limi
0203004	水牛	buffalo	^{L}dringu
0203005	黃牛	the common yellow cattle	^{R}g'u
0203006	(牛)鬥角	to gore	^{F}fukər
0203007	牛犢子	calf	^{L}ngumidju
0203008	(公)豬	pig	^{R}vako
0203009	母豬	sow	^{R}vami

0203010	種豬	breeding boar, sire pig	ᴿvasu
0203011	小豬	shoat, piglet	ᴸvahũ
0203014	羊	sheep	ᴸyo
0203015	山羊	goat	ᴿchə
0203016	馬	horse	ᴸmo
0203017	母馬	mare	ᴿmomi
0203018	驢	ass, donkey	ᴿngodru
0203020	狗	dog	ᴴchi
0203021	母狗	bitch	ᴿchimi
0203022	獵狗	hunting dog	ᴿchimər
0203024	猫	cat	ᴿhala
0203025	猫叫	to mew	ᴿhalamərmər
0203026	公鷄	cock	ᶠrapo
0203027	閹鷄	capon	ᶠrasho
0203028	小公鷄	young cock	ᶠrapudri
0203029	鷄冠	cockscomb	ᶠramomo
0203035	下蛋	to lay eggs	ᶠragugu
0203037	孵卵、抱小鷄	to hatch	ᶠrafu
0203042	鴨子	duck	ᴸɛ
0203044	鵝	goose	ᴸə
0204000	爬虫、昆虫	insects	ᴴbu
0204008	蜜蜂	bee	ᴴbzũbu
0204011	蜂窩	honeycomb, beehive	ᶠbzupu
0204012	蜂蜜	honey	ᶠbzudra
0204013	黄蜂	wasp	ᶠbzuloho
0204014	蝴蝶	butterfly	ᶠbalala
0204015	毛蟲	caterpillar	ᴸbuyeye
0204016	蜻蜓	dragonfly	ᴸdridri
0204018	螢火蟲	firefly	ᴸabumyaci
0204019	蟋蟀	cricket	ᴸabudjata
0204020	蒼蝇	fly	ᴿlapər
0204025	蚊子	mosquito	ᴸtsolubyanga
0204026	（蚊子）叮	（mosquito）to bite	ᴿchedju
0204034	螳螂	praying mantis	ᴿbodjo
0204049	蝨子	louse	ᴴshu
0204051	跳蚤	flea	ᴸthozu
0204054	蛔蟲	intestinal worm	ᶠbzucər
0205051	青蛙	green frog	ᴿpami
0206003	打獵	to hunt	ᴿshuchie
0206008	放牛	to tend cattle	ᴿg'əlu
0206011	趕豬	to tend pigs	ᴸvatapa
0300002	（藤）蔓延	to creep	ᴸg'a
0300003	種子	seed	ᴿdzɨ
0300008	樹	tree	ᴿshipo

0300021	葉	leaf	ᴿshipsupsu
0300024	花	flower	ᴸvɛ
0300044	豆子	bean	ᴸnu
0301004	竹	bamboo	ᴸma
0301005	竹筍	bamboo-shoot	ᴸmadrudju
0301015	松樹	pine	ᴸthobo
0303000	穀物	grains	ᴿdzɨ
0303008	大米	hulled rice	ᴴtrhu
0303011	糠	rice husk	ᴿnyo
0303013	麥子	wheat	ᴴsulu
0303014	蕎麥	buckwheat	ᴸyimu
0303015	稗子	tares	ᴸyakha
0303018	麵粉	wheat flour	ᴸdjovi
0303020	小米	millet	ᴴyugu
0304000	蔬菜	vegetables	ᴸyochy
0304003	馬鈴薯	potato	ᴿyayu
0304024	黃瓜	cucumber	ᴸbyako
0304030	蘿蔔	turnip	ᴸlibi
0304032	茄子	eggplant	ᴸngatsu
0304058	葱	green onion	ᴿfu
0304059	洋葱	onion	ᴸfuluphe
0304061	辣椒	pepper	ᴿXucio
0305000	水果	fruits	ᴸthomoliko
0305002	桃兒	peach	ᴿbi
0305009	柑	tangerine	ᴸhyolo
0306006	除草	to weed	ᴸdromər
0306008	施肥	to fertilize	ᴸdritri
0306011	種地	to plow the field	ᴸdrogi
0306025	打穀子	to thresh	ᶠdzringa
0306038	剝皮	to peel	ᴿzrikunyu
0306039	削皮	to peel with a peeler	ᴿzrakonyu
0401003	早飯	breakfast	ᴿi
0401004	午飯	noon meal, lunch	ᴿdogadzɨ
0401005	晚飯	evening meal, dinner	ᴸhephudradzɨ
0402016	（豬）肚	(pig) stomach	ᴸhĩbi
0402020	（豬）肝	(pork) liver	ᶠshivu
0402021	（豬）肺	lungs	ᴿtsuphu
0402022	肚子	tripe	ᴸhĩbi
0402023	（牛）尾	tail	ᴸmər
0402027	牛肉	beef	ᴸg'əsri
0402029	羊肉	mutton	ᴸtsusri
0402055	木耳	dried fungus	ᴿmuyi
0403009	包子	round dumpling	ᴿlaba
0403029	瓜子	melon seed	ᴿbyakozɨ

0404002	油	oil	ꜝyikɨ
0404010	糖	sugar	ꜞshabzu
0404029	花椒	wild pepper	˻dju
0405001	開水	boiling water	ꜝndruchi
0405002	茶	tea	ꜞikha
0405008	牛奶	milk	˻ngunyanya
0405009	紙烟	cigarette	ꜛya
0405010	抽烟	to smoke	ꜝyandri
0406002	淘米	to wash rice	˻trutshɨ
0406080	蒸	to steam	ꜞni
0406084	烤	to roast	ꜞng'a
0406091	半生不熟	half-cooked	ꜝmamiamtso
0406072	煮（用水煮）	to boil	ꜝtshɨdju
0406075	炒	to stir fry, to fry	ꜞhɯhɯ
0406077	爆	to pop	ꜞbu
0406079	炸	to deep-fry	ꜞtra
0406095	水開了	(water) boils	ꜝndzrutshudju
0406096	煮湯	to cook soup	ꜝdjuca
0703012	劈	to split	ꜝkhu
0703013	刺	to prick	ꜞngo
0703014	穿	to pierce	˻za
0703015	錘子	hammer	˻lantu
0703017	斧頭	axe	ꜞvumi
0703018	砍	to chop with an axe	ꜞnda
0703028	錐	awl	ꜞndju
0703035	釘子	nail	ꜝshudzubzu
0703041	扁担	carrying pole	ꜝvasu
0703044	輪子	wheel	˻djosu
0703045	滾	to roll	ꜝpulili
0703048	鋤頭	hoe	ꜞchieku
0703054	棍子	stick	˻shikodjər
0703055	棍打	to beat (with a stick)	˻shikozrembo
0703056	鞭子	whip	˻bachər
0703057	鞭打、抽	to whip	˻bachərmbo
0703058	繩索	ropes, cordage	˻kuzri
0703060	麻繩	rope	˻sakhɯdjə
0703061	打繩	to twist ropes	˻sakhɯdjəmbo
0703062	桶	pail	ꜝkhuzu
0703063	提桶	hand bucket	ꜝkhozula
0703064	桶杷子	crossbar at the top of a Chinese bucket	ꜝkhozukɔ
0703066	籃	basket	ꜞkha
0703067	提籃	small hand basket	ꜝbantəji
0703068	漏斗	funnel	ꜝvũngasukajɨ

0703071	火柴	matches		ᴿmi
0703072	劃火柴	to light a match		ᴿmitrhɨ
0703073	草	straw		ᴿdju
0703074	板	board		ᴿsipia
0703075	鐵絲	wire		ᶠshuji
0703076	木頭	wood		ᴿshi
0703077	瓦	tile		ᴿgolu
0703079	漆	lacquer		ᴿhɨ̄su
0703084	象牙	ivory		ᶠlɨ̄ndjophukohu
0703085	窯	kiln		ᴿguluvusutsoho
0703088	網	net		ᴿphichu
0703089	網眼	mesh		ᴿphichuluku
0703090	鋸木屑	sawdust		ᴸshivivi
0703092	修理	to repair		ᴿshɨshɨ
0801007	路	road		ᴸdjugu
0801008	走路	to walk on foot		ᴸdjugubər
0801009	築路	to build a road		ᴸdjugushɨshɨ
0801010	三叉路	forked road		ᴸdjuguqhaqha
0801011	十字路	crossroad		ᴸdjuguvivi
0801012	路口	entrance to a road/street		ᴸdjuguqolumi
0801013	馬路	macadam road		ᶠmodjugu
0801014	人行道	sidewalk		ᴸtshodjugu
0801018	巷	lane, an alley		ᴿkhoyu
0801019	死巷	dead end street		ᴿkhoyutsukata
0801020	小徑	path		ᴴdjuguafofo
0801021	橋	bridge		ᴿnzo
0801022	過橋	to cross a bridge		ᶠnzonbər
0801024	吊橋	suspension bridge		ᶠshunzo
0801025	架橋	temporary bridge		ᶠnzochie
0801027	鄉村	village		ᴿfukər
0802003	人民	people		ᴸtshoXo
0802004	亡國	destruction of a nation		ᴿshogo
0802006	賣國	to betray one's country		ᴸtrhɨ
0802014	納稅	to pay tax		ᴸbazrɨdjabu
0802015	團結	to unite		ᴿdzɨdzɨ
0803000	地名	local place names		ᶠdjumi
0901001	買賣	trade		ᶠvulamu
0901003	買	to buy		ᴴhɛ
0901004	賣	to sell		ᴴchi
0901005	好賣	it sells well		ᴿtrhɨhə
0901006	合伙	to go into partnership		ᴿyoko
0901007	本錢	capital		ᴸbazrɨ
0901008	賺錢	to gain/to earn money		ᴸbazrɨkondjo
0901010	賠錢	to lose money in business		ᶠlitrhɨ

0901011	還本	to balance sale with capital	ᴸbazriyahɛ
0901012	開消	expenses	ᴿdju
0901019	商店	shop	ᴸqədjitrhizrɛ
0901020	開舖子	to open a shop	ᴸqədjitrhi
0901021	開張	newly open	ᴴtrhi
0901027	上貨	to unload goods	ᴸqədjidji
0901028	下貨	to load goods	ᴸqədjila
0901029	門面	shop front	ᴿkobo
0901030	字號	store name	ᴿdjigimidju
0901033	廣告	advertisement	ᴸgu
0901036	招貼	posters, notices	ᴸdrog'ashu
0901038	要價	to make a quotation	ᴸphuhŭ
0901039	還價	to make an offer	ᴿphuganga
0901040	多少錢	how much (asking for price)	ᴸbadjibabuta
0901046	簽字	to sign	ᴸdjigidjinyu
0901048	雇客	customer	ᴸqədjihɛsu
0901053	發財	to prosper by becoming wealthy	ᶠsukər
0901054	橫財	windfall	ᶠmazusubədji
0901055	發達	to advance, develop (business, wealth, etc.)	ᶠsukagədjə
0902014	米棧	shop selling rice	ᴿchuhɛdji
0902015	買米、糴米	to buy rice	ᴿchuhɛ
0902016	賣米、糶米	to sell rice	ᴿchutri
0902017	油房	shop selling (cooking) oil	ᶠikii
0902020	鹽店	shop selling salt	ᴸchichire
0902021	肉店	meat shop	ᴸshichire
0902022	買肉	to buy meat	ᴿshihɛsu
0902024	酒坊	wine shop	ᶠvuchire
0902029	布庄	piece goods store	ᴸvuzrechire
0902031	書店	bookshop	ᴸdjigichire
0902032	金店	gold shop	ᴴhɛchire
0902033	飯館	eating house, restaurant	ᴿdzichire
0902034	茶館	teahouse	ᴴikhachire
0902035	酒館	wine shop, a restaurant	ᴴvuchire
0902036	叫菜	to order food in a restaurant	ᶠtidjochucilusuhe
0902037	算帳	to settle a restaurant bill	ᴸbadjihabuta
0902040	找房子	to go house hunting	ᴿishu
0903006	一塊錢	a dollar	ᴸdadjicimər
0903007	一毛錢	a dime	ᴸdadjicitu
0903008	一分錢	a cent	ᴸdadjihĭ
0903013	借（錢）	to lend, to borrow (money)	ᴸnyi
0903014	欠（錢）	to owe (money)	ᴿzo
0903016	還（錢）	to return (money)	ᴸli
0904014	量（米）	to measure (rice)	ᶠchudjo

0904015	量（布）	to measure（cloth）	ᶠvudjandja
0904017	斤	catty	ᴿkhə
0904018	兩	tael	ᶠlo
0904020	斗	peck, a dry measure（316c. in.）	ᴿqa
0904024	丈	measure of 10 feet	ᴸpsʉ
1001001	話	language	ᴿdioma
1001012	問	to ask	ᶠkotshʉ
1001013	答	to answer	ᴸlisho, ᴸlingu
1001017	不做聲	to be silent	ᶠmashatshʉ
1001018	叫	to call	ᴸgahũ
1001019	喊	to shout	ᴸndo
1001024	信	letter	ᴸndjigi
1001025	寫信	to write a letter	ᴸndjigindji
1001030	寄信	to mail a letter	ᴸndjigibu
1001032	電話	telephone	ᴸdiɛnhua
1001033	打電話	to telephone	ᴸdiɛnhuaga
1001034	接電話	to receive a telephone call	ᴸdiɛnhuandhi
1001035	聽電話	to answer a telephone call	ᴸdiɛnhuabahĩ
1001036	報紙	newspaper	ᴸndjigi
1002000	旅行	travelling	ᴿkala
1002001	出門、旅行	to travel	ᴿkalabu
1002008	路費	travelling expenses	ᴸndhuguphu
1002015	回家	to go home	ᶠyokolibu
1003008	人力車	rickshaw	ᴸtshokapisuchezi
1003010	脚踏車	bicycle	ᴿkcichithusuchezi
1003012	三輪車	tricycle	ᴴsolupulilisuchezi
1003018	上車	to get onto a cart	ᶠchetsulobu
1003019	下車	to dismount from a cart	ᶠchetsuzadia
1003027	船	ship, boat	ᴿgu
1003028	船頭	bow	ᴸgug'uzre
1003029	船尾	stern	ᴸgumərpo
1003030	船身	body of a boat	ᴸgugumi
1003033	劃船	to row a boat	ᴿguci
1003050	坐船	to go by boat	ᴿgundzu
1101007	上學	to go to school	ᴸdjigisobu
1101008	放學	to dismiss school	ᴸdjigiphuko
1101025	畢業	to graduate	ᴸsoshica
1101027	教書	to teach	ᴿdjigiso
1101031	識字	literate	ᴸmidjusʉ
1101032	不識字	illiterate	ᴸmidjumasʉ
1101033	念書	to study	ᴿdjigipi
1101036	看書	to read a book	ᴿdjigilu
1101049	寫字	to write	ᴸmidjudji
1101053	寫錯字	to write the wrong characters	ᴸdjilamadji

1102017	鉛筆	pencil	ᴸbucadji
1103001	玩	to play	ᴿkala
1103002	玩泥沙	mud playing	ᴿdjivika
1103003	玩具	toy	ᴿkalasukadji
1103029	聊天	to gossip	ᴿdiomasu
1103045	歌兒	song	ᴸga
1103054	笛子	flute	ᴿfuji
1103055	吹笛子	to play the flute	ᴿfujifu
1103058	喇叭	trumpet	ᴿsalatsu
1103059	吹喇叭	to blow the trumpet	ᴿsalatsufu
1103060	鑼	gong	ᶠdzidzi
1103066	跳舞	to dance	ᴿlopər
1103081	電影	movies	ᴸdiadjaga
1103082	看電影	to watch the movie	ᴸdiadjagalu
1103088	贏	to win	ᴸg'a
1103089	輸	to lose	ᴸmag'a
1201000	鬼神	cults	ᴸtsər
1201001	老天爺	god	ᶠmnaka
1201002	神	deity	ᶠnyuhla
1201003	拜神	to worship god	ᶠnuvu
1201023	佛	buddha	ᴿphusa
1201026	念經	to chant sacred books	ᴸbi
1201033	跳神	to shamanize	ᴴchərmichu
1201039	念咒	to recite incantations	ᴿndji
1201042	算命	to tell fortune	ᶠlutratra
1201059	吉祥	auspicious	ᶠtrashidele
1202002	炮仗	firecrackers	ᴸqa
1202003	放鞭炮	to crack firecrackers	ᶠhopərqa
1202006	過年	to observe the New Year	ᴸkhushi
1203006	娶	to take a wife	ᴴhɛ
1203007	嫁	to take a husband	ᴴvərtshu
1203008	結婚的日子	wedding day	ᴴvərtshusucinyi
1203011	新郎	groom	ᴴvərtsho
1203012	新娘	bride	ᴴvərmi
1203026	生日	birthday	ᴿdjosuhatha
1203027	做生日	to celebrate birthday	ᴿdjosushinyiko
1203032	壽衣	grave clothes	ᴿmotho
1203041	埋葬	to inter, to bury	ᴸmodri
1204005	交朋友	to make friends	ᴸyokosu
1204006	介紹	to introduce	ᴸdhingutaco
1204014	主人	host	ᶠyohokosu
1204015	客人	guest	ᴸvər
1204020	禮物	gift, present	ᴸkadji
1204022	請客	to invite guests, to give a party	ᴸvərndo

1204023	送客	to see a visitor off	^{L}vərpu
1204024	作客	to be a guest	^{L}vərmu
1204030	入座	to seat at a dinner table	^{F}ndzundjandzu
1204031	上菜	to start serving a banquet	^{R}djochɿ
1204032	勸酒	to pledge in wine	^{H}vutandzri
1204036	你好	"how are you"	^{L}nondzu
1204037	請問	"may I ask"	^{F}makotshʉ
1204038	勞駕	"I have troubled you"	^{R}laulo
1204042	對不起	"excuse me"	^{L}mandu
1204043	別見笑	"don't laugh at me -- my ignorance"	^{L}tadjidji
1204044	借光	"allow me to pass"	^{L}ngamakotacibʉsɿ
1204045	別客氣	"do not stand on ceremony"	^{L}vatamu
1204046	請坐	"please have a seat"	^{F}tandzu
1204047	留歩	"don't trouble yourself to come out"	^{R}hīta
1301000	身體、生理	body parts and functions	^{L}gumi
1301001	身體	body	^{L}gumi
1301002	毛	body hair	^{L}djohū
1301003	皮	skin	^{R}djiqa
1301004	皺紋	wrinkle	^{R}djiqata
1301005	痣	mole	^{L}mina
1301006	骨	bone	^{L}shizrika
1301007	髓	marrow	^{R}bintu
1301009	肉	flesh	^{L}shi
1301011	血	blood	^{L}shie
1301012	流血	to bleed	^{L}shiedjudju
1301013	眼水	tears caused by smoke, etc.	^{F}myabu
1301014	汗	sweat	^{R}kulu
1301015	流汗	to sweat	^{R}kuludjudju
1301016	垢	body dirt	^{R}shichu
1301019	泡	blister	^{R}lapu
1301021	膿	pus	^{R}nbər
1301022	釀膿	to suppurate	^{R}nbərdjudju
1301023	呼吸	to breathe	^{L}sadjudju
1301026	喘氣	to pant	^{R}haphər
1301028	打瞌睡	to doze	^{L}yangərngər
1301029	頭	head	^{F}g'ūdjə
1301030	頭頂	top of the head	^{R}lopu
1301031	頭垢	dandruff	^{R}lopuko
1301036	秃頭	bald-headed	^{F}lohomandji
1301038	腦漿	brain	^{R}g'ūhudjə
1301040	前額	forehead	^{R}lophu
1301041	臉	face	^{L}phumi

1301042	眉毛		eyebrow	ᶠmyachohŭ
1301043	眼睛		eyes	ᶠmyalu
1301044	眼皮		eyelid	ᶠmyadjiku
1301045	單眼皮		single eyelid	ᶠmyadjikudjici
1301046	雙眼皮		double eyelid	ᶠmyadjikunyici
1301047	睫毛		eyelash	ᶠmyachohŭ
1301049	眼珠		eyeball	ᶠmyasubulu
1301059	耳朵		ears	ᴸhĭmpər
1301062	耳孔		aperture of the ear	ᴸhĭkū
1301065	鼻子		nose	ᴿnyaga
1301067	鼻孔		nostril	ᴿnyagaluku
1301068	鼻涕		mucus from the nose	ᴸnyamba
1301069	流鼻涕		to have a running nose	ᴸnyambadjudju
1301073	打鼾		to snore	ᴸnyambachi
1301074	嘴		mouth	ᴸkotso
1301076	嘴唇		lips	ᴸnipsidjə
1301077	舌頭		tongue	ᴿi
1301081	唾液		saliva	ᴸtsidjər
1301083	痰		phlegm	ᴿzikər
1301084	吐痰		to spit	ᴿzidzəphi
1301085	小舌		uvula	ᴸidji
1301086	牙		teeth	ᴸhə
1301097	胡子		beard	ᴸaco
1301098	胡鬚		mustache	ᴸaco
1301100	下巴		chin	ᶠmyakandju
1301107	喉〈0918〉		throat	ᴸtshukuta
1301109	肩膀		shoulder	ᶠkərbulu
1301110	夾肢窩		armpit	ᴸyadiakhər
1301111	手		hand	ᴸyaka
1301112	右手		right-hand	ᴿig'ər
1301113	左手		left-hand	ᴸlag'ər
1301114	胳臂		arm	ᴸlabudjər
1301115	胳臂肘		elbow	ᴸakərtsha
1301118	手腕子		wrist	ᴸlatsĭ
1301120	手背		back of the hand	ᴸlakadyumu
1301121	手掌		palm	ᴸlapsu
1301122	手指頭		finger	ᴸlami
1301123	手節		knuckles	ᴸlamitshi
1301124	虎口		space between the thumb and forefinger	ᴸlakər
1301125	手縫		spaces between fingers	ᴸlamikərkər
1301126	指尖		finger tips	ᴸlamigodja
1301127	指甲		fingernail	ᴸlamidjiku
1301128	大姆指		thumb	ᶠanimo

1301129	小指	little finger	ꜝakhadji
1301130	食指	index finger	ꜜalele
1301131	中指	middle finger	ꜝalele
1301132	無名指	ring finger, the 3rd finger	ꜜdrokhadji
1301138	拳頭	fist	ꜜgutshilu
1301139	胸	chest	ᴿgohlu
1301144	肺	lungs	ᴿtshɯphɯ
1301145	胃	stomach	ᴿdjudja
1301146	腰	waist	ᴿdju
1301148	肚臍	navel	ᴿdjaku
1301149	臍帶	umbilical cord	ᴿdjapər
1301150	肝	liver	ꜝchibu
1301151	胆	gall bladder	ꜜnchi
1301152	腎	kidneys	ᴿfulu
1301155	腸	intestines	ᴿutiti
1301157	背骨	backbone	ꜝXodjə
1301161	尿	urine	ꜜmbər
1301162	大便	shit	ꜝkhi
1301164	放屁	to expel intestinal gas	ᴿkhichi
1301165	男生殖器	male organ (common term)	ꜜniho
1301166	男生殖器（隱語）	male organ (euphemistic term)	ꜜniho
1301167	男生殖器（兒語）	male organ (baby term)	ꜜniho
1301168	夢遺	to have nocturnal emissions	ᴿnbudzə
1301169	女生殖器	vulva (common term)	ꜝpapa
1301170	女生殖器（兒語）	vulva (baby term)	ꜝpapa
1301171	女生殖器（隱語）	vulva (euphemistic term)	ꜝpapa
1301172	子宮	uterus	ꜜziko
1301175	月經	menstruation	ꜝshidjudju
1301176	性交	sexual intercourse (common term)	ᴿlaci
1301177	性交（隱語）	sexual intercourse (euphemistic term)	ᴿlaci
1301178	懷孕	to be pregnant	ꜜlakupa
1301184	腿	the leg	ꜝbuyu
1301185	大腿	thigh	ꜜguluchi
1301186	膝蓋	kneecap	ꜜshichie
1301190	脚	foot	ꜜshiqa
1301195	脚底	sole of the foot	ᴿbapsɯ
1301202	聲音	voice	ꜜkho
1301203	肋骨	ribs	ꜝXodjə
1301205	背	back	ᴿdju
1301206	肛門	anus	ꜜchiku
1301207	陰莖	penis	ꜜniho
1301208	陰囊	scrotum	ꜜlithidjika
1301209	睾丸	testicles	ꜜlithi

1301210	精液	sperm, semen	ᴿndodje
1302001	點頭	to nod	ꜝg'odjətangər
1302002	搖頭	to shake the head	ꜝg'odjədjudju
1302003	抬頭	to raise the head	ꜝg'odjəlotshʉ
1302004	低頭	to droop the head	ꜝg'odjəkʉkʉ
1302005	回頭	to turn the head	ꜝg'odjəndjo
1302008	皺眉	to knit the eyebrows	ꜝmyalutsʉmər
1302009	看	to see	ᴸlu
1302010	開眼	to open the eyes	ꜝmyalupo
1302011	閉眼	to close the eyes	ꜝmyalumərmər
1302020	聽	to hear	ᴿbahĩ
1302021	聞	to smell	ᴿhĩhĩ
1302030	吸	to suck	ᴿthi
1302031	咬	to bite	ᴸchʉ
1302034	齦（骨頭）	to gnaw at a bone	ᴸkhər
1302036	舐	to lick with blade of tongue	ꜝya
1302042	含	to hold in the mouth	ᴿhtshita
1302043	吞	to swallow	ꜝniphi
1302044	哽	to choke with food	ᴸdzikata
1302046	噴	to spurt	ᴿXota
1302047	吹	to blow	ᴴfu
1302048	吐口水	to spit	ᴴphi
1302050	吐舌頭	to stick out the tongue	ᴿĩdhi
1302051	挑	to shoulder	ᴸchi
1302054	腋下夾	to tug under the arm	ᴸyedjekərkərnita
1302056	揮手	to wave the hand	ᴸlakaphala
1302060	伸手	to stretch out the hand	ᴸlakandhi
1302061	拍手	to clap the hands	ᴸlakanganga
1302064	握手	to shake hands	ᴸlakasoso
1302066	指	to point	ᴸdiathatha
1302067	數手指頭	to count with the fingers	ᴸlanika
1302068	彈指	to snap the fingers	ᴸlanisa
1302069	折指頭關節	to crack the knuckles	ᴸlanisachie
1302070	拿	to hold with the hand	ᴸla
1302071	拈	to take in the fingers	ᴿkani
1302093	擦	to rub in	ᴸzo
1302095	按	to press down	ᴸtrhi
1302106	推	to push	ᴿtsho
1302107	拉	to pull	ꜝkapi
1302115	撈	to fish out	ꜝg'a
1302151	包	to wrap	ᴿzrabu
1302178	坐	to sit	ꜝndzu
1302179	坐下	to sit down	ᴸmindzuti
1302180	坐起來	to sit up	ᴸlotsrhi

1302181	站	to stand	ᴸhĩ
1302203	跳	to jump	ᴸlopər
1303001	洗臉	to wash face	ᴸphomitsʉ
1303003	洗澡	to take a bath	ᴿgumitshʉ
1303011	牙刷	toothbrush	ᴴhətshʉ
1303015	漱口	to rinse the mouth	ᴴkotsoii
1303018	揩（屁股）	to clean the bottom	ᴿdjubikuku
1303020	梳子	comb	ᴿg'upʉ
1303025	辮子	pigtail	ᶠg'opərngu
1303028	剪頭髪（男）	to have a haircut (male)	ᶠg'odjəkər
1303029	剪頭髪（女）	to have a haircut (female)	ᶠg'odjəkər
1303030	剃頭	to shave the head	ᶠg'odjəchu
1400000	生老病死	life, sickness, and death	ᴿdjolɛlamog'olɛshoko
1401001	生命	life	ᴿtshoko
1401002	一生、一輩子	to whole life	ᴿcidzɿ
1401004	出生	to be born	ᴿdjo
1401005	活	lining, to be alive	ᴿsadzɿ
1401006	養孩子	to raise children	ᴿlakhʉg'umər
1401007	看（孩子）	to watch the children	ᴿlakhʉg'ulu
1401008	（年紀）小	young in age	ᶠpəratsʉtsʉ
1401009	長大	to grow	ᶠdhudiodju
1401010	大了	to be grown up	ᶠdiodju
1401011	老了	to get old	ᶠlamo
1401013	休息	to rest	ᶠnyi
1401014	睡覺	to sleep	ᴿndju
1401015	睡午覺	to take a nap	ᴿnikondju
1401016	做夢	to dream	ᴿima
1401017	說夢話	to talk in sleep	ᴸimasʉsʉshu
1401022	死	to die	ᴿshoko
1401024	上吊	to hang oneself	ᶠg'etsʉ
1401027	僵屍	corpse	ᴴtshomo
1401030	歲	year old	ᴸpər
1402001	病	disease	ᴴmgo
1402003	大病、重病	serious illness	ᴴmgogə'djə
1402010	頭痛	to have headache	ᴴg'django
1402011	頭暈	to feel dizzy	ᴴg'djandzro
1402012	眼花	eyesight blurred	ᴴmyalukobʉ
1402016	耳朵聾	deaf	ᴸhĩbu
1402019	拔牙	to remove teeth	ᴸhəkərpu
1402021	打嗝	to hiccough	ᴸgəti
1402028	心跳	nervous, palpitating heart	ᴿnimilupər
1402034	拉肚子	to have diarrhea	ᴸhĩbishu
1402042	發燒	to have fever	ᴸgumichi
1402063	生蝨子	to have lice	ᶠshuba

1402080	鼻血		nosebleed	ᴸnyanngashi
1402082	便秘		constipation	ᴸmimi
1403000	醫藥		medicine and cure	ᴸtshʉgʉ
1403002	看醫生		to visit a doctor	ᴴngolu
1403009	藥		medicine	ᴸtshʉgʉ
1404007	當兵		to become a soldier	ᴸmamu
1404010	敵人		enemy	ᴸtshomaphio
1404011	戰場		battlefield	ᴸqaqandjozre
1404018	槍		gun	ᴿnyacu
1404020	子彈		bullet	ᴸdzolu
1404024	攻		to attack	ᴿtshʉta
1404025	守		to guard	ᴿlodia
1404026	進		to advance	ᴿtshʉta
1404027	退		to retreat	ᴸdjudju
1501002	姓		to be surnamed	ᴸshi
1501003	名字		name	ᴿmi
1501007	稱呼		to call, to designate	ᴴhatamudo
1501009	算		to count as	ᴿsa
1501010	出身		origin	ᴿndro
1501011	老家		native village	ᶠyoqolamu
1501012	家		home	ᶠyoqo
1501013	地址		address	ᶠdjudjə
1502001	祖先		ancestor	ᶠnuha
1502002	親戚		relatives	ᴸvudji
1502003	近親		close relatives	ᴸvudjiadjudju
1502004	遠親		distant relatives	ᴸvudjidiakhu
1502005	親		close (in relationship)	ᴸadjudju
1502006	疏		distant (in relationship)	ᶠdiakhu
1502009	長輩		senior generation	ᴸlochi
1502010	曾祖父		great-grandfather	ᴸloavu
1502011	曾祖母		great-grandmother	ᴸloayi
1502012	爺爺		paternal grandfather (address term)	ᴸavu
1502013	祖父		paternal grandfather (quoting term)	ᴸavu
1502014	奶奶		paternal grandmother (address term)	ᴸayi
1502015	祖母		paternal grandmother (quoting term)	ᴸayi
1502017	爸爸		father (address term)	ᶠadia
1502018	父親		father (quoting term)	ᶠadia
1502019	媽媽		mother (address term)	ᴿama
1502020	母親		mother (quoting term)	ᴿama
1502021	後母（對稱）		stepmother (address term)	ᶠalili
1502022	後母（指稱）		stepmother (quoting term)	ᶠalili
1502023	公公（對稱）		husband's father (address term)	ᶠaphʉ
1502024	公公（指稱）		husband's father (quoting term)	ᶠaphʉ
1502025	婆婆（對稱）		husband's mother (address term)	ᶠani

1502026	婆婆（指稱）	husband's mother (quoting term)	ᶠani
1502027	叔伯	paternal uncles	ᴸavomo
1502028	伯父（對稱）	father's elder brother (address term)	ᴸaomodiodji
1502029	伯父（指稱）	father's elder brother (quoting term)	ᴸaomodiodji
1502030	伯母	father's elder brother's wife	ᴿlilidədji
1502032	婶母	father's younger brother's wife	ᴿayi
1502033	姑父	father's sister's husband	ᶠaphʉ
1502040	岳父	wife's father (address term)	ᴸavu
1502042	岳母	wife's mother (address term)	ᴸadzɨ
1502050	丈夫	husband	ᴿmolu
1502051	妻子	wife	ᴸmbər
1502052	正房	legal wife	ᴿimi
1502053	偏房	concubine	ᴸidji
1502054	兄弟	brothers	ᴿgodji
1502055	同胞兄弟	uterine brothers	ᴸzaiyagodhi
1502056	〈1187〉〈1222〉	wives of brothers	ᶠmitrhihami
1502057	哥哥（對稱）	elder brother (address term)	ᶠapo
1502058	哥哥（指稱）	elder brother (quoting term)	ᶠapo
1502059	嫂子	elder brother's wife	ᶠmitrhi
1502060	弟弟	younger brother (quoting term)	ᴿgodhi
1502061	姐妹	sisters	ᴸayagodhi
1502063	姐姐	elder sister	ᴸaya
1502064	姐夫	elder sister's husband	ᶠapo
1502065	妹妹	younger sister (quoting term)	ᴿgədri
1502067	大伯子	husband's elder brother	ᴸzagəma
1502068	小叔子	husband's younger brother	ᴸgodrimo
1502069	大姑子	husband's elder sister	ᴸayamo
1502070	小姑子	husband's younger sister	ᴸgodrimo
1502075	堂兄弟	siblings of father's brothers	ᶠadiazeagodhi
1502076	表兄弟	siblings of father's sisters, of mother's brothers and sisters, cousins	ᴸavudhimi
1502079	晚輩	junior generation	ᴸmichie
1502081	養子	foster son	ᶠdzingume
1502083	媳婦	son's wife	ᴸtrhi
1502085	女兒	daughter	ᴿzimi
1502086	女婿	daughter's husband	ᶠzavu
1502087	姪兒	brother's son	ᶠzriga
1502088	姪女	brother's daughter	ᴿzumi
1502091	孫子	son's son	ᴸzubu
1502092	孫女	son's daughter	ᴸzubumi
1502096	家眷、家人	family	ᶠyokokotsho
1503004	結拜兄弟	sworn brothers	ᴸzayegodhishu
1503005	同鄉	people from the same native	ᴿdzigadhi

			village	
1503007	同學		schoolmate	ᶠsodziyokho
1503008	朋友		friend	ᴿyokho
1503009	老朋友		intimate friend	ᴿyokholamo
1503010	鄰居		neighbor	ᴿfukər
1600002	小孩子		child	ᴿlakhu
1600003	男孩子		boy	ᴴji
1600004	女孩子		girl	ᶠzrimi
1600005	小伙子		young man	ᴸmoloji
1600006	男人		male	ᴸmoloji
1600008	單身漢		bachelor	ᴸtsondjukalala
1600009	鰥夫		widower	ᴸbushokoni
1600010	女人		female	ᴿzumi
1600011	姑娘		unmarried young woman	ᴸzumiphiadjudju
1600012	女人（已婚）		married woman	ᴸazumo
1600013	老處女		old maid	ᴿayimi
1600014	再婚的女人		woman who remarries	ᴿzumilivatshə
1600015	孕婦		pregnant woman	ᴿlakhupa
1600016	寡婦		widow	ᴿmolushokoni
1600017	老頭兒		old man	ᴿudzi
1600018	老太婆		old woman	ᴿayimi
1600019	頭胎		first born	ᴿtsoshitsolodro
1600020	老幺		youngest child	ᶠlimər
1600021	雙胞胎		twin	ᴸchidju
1600022	獨生子		single child	ᴿchiya
1600023	遺腹子		posthumous child	ᴸchidji
1600028	敗家子		son who ruins the family	ᴿtshoəkhrbər
1600031	自己人		in-group	ᴸyobyokotsho
1600032	外人		outsider	ᶠsutsho
1600036	本地人		aboriginal	ᶠtukutsho
1600037	外省人		person from another province	ᶠnuakotsho
1700026	老師		teacher	ᶠsomi
1700027	學生		student	ᴸsodji
1700031	地主		landowner	ᶠdzibashiphi
1700032	放牛的		cattle tender	ᴸg'ushosu
1700033	放豬的		pig tender	ᴸvatsrisu
2003002	香		fragrant	ᴴbi
2003003	新鮮		(food) fresh	ᶠshitsha
2003004	臭		bad smell	ᶠbiniphu
2003005	（肉）臭		(meat) rotten	ᴸvashibini
2003006	（火腿）臭		(ham) stale smell	ᴴragubini
2004001	樣子		shape	ᴿi
2300000	時間		time	ᴸhatha
2300001	時候		time	ᴸhathacithu

2300002	四季	four seasons	ᴸndzʉbər
2300010	年	year	ᴴkhu
2300012	今年	this year	ᶠpsʉvər
2300013	明年	next year	ᶠsoni
2300014	後年	year after next	ᶠnoni
2300015	去年	last year	ᴸini
2300016	前年	year before last	ᴸshini
2300017	年初	beginning of the year	ᶠkug'u
2300018	年底	end of the year	ᶠkumər
2300019	一年到頭	all year round	ᶠkudjiligundjo
2300020	天干	ten heavenly stems	ᶠmufu
2300044	月	month	ᴸhlɛ
2300048	這個月	this month	ᶠdihlɛ
2300049	上個月	last month	ᶠG'oacihlɛ
2300050	下個月	next month	ᶠmərcihlɛ
2300051	月初	beginning of the month	ᴸhlɛG'oa
2300052	月中	middle of the month	ᴸhlɛkadju
2300053	月底	end of the month	ᴸhlɛmər
2300054	初一	first day of the lunar month	ᴸhlɛcini
2300055	十五	15th day of the lunar month	ᴸXogani
2300056	天	day	ᴿhata
2300057	今天	today	ᴿtani
2300058	明天	tomorrow	ᴸshugu
2300059	後天	day atrer tomorrow	ᶠnosho
2300060	大後天	day after day after tomorrow	ᶠnonyisho
2300061	昨天	yesterday	ᶠzʉnyi
2300062	前天	day before yesterday	ᴸshinyi
2300063	大前天	day before day before yesterday	ᴿshicinyi
2300064	今天早上	this morning	ᴿdasho
2300065	明天早上	tomorrow morning	ᴿshugunadje
2300066	今天晚上	this evening	ᴸtahũ
2300067	明天晚上	tomorrow evening	ᶠsohũ
2300068	後天晚上	day after tomorrow evening	ᶠnosohũgu
2300069	昨天晚上	yesterday evening	ᶠyuhũ
2300070	前天晚上	day before yesterday evening	ᴿshihũ
2300071	白天	daytime	ᶠhiminigu
2300072	夜間	nighttime	ᴸhũkhu
2300073	整天	whole day	ᴸdjinimu
2300076	天亮、黎明	dawn	ᶠmyando
2300078	日出	sunrise	ᶠhimidjudju
2300079	早晨	morning	ᴸnyadzi
2300080	上午	before noon	ᴿnikhu
2300081	中午	noon	ᴿnikhu
2300082	下午	afternoon	ᴸhũ

2300083	傍晚		sunset	ᴸhŭkhu
2300084	晚上		evening	ᴸhŭngu
2300085	半夜		midnight	ᴸhŭngudjiti
2300086	隔一天		every other day	ᴸcinika
2300087	隔夜		overnight	ᴸcihaka
2300088	過夜		to stay overnight	ᴿtaha
2300091	鐘頭、小時		hour	ᴴthu
2300092	點鐘		o'clock	ᴴthu
2300093	五分鐘		numeral on the face of the clock	ᴸngahĩ
2300094	幾月幾號（今天幾號）		(to tell date) "what day is today?"	ᶠhanihɛᴸhanini
2300095	問時候（幾點鐘）		(to tell time) "what time is it?"	ᴸhanithu
2401001	地方		place	ᶠdzuva
2401008	中心		central	ᴸkadju
2401011	裡面		inside	ᴿkolo
2401013	外面		outside	ᴿikhədjə
2401015	上面		above	ᴸdiomu
2401018	下面		below	ᴿahi
2401024	附近		around	ᴸandjundju
2401025	周圍		surrounding	ᴿkudro
2401026	對面		opposite	ᴿruta
2401039	遠		far	ᶠdiaku
2401040	近		near	ᴸandjondjo
2402003	開始		to start	ᴸamimu
2402005	完		to end	ᴿshica
2402006	從、打		from	ᴸdam
2402007	來		to come	ᴴlo
2402008	去		to go	ᴸdju
2402009	上		to ascend	ᴸlaga
2402010	下		to descend	ᴸmiag
2402011	進		to enter	ᴴdia
2402012	出		to exit	ᴿdjudju
2402013	回		to return	ᴿlidia
2402014	過		to cross	ᴸnbər
2500000	存現		copula, existential	ᴸndjo
2500003	有		existential verb, to have	ᴸdzi
2500005	不見了		to disappear	ᴸmandohər
2600001	所有、全部		all	ᴸyahamu
2600002	每		every	ᴿmuta
2600003	很久		very long (in time)	ᶠG'oatha
2600004	整個		whole	ᴸdjilumu
2600005	一半		half	ᴸdjimopha
2600006	大半		greater half	ᶠdiadjimopha
2600007	小半		smaller half	ᴸatsʉtsʉmopha
2600008	一個半		one and a half	ᴿdzilumopha

2600012	増加	to increase	ᶠdrodro
2600019	一	one	ᴸci
2600020	二	two	ᴸni
2600021	三	three	ᴸso
2600022	四	four	ᴸzi
2600023	五	five	ᴸnga
2600024	六	six	ᴸqhu
2600025	七	seven	ᴸsi
2600026	八	eight	ᴸhĩ
2600027	九	nine	ᴸnggu
2600028	十	ten	ᴸhĩXo
2600037	十多個、十來個	ten odd	ᴸXohanilu
2600040	頭一個	the first one	ᴸdroG'ogocilu
2600041	最後一個	the last one	ᶠmərgocilu
2700012	人人	everyone, all	ᴴtshocigumta
2700017	各自	individually	ᴸyokoyo
2700027	這些	these	ᶠtitsa
2700028	那些	those	ᶠchitsa
2700029	這兒	here	ᴸtamu
2700030	那兒	there	ᴸchimu
2700038	什麼	what?	ᶠhũtsa
2700040	哪兒	where?	ᶠashadia
2700044	爲什麼	why?	ᴿhomolɛ
2700046	幾個？（十個以内）	how much/how many (less than ten)	ᴸhabuta
2700047	多少？（十個以上）	how much/how many (more than ten)	ᴸhabuta
2700048	多久	how long (in time)	ᴸhakhudjə
2700049	一些	some (number)	ᴿyabu
2700050	一點兒	a little, some (quantity)	ᴸnikadji
2700051	一會兒	a little while	ᴸdrithadri
2800005	再	again	ᴿtsai
2800006	另外	additionally	ᴸtali
2800018	暫時、暫且	temporarily	ᶠthanshi
2800020	永遠、永久	forever	ᴸdzimimuta
2800022	後來	later	ᴿmərdia

英語＝漢語＝ナムイ語順

英語	漢語	ナムイ語	項目番号
"allow me to pass"	借光	ᴸngamakotacibusi	1204044
"do not stand on ceremony"	別客氣	ᴸvatamu	1204045
"don't laugh at me -- my ignorance"	別見笑	ᴸtadjidji	1204043
"don't trouble yourself to come"	留歩	ᴿhĩta	1204047

English	Chinese	Transcription	Code
out"			
"excuse me"	對不起	ᴸmandu	1204042
"how are you"	你好	ᴸnondzu	1204036
"I have troubled you"	勞駕	ᴿlaulo	1204038
"may I ask"	請問	ᶠmakotshʉ	1204037
"please have a seat"	請坐	ᶠtandzu	1204046
(animals) to give birth to the young	(動物) 產子	ᴸzupzudja	200001
(food) fresh	新鮮	ᶠshitsha	2003003
(ham) stale smell	(火腿) 臭	ᴴragubini	2003006
(meat) rotten	(肉) 臭	ᶠvashibini	2003005
(mosquito) to bite	(蚊子) 叮	ᴿchedju	204026
(pig) stomach	(豬) 肚	ᴸhĭbi	402016
(pork) liver	(豬) 肝	ᶠshivʉ	402020
(to tell date) "what day is today?"	幾月幾號 (今天幾號)	ᴸhanihɛᴸhanini	2300094
(to tell time) "what time is it?"	問時候 (幾點鐘)	ᴸhanithu	2300095
(water) boils	水開了	ᴸndzrutshudju	406095
(water) to wash	(水) 沖	ᶠzuzri	102038
(wind) to blow	(風) 吹	ᴴfu	101028
15th day of the lunar month	十五	ᴸXogani	2300055
a cent	一分錢	ᴸdadjihĭ	903008
a dime	一毛錢	ᴸdadjicitu	903007
a dollar	一塊錢	ᴸdadjicimər	903006
a little while	一會兒	ᴸdrithadri	2700051
a little, some (quantity)	一點兒	ᴸnikadji	2700050
aboriginal	本地人	ᶠtukutsho	1600036
above	上面	ᴸdiomu	2401015
additionally	另外	ᴸtali	2800006
address	地址	ᶠdjudjə	1501013
advertisement	廣告	ᴸgu	901033
afternoon	下午	ᴸhũ	2300082
again	再	ᴿtsai	2800005
against the current	逆水	ᶠndrudzər	103010
against the wind	頂風	ᶠmuzukata	103003
all	所有、全部	ᴸyahamu	2600001
all year round	一年到頭	ᶠkudjɨligundjo	2300019
ancestor	祖先	ᶠnuha	1502001
animals	動物	ᴸkozra	200000
anus	肛門	ᴸchiku	1301206
aperture of the ear	耳孔	ᴸhĭkũ	1301062
arm	手臂	ᴸlabudjər	1301114
armpit	夾肢窩	ᴸyadiakhər	1301110
around	附近	ᴸandjundju	2401024
ass, donkey	驢	ᴿngodru	203018

auspicious	吉祥	ᶠtrashidele	1201059
awl	錐	ᴿndju	703028
axe	斧頭	ᴿvumi	703017
bachelor	單身漢	ᴸtsondjukalala	1600008
back	背	ᴿdju	1301205
back of the hand	手背	ᴸlakadyumu	1301120
backbone	背骨	ᶠXodjə	1301157
bad smell	臭	ᶠbiniphu	2003004
badger	貉	ᴿvaphu	201018
bald-headed	禿頭	ᶠlohomandji	1301036
bamboo	竹	ᴸma	301004
bamboo-shoot	竹笋	ᴸmadrudjɨ	301005
basket	籃	ᴿkha	703066
bat	蝙蝠	ᴿhadru	202033
battlefield	戰場	ᴸqaqandjozre	1404011
bean	豆子	ᴸnu	300044
bear	熊	ᴴvu	201015
beard	胡子	ᴸaco	1301097
beast	禽獸	ᶠbikodra	201001
beasts	走獸	ᶠbikodra	201000
bee	蜜蜂	ᴴbzũbu	204008
beef	牛肉	ᴸg'əsri	402027
before noon	上午	ᴿnikhu	2300080
beginning of the month	月初	ᶠhlεG'oa	2300051
beginning of the year	年初	ᶠkug'u	2300017
below	下面	ᴿahi	2401018
bicycle	脚踏車	ᴿkcichithusuchez i	1003010
bird	鳥	ᴸgidjibi	202001
birthday	生日	ᴿdjosuhatha	1203026
bitch	母狗	ᴿchimi	203021
blister	泡	ᴿlapu	1301019
blood	血	ᴸshie	1301011
board	板	ᴿsipia	703074
body	身體	ᴸgumi	1301001
body dirt	垢	ᴿshichu	1301016
body hair	毛	ᴸdjohũ	1301002
body of a boat	船身	ᴸgugumi	1003030
body parts and functions	身體、生理	ᴸgumi	1301000
boiling water	開水	ᶠndruchi	405001
bone	骨	ᴸshizrika	1301006
bookshop	書店	ᴸdjigichire	902031
bottom of water	水底	ᴸndzrukolo	102034
bow	船頭	ᴸgug'uzre	1003028
boy	男孩子	ᴴji	1600003

193

brain	腦漿	ᴿg'ʉ̄hudjə	1301038
breakfast	早飯	ᴿi	401003
breeding boar, sire pig	種豬	ᴿvasu	203010
bride	新娘	ᴴvərmi	1203012
bridge	橋	ᴿnzo	801021
bright	亮	ᴿdohɛji	101022
brothers	兄弟	ᴿgodji	1502054
brother's daughter	姪女	ᴿzumi	1502088
brother's son	姪兒	ꜝzriga	1502087
buckwheat	蕎麥	ᴸyimu	303014
buddha	佛	ᴿphusa	1201023
buffalo	水牛	ᴸdringu	203004
bullet	子彈	ᴸdzolu	1404020
butterfly	蝴蝶	ꜝbalala	204014
calf	牛犢子	ᴸngumidju	203007
capital	本錢	ᴸbazri	901007
capon	閹鷄	ꜝrasho	203027
carrying pole	扁担	ꜝvasu	703041
cat	猫	ᴿhala	203024
caterpillar	毛蟲	ᴸbuyeye	204015
cattle tender	放牛的	ᴸg'ʉshosu	1700032
catty	斤	ᴿkhə	904017
cave	山洞	ꜝluku	102028
central	中心	ᴸkadju	2401008
chest	胸	ᴿgohlu	1301139
child	小孩子	ᴿlakhʉ	1600002
chin	下巴	ꜝmyakandju	1301100
cigarette	紙烟	ᴴya	405009
claw	爪子	ᴸtritri	200006
cliff	山巖	ᴿzraku	102022
climate	水土	ꜝndrudzuva	101072
close (in relationship)	親	ᴸadjudju	1502005
close relatives	近親	ᴸvudjiadjudju	1502003
cloud	雲彩	ᴿdruva	101047
cloudy day	陰天	ꜝmatsa	101069
cock	公鷄	ꜝrapo	203026
cockscomb	鷄冠	ꜝramomo	203029
comb	梳子	ᴿg'upʉ	1303020
concubine	偏房	ᴿidji	1502053
constipation	便秘	ᴸmimi	1402082
copper	銅	ᴴki	102074
copula, existential	存現	ᴸndjo	2500000
corpse	僵屍	ᴴtshomo	1401027
cow	母牛	ᴿlimi	203003

crack	縫	ᴸzrakərkər	102031
cricket	蟋蟀	ᴸabudjata	204019
crossbar at the top of a Chinese bucket	桶杷子	ꜰkhozukɔ	703064
crossroad	十字路	ᴸdjuguvivi	801011
crow	烏鴉	ꜰlaqo	202015
cucumber	黃瓜	ᴸbyako	304024
cults	鬼神	ᴸtsər	1201000
customer	雇客	ᴸqadjihɛsu	901048
dandruff	頭垢	ᴿlopuko	1301031
daughter	女兒	ᴿzimi	1502085
daughter's husband	女婿	ꜰzavu	1502086
dawn	天亮、黎明	ꜰmyando	2300076
day	天	ᴿhata	2300056
day after day after tomorrow	大後天	ꜰnonyisho	2300060
day after tomorrow evening	後天晚上	ꜰnosohŭgu	2300068
day atrer tomorrow	後天	ꜰnosho	2300059
day before day before yesterday	大前天	ᴿshicinyi	2300063
day before yesterday	前天	ᴸshinyi	2300062
day before yesterday evening	前天晚上	ᴿshihŭ	2300070
daytime	白天	ꜰhiminigu	2300071
dead end street	死巷	ᴿkhoyutsɯkata	801019
deaf	耳朵聾	ᴸhĭbu	1402016
deer	鹿	ᴸche	201012
deity	神	ꜰnyuhla	1201002
destruction of a nation	亡國	ᴿshogo	802004
dike	堤防	ndupadrɨ	103017
disease	病	ᴴmgo	1402001
distant (in relationship)	疏	ꜰdiakhu	1502006
distant relatives	遠親	ᴸvudjidiakhu	1502004
ditch	溝渠	ᴿkabodre	103023
dog	狗	ᴴchi	203020
domestic animals	家畜	ᴸkodjer	203000
double eyelid	雙眼皮	ꜰmyadjikunyici	1301046
dragon	龍	ꜰlodre	200012
dragonfly	蜻蜓	ᴸdridri	204016
dried fungus	木耳	ᴿmuyi	402055
drizzle	小雨	ᴴhĭLatsɯtsɯ	101041
drought	天旱	ꜰndzrivakapa	101071
duck	鴨子	ᴸɛ	203042
dust	末子	ᴿdjapər	102096
dust	灰塵	ᴸdzrikavi	102093
ears	耳朵	ᴸhĭmpər	1301059
earth, fire	地理、火	ꜰdzuva, ꜰmi	102000

195

earthquake	地震	ᶠdzuvuliɛ	102004
eating house, restaurant	飯舘	ᴿdzichire	902033
egg	蛋	ᴿrangu	202010
eggplant	茄子	ᴸngatsʉ	304032
eight	八	ᴸhĩ	2600026
elbow	手臂肘	ᴸakərtsha	1301115
elder brother (address term)	哥哥（對稱）	ᶠapo	1502057
elder brother (quoting term)	哥哥（指稱）	ᶠapo	1502058
elder brother's wife	嫂子	ᶠmitrhi	1502059
elder sister	姐姐	ᴸaya	1502063
elder sister's husband	姐夫	ᶠapo	1502064
elephant	象	ᴴlinbuchu	201010
embankment	水壩	ᶠndrutogo	103016
end of the month	月底	ᴸhlɛmər	2300053
end of the year	年底	ᶠkumər	2300018
enemy	敵人	ᴸtshomaphio	1404010
entrance to a road/street	路口	ᴸdjuguqolumi	801012
evening	晚上	ᴸhũngu	2300084
evening meal, dinner	晚飯	ᴸhephudradzi	401005
every	每	ᴿmuta	2600002
every other day	隔一天	ᴸcinika	2300086
everyone, all	人人	ᴴtshocigumta	2700012
existential verb, to have	有	ᴸdzɨ	2500003
expenses	開消	ᴿdju	901012
eyeball	眼珠	ᶠmyasubulu	1301049
eyebrow	眉毛	ᶠmyachohũ	1301042
eyelash	睫毛	ᶠmyachohũ	1301047
eyelid	眼皮	ᶠmyadjiku	1301044
eyes	眼睛	ᶠmyalu	1301043
eyesight blurred	眼花	ᴴmyalukobu	1402012
face	臉	ᴸphumi	1301041
family	家眷、家人	ᶠyokokotsho	1502096
far	遠	ᶠdiaku	2401039
father (address term)	爸爸	ᶠadia	1502017
father (quoting term)	父親	ᶠadia	1502018
father's elder brother (address term)	伯父（對稱）	ᴸaomodiodji	1502028
father's elder brother (quoting term)	伯父（指稱）	ᴸaomodiodji	1502029
father's elder brother's wife	伯母	ᴿlilidədji	1502030
father's sister's husband	姑父	ᶠaphʉ	1502033
father's younger brother's wife	婶母	ᴿayi	1502032
feather	羽毛	ᴸgidjihũ	202004
female	女人	ᴿzumi	1600010

finch, oriole	黄鶯	ᴿalayu	202022
fine day, nice day	晴天	ᴸhimichi	101068
finger	手指頭	ᴸlami	1301122
finger tips	指尖	ᴸlamigodja	1301126
fingernail	指甲	ᴸlamidjiku	1301127
fire	火	ᶠmi	102098
firecrackers	炮仗	ᴸqa	1202002
firefly	螢火蟲	ᴸabumyaci	204018
first born	頭胎	ᴿtsoshitsolodro	1600019
first day of the lunar month	初一	ᴸhlɛcini	2300054
fist	拳頭	ᴸgutshilu	1301138
five	五	ᴸnga	2600023
flame	火焰	ᶠmindje	102108
flea	跳蚤	ᴸthozu	204051
flesh	肉	ᴸshi	1301009
fleshy part of bird's tail	尾椎	ᴸmadrio	202011
flood	大水	ᶠzudiadju	102039
flower	花	ᴸvɛ	300024
flute	笛子	ᴿfuji	1103054
fly	蒼蠅	ᴿlapər	204020
foam, froth	泡沫	ᴸzriba	102097
fog, mist	霧	ᴿgɛra	101050
foot	脚	ᴸshiqa	1301190
foot of a hill	山脚	ᴴgakudjamər	102017
ford	渡口	ᶠzug'odza	102066
forehead	前額	ᴿlophu	1301040
forever	永遠、永久	ᴸdzimimuta	2800020
forked road	三叉路	ᴸdjuguqhaqha	801010
foster son	養子	ᶠdzingume	1502081
four	四	ᴸzi	2600022
four seasons	四季	ᴸndzubər	2300002
fowl	飛禽	ᴿbi	202000
fox	狐狸	ᴿdya	201006
fox, wildcat	野貓	ᴸndu	201008
fragrant	香	ᴴbi	2003002
friend	朋友	ᴿyokho	1503008
from	從、打	ᴸdam	2402006
frost	霜	ᴿmuphə	101056
fruits	水果	ᴸthomoliko	305000
funnel	漏斗	ᶠvũngasukaji	703068
gall bladder	胆	ᴸnchi	1301151
gift, present	禮物	ᴸkadji	1204020
girl	女孩子	ᶠzrimi	1600004
goat	山羊	ᴿchə	203015

god	老天爺	ᶠmnaka	1201001
gold	金子	ᶠhɛ	102072
gold shop	金店	ᴴhɛchire	902032
gong	鑼	ᶠdzidzi	1103060
goose	鵝	ᴸə	203044
gorge	山澗	ᴸzraluku	102027
grains	穀物	ᴿdzi	303000
grave clothes	壽衣	ᴿmotho	1203032
greater half	大半	ᶠdiadjimopha	2600006
great-grandfather	曾祖父	ᴸloavu	1502010
great-grandmother	曾祖母	ᴸloayi	1502011
green frog	青蛙	ᴿpami	205051
green onion	蔥	ᴿfu	304058
groom	新郎	ᴴvərtsho	1203011
ground	地上	ᶠdzuvaphu	102003
guest	客人	ᴸvər	1204015
gun	槍	ᴿnyacu	1404018
hail	冰雹	ᶠndro	101060
half	一半	ᴸdjimopha	2600005
half-cooked	半生不熟	ᶠmamiamtso	406091
halfway up a mountain	山半腰	ᴴgakudjiti	102016
hammer	錘子	ᴸlantu	703015
hand	手	ᴸyaka	1301111
hand bucket	提桶	ᶠkhozula	703063
hawk	老鷹	ᴿga	202012
head	頭	ᶠg'ŭdjə	1301029
heavy rain	大雨	ᴴhĭdiaᶠdzumudru	101040
herd	群	ᴿdziphi	200013
here	這兒	ᴸtamu	2700029
heron	蒼鷺	ᴸanya	202032
hill	山	ᴿdzəbi	102014
hill without vegetation	童山	ᴿzrandi	102021
hoe	鋤頭	ᴿchieku	703048
hole	窟窿	ᶠluku	102029
home	家	ᶠyoqo	1501012
honey	蜂蜜	ᶠbzudra	204012
honeycomb, beehive	蜂窩	ᶠbzupu	204011
hoof	蹄子	ᴸkalu	200008
horizon	天邊	ᶠmnakhazrime	101004
horn	角	ᶠkukɛr	200009
horse	馬	ᴸmo	203016
host	主人	ᶠyohokosu	1204014
hour	鐘頭、小時	ᴴthu	2300091
how long (in time)	多久	ᴸhakhudjə	2700048

how much (asking for price)	多少錢	ᴸbadjibabuta	901040
how much/how many (less than ten)	幾個？（十個以内）	ᴸhabuta	2700046
how much/how many (more than ten)	多少？（十個以上）	ᴸhabuta	2700047
hulled rice	大米	ᴴtrhu	303008
hunting dog	獵狗	ᴿchimər	203022
husband	丈夫	ᴿmolu	1502050
husband's elder brother	大伯子	ᴸzagəma	1502067
husband's elder sister	大姑子	ᴸayamo	1502069
husband's father (address term)	公公（對稱）	ᶠaphʉ	1502023
husband's father (quoting term)	公公（指稱）	ᶠaphʉ	1502024
husband's mother (address term)	婆婆（對稱）	ᶠani	1502025
husband's mother (quoting term)	婆婆（指稱）	ᶠani	1502026
husband's younger brother	小叔子	ᴸgodrimo	1502068
husband's younger sister	小姑子	ᴸgodrimo	1502070
ice	冰	ᴸndzrundzru	102036
illiterate	不識字	ᴸmidjumasʉ	1101032
index finger	食指	ᴸalele	1301130
individually	各自	ᴸyokoyo	2700017
in-group	自己人	ᴸyobyokotsho	1600031
insects	爬虫、昆虫	ᴴbu	204000
inside	裡面	ᴿkolo	2401011
intestinal worm	蛔蟲	ᶠbzucər	204054
intestines	腸	ᴿutiti	1301155
intimate friend	老朋友	ᴿyokholamo	1503009
it rains	下雨	ᶠhĭdru	101037
it sells well	好賣	ᴿtrhihə	901005
it thunders	打雷	ᶠmuvomərmər	101065
ivory	象牙	ᶠlĩndjophukohʉ	703084
junior generation	晚輩	ᴸmichie	1502079
kidneys	腎	ᴿfulu	1301152
kiln	窯	ᴿguluvusʉtsoho	703085
kneecap	膝蓋	ᴸshichie	1301186
knuckles	手節	ᴸlamitshi	1301123
lacquer	漆	ᴿhĩsu	703079
lake	湖	ᴿbotho	102063
landowner	地主	ᶠdzɩbashiphi	1700031
landslide	山崩	ᴸdravibyo	102019
lane, an alley	巷	ᴿkhoyu	801018
language	話	ᴿdioma	1001001
last month	上個月	ᶠG'oacihlɛ	2300049
last year	去年	ᴸini	2300015
later	後來	ᴿmərdia	2800022

199

English	Chinese	Phonetic	Code
leaf	葉	^{R}shipsupsu	300021
left-hand	左手	^{L}lag'ər	1301113
legal wife	正房	^{R}imi	1502052
leopard	豹子	^{L}dje	201004
letter	信	^{L}ndjigi	1001024
life	生命	^{R}tshoko	1401001
life, sickness, and death	生老病死	^{R}djolɛlamog'olɛshoko	1400000
light	光	^{R}zo	101020
lightning	閃電	^{F}muərzupa	101062
lining, to be alive	活	^{R}sadzɨ	1401005
lion	獅子	^{R}trhala	201003
lips	嘴唇	^{L}nipsidjə	1301076
literate	識字	^{L}midjusu	1101031
little finger	小指	^{F}akhadji	1301129
liver	肝	^{F}chibu	1301150
livestock	牲口	^{F}mo	203001
local place names	地名	^{F}djumi	803000
louse	蝨子	^{H}shu	204049
lower course of a river	下流	^{F}ndrumər	102111
lungs	（豬）肺	^{R}tsuphu	402021
lungs	肺	^{R}tshuphu	1301144
macadam road	馬路	^{F}modjugu	801013
magpie	喜鵲	^{R}chacha	202016
male	男人	^{L}moloji	1600006
male organ (baby term)	男生殖器（兒語）	^{L}niho	1301167
male organ (common term)	男生殖器	^{L}niho	1301165
male organ (euphemistic term)	男生殖器（隱語）	^{L}niho	1301166
mare	母馬	^{R}momi	203017
married woman	女人（已婚）	^{L}azumo	1600012
marrow	髓	^{R}bintu	1301007
matches	火柴	^{R}mi	703071
measure of 10 feet	丈	^{L}psu	904024
meat shop	肉店	^{L}shichire	902021
medicine	藥	^{L}tshugu	1403009
medicine and cure	醫藥	^{L}tshugu	1403000
melon seed	瓜子	^{R}byakozɨ	403029
menstruation	月經	^{F}shidjudju	1301175
mesh	網眼	^{R}phichuluku	703089
middle finger	中指	^{F}alele	1301131
middle of the month	月中	^{L}hlɛkadju	2300052
midnight	半夜	^{L}hũngudjiti	2300085
mildew, mold	霉	^{R}phohoto	102092
milk	牛奶	^{L}ngunyanya	405008
millet	小米	^{H}yugu	303020

mole	痣	ᴸmina	1301005
monkey	猴子	ᴸmi	201016
month	月	ᴸhlɛ	2300044
moon	月亮	ᴿdawa	101011
moonlight	月光	ᴿdawaᴴzo	101015
morning	早晨	ᴸnyadzɨ	2300079
mosquito	蚊子	ᴸtsolubyanga	204025
mother（address term）	媽媽	ᴿama	1502019
mother（quoting term）	母親	ᴿama	1502020
mound	小山	ᴸgakuatsʉtsʉ	102020
mouse	老鼠	ᴿha	201022
mouth	嘴	ᴸkotso	1301074
movies	電影	ᴸdiadjaga	1103081
mucus from the nose	鼻涕	ᴸnyamba	1301068
mud	泥（濕的）	ᴿyaki	102008
mud playing	玩泥沙	ᴿdjɨvika	1103002
mustache	胡鬚	ᴸaco	1301098
mutton	羊肉	ᴸtsʉsri	402029
nail	釘子	ᶠshudzʉbzu	703035
name	名字	ᴿmi	1501003
native village	老家	ᶠyoqolamu	1501011
nature, natural phenomena	自然、自然現象		100000
navel	肚臍	ᴿdjaku	1301148
near	近	ᴸandjondjo	2401040
neighbor	鄰居	ᴿfukər	1503010
nervous, palpitating heart	心跳	ᴿnimilupər	1402028
net	網	ᴿphichu	703088
newly open	開張	ᴴtrhi	901021
newspaper	報紙	ᴸndjigi	1001036
next month	下個月	ᶠmərcihlɛ	2300050
next year	明年	ᶠsoni	2300013
night falls	天黑了	ᴴnahũ	101003
nighttime	夜間	ᴸhŭkhu	2300072
nine	九	ᴸnggu	2600027
noon	中午	ᴿnikhu	2300081
noon meal, lunch	午飯	ᴿdogadzɨ	401004
nose	鼻子	ᴿnyaga	1301065
nosebleed	鼻血	ᴸnyanngashi	1402080
nostril	鼻孔	ᴿnyagaluku	1301067
numeral on the face of the clock	五分鐘	ᴿngahĩ	2300093
obscure, dark	暗	ᴿnahu	101024
o'clock	點鐘	ᴴthu	2300092
oil	油	ᶠyiki	404002

old maid	老處女	^{R}ayimi	1600013
old man	老頭兒	^{R}udzɨ	1600017
old woman	老太婆	^{R}ayimi	1600018
on fire, to catch fire	着火	^{F}mimakalihu	102100
one	一	^{L}ci	2600019
one and a half	一個半	^{R}dzɨlumopha	2600008
onion	洋葱	^{L}fuluphe	304059
opposite	對面	^{R}ruta	2401026
origin	出身	^{R}ndro	1501010
outside	外面	^{R}ikhədjə	2401013
outsider	外人	^{F}sutsho	1600032
overnight	隔夜	^{L}cihaka	2300087
ox	公牛	^{R}ligu	203002
pail	桶	^{F}khuzu	703062
palm	手掌	^{L}lapsu	1301121
paternal grandfather (address term)	爺爺	^{L}avu	1502012
paternal grandfather (quoting term)	祖父	^{L}avu	1502013
paternal grandmother (address term)	奶奶	^{L}ayi	1502014
paternal grandmother (quoting term)	祖母	^{L}ayi	1502015
paternal uncles	叔伯	^{L}avomo	1502027
path	小徑	^{H}djuguafofo	801020
peach	桃兒	^{R}bi	305002
peacock	孔雀	^{R}suphie	202026
peak	山頂	^{H}gakuBu	102015
peck, a dry measure (316c. in.)	斗	^{R}qa	904020
pencil	鉛筆	^{L}bucadji	1102017
penis	陰莖	^{L}niho	1301207
people	人民	^{L}tshoXo	802003
people from the same native village	同鄉	^{R}dzigadhi	1503005
pepper	辣椒	^{R}Xucio	304061
person from another province	外省人	^{F}nuakotsho	1600037
pheasant	雉、野鷄	^{R}he	202030
phlegm	痰	^{R}zikər	1301083
piece goods store	布庄	^{L}vuzrechire	902029
pig	(公) 豬	^{R}vako	203008
pig tender	放豬的	^{L}vatsrisu	1700033
pigeon	鴿子	^{R}thoyie	202018
pigtail	辮子	^{F}g'opərngu	1303025
pine	松樹	^{L}thobo	301015
pitch dark	黑	^{L}nakhi	101025
place	地方	^{F}dzuva	2401001
pond	池塘	^{R}chithang	102067
porcupine	刺蝟	^{R}phu	201019

posters, notices	招貼	ᴸdrog'ashu	901036
posthumous child	遺腹子	ᴸchidji	1600023
potato	馬鈴薯	ᴿyayu	304003
powder	粉	ᴿdrovɛ	102095
praying mantis	螳螂	ᴿbodjo	204034
pregnant woman	孕婦	ᴿlakhʉpa	1600015
pus	膿	ᴿnbər	1301021
rabbit	兔子	ᴿtoli	201021
rain	雨	ᴿhĩ	101036
rainbow	虹	ᴿgan	101046
raindrop	雨點	ᴸhĩlulu	101044
rainy day	下雨天	ᶠhidru	101070
ravine, pit	山坑	ᴸzraku	102026
relatives	親戚	ᴸvudji	1502002
ribs	肋骨	ᶠXodjə	1301203
rice husk	糠	ᴿnyo	303011
rickshaw	人力車	ᴸtshokapisuchez i	1003008
right-hand	右手	ᴿig'ər	1301112
ring finger, the 3rd finger	無名指	ᴸdrokhadji	1301132
river	河	ᴿhanji	102064
river bank	河岸	ᴸchibu	102065
river-bed	河床	ᴿkapo	102112
road	路	ᴸdjugu	801007
rock	大石頭	ᴸlupuᴸdiaposu	102011
roedeer	馴鹿	ᴸlo	201013
rope	麻繩	ᴸsakhʉdjə	703060
ropes, cordage	繩索	ᴸkuzri	703058
rosy clouds, rosy sunset	晚霞	ᴿdruvaluta	101049
round dumpling	包子	ᴿlaba	403009
saliva	唾液	ᴸtsidjər	1301081
sand	沙	ᴸdjevivi	102013
sandy beach	沙灘	ᴸdjevivie	102060
sawdust	鋸木屑	ᴸshivivi	703090
schoolmate	同學	ᶠsodziyokho	1503007
scrotum	陰囊	ᴸlithidjika	1301208
seed	種子	ᴿdzi	300003
senior generation	長輩	ᴸlochi	1502009
serious illness	大病、重病	ᴴmgogə'djə	1402003
seven	七	ᴸsi	2600025
sexual intercourse (common term)	性交	ᴿlaci	1301176
sexual intercourse (euphemistic term)	性交（隱語）	ᴿlaci	1301177
shadow	影	ᴿnahũ	101026
shape	樣子	ᴿi	2004001

English	Chinese	Transcription	Code
sheep	羊	ᴸyo	203014
ship, boat	船	ᴿgu	1003027
shit	大便	ꟳkhi	1301162
shoat, piglet	小豬	ᴸvahū	203011
shop	商店	ᴸqədjitrhizrɛ	901019
shop front	門面	ᴿkobo	901029
shop selling (cooking) oil	油房	ꟳikii̇	902017
shop selling rice	米棧	ᴿchuhɛdji	902014
shop selling salt	鹽店	ᴸchichire	902020
shoulder	肩膀	ꟳkərbulu	1301109
shower	驟雨	ꟳkhumdju	101042
siblings of father's brothers	堂兄弟	ꟳadiazeagodhi	1502075
siblings of father's sisters, of mother's brothers and sisters, cousins	表兄弟	ᴸavudhimi	1502076
sidewalk	人行道	ᴸtshodjugu	801014
silver	銀子	ꟳngu	102073
single child	獨生子	ᴿchiya	1600022
single eyelid	單眼皮	ꟳmyadjikudjici	1301045
sisters	姐妹	ᴸayagodhi	1502061
six	六	ᴸqhu	2600024
skin	皮	ᴿdjiqa	1301003
sky	天空	ꟳmnakha	101001
slope of a hill	山坡	ᴸdrivapopo	102018
small hand basket	提籃	ꟳbantəji	703067
smaller half	小半	ᴸatsɨtsɨmopha	2600007
smoke	烟	ꟳmikhu	102106
snow	雪	ꟳvie	101057
soft core of the young antler of the deer	茸	ᴸchiekuqa	200010
soil, earth	土（乾的）	ᴸdri	102007
sole of the foot	脚底	ᴿbapsɨ	1301195
some (number)	一些	ᴿyabu	2700049
son who ruins the family	敗家子	ᴿtshoəkhrbər	1600028
song	歌兒	ᴸga	1103045
son's daughter	孫女	ᴸzubumi	1502092
son's son	孫子	ᴸzubu	1502091
son's wife	媳婦	ᴸtrhi	1502083
sow	母豬	ᴿvami	203009
space between the thumb and forefinger	虎口	ᴸlakər	1301124
spaces between fingers	手縫	ᴸlamikərkər	1301125
sparrow	麻雀	ᴸlandridri	202017
sperm, semen	精液	ᴿndodje	1301210

spring	泉	ᴿranzɨ	102070
star	星	ᴿdri	101016
stepmother（address term）	後母（對稱）	ᶠalili	1502021
stepmother（quoting term）	後母（指稱）	ᶠalili	1502022
stern	船尾	ᴸgumərpo	1003029
stick	棍子	ᴸshikodjər	703054
stomach	胃	ᴿdjudja	1301145
stone	石頭	ᴸlupu	102010
store name	字號	ᴿdjigimidju	901030
straw	草	ᴿdju	703073
stream	溪	ᴿkaboatsʉtsʉ	102068
student	學生	ᴸsodji	1700027
sugar	糖	ᴿshabzu	404010
sun	太陽	ᴿhĩmĩ	101005
sunrise	日出	ᶠhimidjudju	2300078
sunset	傍晚	ᴸhŭkhu	2300083
surface of water	水面	ᴸndzrudimu	102033
surrounding	周圍	ᴿkudro	2401025
suspension bridge	吊橋	ᴸshunzo	801024
swallow	燕子	ᴿbibaba	202014
swamp	濕地、沼澤	ᶠnzushubi	102006
sweat	汗	ᴿkulu	1301014
sworn brothers	結拜兄弟	ᴸzayegodhishu	1503004
tael	兩	ᶠlo	904018
tail	（牛）尾	ᴸmər	402023
tail	尾巴	ᴿmərpo	200004
tangerine	柑	ᴸhyolo	305009
tares	稗子	ᴸyakha	303015
tea	茶	ᴿikha	405002
teacher	老師	ᶠsomi	1700026
teahouse	茶舘	ᴴikhachire	902034
tears caused by smoke, etc.	眼水	ᶠmyabu	1301013
teeth	牙	ᴸhə	1301086
telephone	電話	ᴸdiɛnhua	1001032
temporarily	暫時、暫且	ᶠthanshi	2800018
temporary bridge	架橋	ᶠnzochie	801025
ten	十	ᴸhĩXo	2600028
ten heavenly stems	天干	ᶠmufu	2300020
ten odd	十多個、十來個	ᴸXohanilu	2600037
testicles	睾丸	ᴸlithi	1301209
the clouds disperse	雲散	ᴸyokoyomu	101048
the common yellow cattle	黃牛	ᴿg'u	203005
the day breaks	天亮了	ᶠmyando	101002
the earth	地	ᶠdzuva	102001

the first one	頭一個	ᴸdroG'ogocilu	2600040
the hail falls	下雹子	ᴿndrodju	101061
the last one	最後一個	ᶠmərgocilu	2600041
the leg	腿	ᶠbuyu	1301184
the rain ceases	晴雨	ᴸliqho	101039
the snow melts	化雪	ᴿviehua	101058
the sun rises	出太陽	ᴿhimiᴿdzruzru	101006
the sun sets	日落	ᴿhimiᴸqhɛ	101007
the wind blows	刮風	ᶠmusudadji	101029
the wind stops	（風）停	ᴿmafu	101030
there	那兒	ᴸchimu	2700030
these	這些	ᶠtitsa	2700027
thigh	大腿	ᴸguluchi	1301185
this evening	今天晚上	ᴸtahū	2300066
this month	這個月	ᶠdihlɛ	2300048
this morning	今天早上	ᴿdasho	2300064
this year	今年	ᶠpsuvər	2300012
those	那些	ᶠchitsa	2700028
three	三	ᴸso	2600021
throat	喉嚨	ᴸtshʉkuta	1301107
thumb	大姆指	ᶠanimo	1301128
thunder	雷	ᶠmuvo	101064
tiger	老虎	ᴿla	201002
tile	瓦	ᴿgolu	703077
time	時候	ᴸhathacithu	2300001
time	時間	ᴸhatha	2300000
to advance	進	ᴿtshʉta	1404026
to advance, develop (business, wealth, etc.)	發達	ᶠsukagədjə	901055
to answer	答	ᴸlisho, ᴸlingu	1001013
to answer a telephone call	聽電話	ᴸdiɛnhuabahī	1001035
to ascend	上	ᴸlaga	2402009
to ask	問	ᶠkotshʉ	1001012
to attack	攻	ᴿtshʉta	1404024
to balance sale with capital	還本	ᴸbazriyahɛ	901011
to be a guest	作客	ᴸvərmu	1204024
to be born	出生	ᴿdjo	1401004
to be grown up	大了	ᶠdiodju	1401010
to be pregnant	懷孕	ᴸlakupa	1301178
to be silent	不做聲	ᶠmashatshʉ	1001017
to be struck by a thunderbolt	雷劈	ᶠmuvoukhi	101066
to be surnamed	姓	ᴸshi	1501002
to beat (with a stick)	棍打	ᴸshikozrembo	703055
to become a soldier	當兵	ᴸmamu	1404007

to betray one's country	賣國	ᴸtrhɨ	802006
to bite	咬	ᴸchu	1302031
to bleed	流血	ᴸshiedjudju	1301012
to blow	吹	ᴴfu	1302047
to blow the trumpet	吹喇叭	ᴿsalatsufu	1103059
to boil	煮（用水煮）	ᶠtshɨdju	406072
to breathe	呼吸	ᴸsadjudju	1301023
to build a road	築路	ᴸdjugushishi	801009
to burn	燒	ᶠmimaka	102099
to buy	買	ᴴhɛ	901003
to buy meat	買肉	ᴿshihɛsu	902022
to buy rice	買米、糴米	ᴿchuhɛ	902015
to call	叫	ᴸgahũ	1001018
to call, to designate	稱呼	ᴴhatamudo	1501007
to celebrate birthday	做生日	ᴿdjosushinyiko	1203027
to chant sacred books	念經	ᴸbi	1201026
to chew the cud	反芻	ᶠdruliga	200011
to choke with food	哽	ᴸdzɨkata	1302044
to chop with an axe	砍	ᴿnda	703018
to clap the hands	拍手	ᴸlakanganga	1302061
to claw	抓	ᴴg'ər	200007
to clean the bottom	揩（屁股）	ᴿdjubikuku	1303018
to climb a hill	爬山	ᴿrabibər	103004
to close the eyes	閉眼	ᶠmyalumərmər	1302011
to come	來	ᴴlo	2402007
to congeal	凝固	ᴸfudrikalanya	102114
to cook soup	煮湯	ᶠdjuca	406096
to count as	算	ᴿsa	1501009
to count with the fingers	數手指頭	ᴸlanika	1302067
to crack	裂	ᶠkərpər	102005
to crack firecrackers	放鞭炮	ᶠhopərqa	1202003
to crack the knuckles	折指頭關節	ᴸlanisachie	1302069
to creep	（藤）蔓延	ᴸg'a	300002
to cross	過	ᴸnbər	2402014
to cross a bridge	過橋	ᶠnzonbər	801022
to dance	跳舞	ᴿlopər	1103066
to deep-fry	炸	ᴿtra	406079
to descend	下	ᴸmiag	2402010
to descend from a hill	下山	ᴸzalidia	103006
to die	死	ᴿshoko	1401022
to disappear	不見了	ᴸmandohər	2500005
to dismiss school	放學	ᴸdjigiphuko	1101008
to dismount from a cart	下車	ᶠchetsuzadia	1003019
to dive	潛水	ᶠndruahyomuchi	103012

ナムイ語語彙集

207

to doze	打瞌睡	ᴸyangərngər	1301028
to dream	做夢	ᴿima	1401016
to dredge a river	疏通水流	ᴿkhərzahusi	103014
to drip	滴	ᴸndrə	101045
to droop the head	低頭	ᶠg'odjəkuku	1302004
to drown	溺	ᶠndruhota	103011
to end	完	ᴿshica	2402005
to enjoy coolness	乘涼	ᴴshushubuyu	103021
to enter	進	ᴴdia	2402011
to exit	出	ᴿdjudju	2402012
to expel intestinal gas	放屁	ᴿkhichi	1301164
to feel dizzy	頭暈	ᴴg'djandzro	1402011
to fertilize	施肥	ᴸdritri	306008
to fish out	撈	ᴸg'a	1302115
to float	浮	ᴸbzu	102042
to flood	泛濫	ᶠzudzudjamo	102041
to flow	（水）流	ᶠzuzaqo	102037
to foam	冒泡	ᶠdzudzuva	102071
to freeze	結冰、凍	ᴸndzrugota	102035
to gain/to earn money	賺錢	ᴸbazrikondjo	901008
to get drenched by the rain	淋雨	ᶠhĩdru	101038
to get old	老了	ᶠlamo	1401011
to get onto a cart	上車	ᶠchetsulobu	1003018
to gnaw at a bone	齦（骨頭）	ᴸkhər	1302034
to go	去	ᴸdju	2402008
to go by boat	坐船	ᴿgundzu	1003050
to go home	回家	ᶠyokolibu	1002015
to go house hunting	找房子	ᴿishu	902040
to go into partnership	合伙	ᴿyoko	901006
to go to school	上學	ᴸdjigisobu	1101007
to go with the wind	順風	ᶠmizufu	103002
to gore	（牛）鬥角	ᶠfukər	203006
to gossip	聊天	ᴿdiomasu	1103029
to graduate	畢業	ᴸsoshica	1101025
to grow	長大	ᶠdhudiodju	1401009
to guard	守	ᴿlodia	1404025
to hang oneself	上吊	ᶠg'etsu	1401024
to hatch	孵卵、抱小鷄	ᶠrafu	203037
to have a haircut (female)	剪頭髮（女）	ᶠg'odjəkər	1303029
to have a haircut (male)	剪頭髮（男）	ᶠg'odjəkər	1303028
to have a running nose	流鼻涕	ᴸnyambadjudju	1301069
to have diarrhea	拉肚子	ᴸhĩbishu	1402034
to have fever	發燒	ᴸgumichi	1402042
to have headache	頭痛	ᴴg'django	1402010

to have lice	生蝨子	ᶠshuba	1402063
to have nocturnal emissions	夢遺	ᴿnbudzə	1301168
to hear	聽	ᴿbahĩ	1302020
to hiccough	打噎	ᴸgəti	1402021
to hold in the mouth	含	ᴿhtshita	1302042
to hold with the hand	拿	ᴸla	1302070
to hunt	打獵	ᴿshuchie	206003
to increase	增加	ᶠdrodro	2600012
to inter, to bury	埋葬	ᴸmodri	1203041
to introduce	介紹	ᴸdhingutaco	1204006
to inundate	淹	ᴿngku	102115
to invite guests, to give a party	請客	ᴸvərndo	1204022
to jump	跳	ᴸlopər	1302203
to knit the eyebrows	皺眉	ᶠmyalutsɯmər	1302008
to lay eggs	下蛋	ᴿragugu	203035
to lend, to borrow (money)	借（錢）	ᴸnyi	903013
to lick with blade of tongue	舐	ᴸya	1302036
to light a match	劃火柴	ᴿmitrhi	703072
to load goods	下貨	ᴸqədjila	901028
to lose	輸	ᴸmag'a	1103089
to lose money in business	賠錢	ᶠlitrhi	901010
to mail a letter	寄信	ᴸndjigibu	1001030
to make a quotation	要價	ᴸphuhũ	901038
to make an offer	還價	ᴿphuganga	901039
to make friends	交朋友	ᴸyokosu	1204005
to measure (cloth)	量（布）	ᶠvudjandja	904015
to measure (rice)	量（米）	ᶠchudjo	904014
to melt	溶解	ᴴdzuduzhua	101059
to mew	猫叫	ᴿhalamərmər	203025
to mount a hill	上山	ᴿrabibər	103005
to navigate	航海	ᴸnguchi	103018
to nod	點頭	ᶠg'odjətangər	1302001
to observe the New Year	過年	ᴸkhushi	1202006
to open a shop	開舖子	ᴸqədjitrhi	901020
to open the eyes	開眼	ᶠmyalupo	1302010
to order food in a restaurant	叫菜	ᶠtidjochucilusuhe	902036
to owe (money)	欠（錢）	ᴿzo	903014
to pant	喘氣	ᴿhaphər	1301026
to pay tax	納稅	ᴸbazridjabu	802014
to peck	啄	ᴿbupa	202007
to peel	剝皮	ᴿzrikunyu	306038
to peel with a peeler	削皮	ᴿzrakonyu	306039
to pierce	穿	ᴸza	703014
to play	玩	ᴿkala	1103001

English	Chinese	Transcription	Code
to play the flute	吹笛子	ᴿfujifu	1103055
to pledge in wine	勸酒	ᴴvutandzri	1204032
to plow the field	種地	ᴸdrogi	306011
to point	指	ᴸdiathatha	1302066
to pop	爆	ᴿbu	406077
to press down	按	ᴸtrhi	1302095
to prick	刺	ᴿngo	703013
to prosper by becoming wealthy	發財	ᶠsukər	901053
to pull	拉	ᶠkapi	1302107
to push	推	ᴿtsho	1302106
to raise children	養孩子	ᴿlakhʉg'umər	1401006
to raise the head	抬頭	ᶠg'odjəlotshʉ	1302003
to read a book	看書	ᴿdjigilu	1101036
to receive a telephone call	接電話	ᴸdiɛnhuandhi	1001034
to recite incantations	念咒	ᴿndji	1201039
to remove teeth	拔牙	ᴸhəkərpu	1402019
to repair	修理	ᴿshishi	703092
to rest	休息	ᶠnyi	1401013
to retreat	退	ᴸdjudju	1404027
to return	回	ᴿlidia	2402013
to return (money)	還（錢）	ᴸli	903016
to rinse the mouth	漱口	ᴴkotsoii	1303015
to roar (as lion)	吼	ᴸndo	201026
to roast	烤	ᴿng'a	406084
to roll	滾	ᶠpulili	703045
to row a boat	划船	ᴿguci	1003033
to rub in	擦	ᴸzo	1302093
to seat at a dinner table	入座	ᶠndzundjandzu	1204030
to see	看	ᴸlu	1302009
to see a visitor off	送客	ᴸvərpu	1204023
to sell	賣	ᴴchi	901004
to sell rice	賣米、糶米	ᴿchutri	902016
to settle a restaurant bill	算帳	ᴸbadjihabuta	902037
to shake hands	握手	ᴸlakasoso	1302064
to shake the head	搖頭	ᶠg'odjədjudju	1302002
to shamanize	跳神	ᴴchərmichu	1201033
to shave the head	剃頭	ᶠg'odjəchu	1303030
to shine	照	ᴿzo	101009
to shoulder	挑	ᴸchɨ	1302051
to shout	喊	ᴸndo	1001019
to sign	簽字	ᴸdjigidjinyu	901046
to sink	沈	ᶠzukuozako	102043
to sit	坐	ᶠndzu	1302178
to sit down	坐下	ᴸmindzuti	1302179

to sit up	坐起來	ᴸlotsrhi	1302180
to sleep	睡覺	ᴿndju	1401014
to smell	聞	ᴿhĩhĩ	1302021
to smoke	抽烟	ᶠyandri	405010
to smoke	燻	ᶠmikhulaha	102107
to snap the fingers	彈指	ᴸlanisa	1302068
to snore	打鼾	ᴸnyambachi	1301073
to spit	吐口水	ᴴphi	1302048
to spit	吐痰	ᴿzɨdzəphi	1301084
to split	劈	ᶠkhu	703012
to spurt	噴	ᴿXota	1302046
to stand	站	ᴸhĩ	1302181
to start	開始	ᴸamimu	2402003
to start serving a banquet	上菜	ᴿdjochi	1204031
to stay overnight	過夜	ᴿtaha	2300088
to steam	蒸	ᴿni	406080
to stick out the tongue	吐舌頭	ᴸĩdhi	1302050
to stir fry, to fry	炒	ᴿhʉhʉ	406075
to stop the flow of water	截水	ᴿkhərta	103013
to stretch out the hand	伸手	ᴸlakandhi	1302060
to study	念書	ᴿdjigipi	1101033
to submerge	丟在水裡	ᶠndruvudjumici	103024
to suck	吸	ᴿthi	1302030
to sun	晒	ᴿhimiᴿg'a	101008
to suppurate	釀膿	ᴿnbərdjudju	1301022
to swallow	吞	ᶠniphi	1302043
to sweat	流汗	ᴿkuludjudju	1301015
to take a bath	洗澡	ᴿgumitshʉ	1303003
to take a husband	嫁	ᴴvərtshʉ	1203007
to take a nap	睡午覺	ᴿnikondju	1401015
to take a wife	娶	ᴴhɛ	1203006
to take in the fingers	拈	ᴿkanɨ	1302071
to talk in sleep	説夢話	ᴸimasʉsʉshu	1401017
to teach	教書	ᴿdjigiso	1101027
to telephone	打電話	ᴸdiɛnhuaga	1001033
to tell fortune	算命	ᶠlutratra	1201042
to tend cattle	放牛	ᴿg'əlu	206008
to tend pigs	養豬	ᴸvatapa	206011
to thresh	打穀子	ᶠdzringa	306025
to travel	出門、旅行	ᴿkalabu	1002001
to tug under the arm	腋下夾	ᴸyedjekərkərnita	1302054
to turn the head	回頭	ᶠg'odjəndjo	1302005
to twinkle	閃鑠	ᶠtsipha	101021
to twist ropes	打繩	ᴸsakhʉdjəmbo	703061

to unite	團結	ᴿdzɨdzɨ	802015
to unload goods	上貨	ᴸqədjidji	901027
to visit a doctor	看醫生	ᴴngolu	1403002
to wag the tail	搖尾	ᴸmakudzabudzru	200005
to walk on foot	走路	ᴸdjugubər	801008
to wash face	洗臉	ᴸphomitshu	1303001
to wash rice	淘米	ᴸtrutshɨ	406002
to watch the children	看（孩子）	ᴿlakhug'ulu	1401007
to watch the movie	看電影	ᴸdiadjagalu	1103082
to wave the hand	揮手	ᴸlakaphala	1302056
to weed	除草	ᴸdromər	306006
to whip	鞭打、抽	ᴸbachərmbo	703057
to whole life	一生、一輩子	ᴿcidzɨ	1401002
to win	贏	ᴸg'a	1103088
to worship god	拜神	ᶠnuvu	1201003
to wrap	包	ᴿzrabu	1302151
to write	寫字	ᴸmidjudji	1101049
to write a letter	寫信	ᴸndjigindji	1001025
to write the wrong characters	寫錯字	ᴸdjilamadji	1101053
today	今天	ᴿtani	2300057
tomorrow	明天	ᴸshugu	2300058
tomorrow evening	明天晚上	ᶠsohu	2300067
tomorrow morning	明天早上	ᴿshugunadje	2300065
tongue	舌頭	ᴿi	1301077
toothbrush	牙刷	ᴸhətshu	1303011
top of the head	頭頂	ᴿlopu	1301030
toy	玩具	ᴿkalasukadji	1103003
trade	買賣	ᶠvulamu	901001
travelling	旅行	ᴿkala	1002000
travelling expenses	路費	ᴸndhuguphu	1002008
tree	樹	ᴿshipo	300008
tricycle	三輪車	ᴴsolupulilisuchez i	1003012
tripe	肚子	ᴸhɨbi	402022
trumpet	喇叭	ᴿsalatsu	1103058
turnip	蘿蔔	ᴸlibi	304030
turtledove	斑鳩	ᴿthoyie	202020
twin	雙胞胎	ᴸchidju	1600021
two	二	ᴸni	2600020
umbilical cord	臍帶	ᴿdjapər	1301149
unmarried young woman	姑娘	ᴸzumiphiadjudju	1600011
upper course of a river	上流	ᶠndrungu	102110
urine	尿	ᴸmbər	1301161
uterine brothers	同胞兄弟	ᴸzaiyagodhi	1502055
uterus	子宮	ᴸziko	1301172

uvula	小舌	ᴸidji	1301085
valley	山谷	ᴿrakhər	102025
vapor, steam	水蒸氣	ᴿsa	102109
vegetables	蔬菜	ᴸyochy	304000
verdigris	銅綠	ꜰhɛdru	102075
very long (in time)	很久	ꜰG'oatha	2600003
village	鄉村	ᴿfukər	801027
voice	聲音	ᴸkhɔ	1301202
vulva (baby term)	女生殖器（兒語）	ꜰpapa	1301170
vulva (common term)	女生殖器	ꜰpapa	1301169
vulva (euphemistic term)	女生殖器（隱語）	ꜰpapa	1301171
waist	腰	ᴿdju	1301146
wasp	黃蜂	ꜰbzuloho	204013
water	水	ᴸndzru	102032
water gate	水閘	ꜰndrukobo	103015
waterfall	瀑布	ꜰzuvudje	102046
wave	波浪	ꜰzuvulie	102051
weather	天氣	ꜰmutsaliqo	101067
wedding day	結婚的日子	ᴴvərtshusucinyi	1203008
what?	什麼	ꜰhūtsa	2700038
wheat	麥子	ᴴsulu	303013
wheat flour	麵粉	ᴸdjovi	303018
wheel	輪子	ᴸdjosu	703044
where?	哪兒	ꜰashadia	2700040
whip	鞭子	ᴸbachər	703056
whole	整個	ᴸdjilumu	2600004
whole day	整天	ᴸdjinimu	2300073
why?	爲什麼	ᴿhomolɛ	2700044
widow	寡婦	ᴿmolushokoni	1600016
widower	鰥夫	ᴸbushokoni	1600009
wife	妻子	ᴸmbər	1502051
wife's father (address term)	岳父	ᴸavu	1502040
wife's mother (address term)	岳母	ᴸadzi	1502042
wild boar	野豬	ᴿbanyo	201014
wild goose	雁	ᴴku	202027
wild pepper	花椒	ᴸdju	404029
wind	風	ꜰmusu	101027
windfall	橫財	ꜰmazusubədji	901054
wine shop	酒坊	ꜰvuchire	902024
wine shop, a restaurant	酒舘	ᴴvuchire	902035
wing	翅膀	ᴸduka	202003
wire	鐵絲	ꜰshuji	703075
with the current	順水	ᴸndruqaqanbər	103009
wives of brothers	妯娌	ꜰmitrhihami	1502056

213

wolf	狼	ᴸdjie	201005
woman who remarries	再婚的女人	ᴿzumilivatshə	1600014
wood	木頭	ᴿshi	703076
woodpecker	啄木鳥	ᴿzumie	202025
world	世界	ᶠnanakayaku	103022
wrinkle	皺紋	ᴿdjiqata	1301004
wrist	手腕子	ᴸlatsĩ	1301118
year	年	ᴴkhu	2300010
year after next	後年	ᶠnoni	2300014
year before last	前年	ᴸshini	2300016
year old	歲	ᴸpər	1401030
yesterday	昨天	ᶠzunyi	2300061
yesterday evening	昨天晚上	ᶠyuhũ	2300069
young cock	小公鷄	ᶠrapudri	203028
young in age	（年紀）小	ᶠpəratsutsu	1401008
young man	小伙子	ᴸmoloji	1600005
younger brother (quoting term)	弟弟	ᴿgodhi	1502060
younger sister (quoting term)	妹妹	ᴿgədri	1502065
youngest child	老幺	ᶠlimər	1600020

ナムイ語＝英語＝漢語順

ナムイ語	英語	漢語	項目番号
ᶠadia	father (address term)	爸爸	1502017
ᶠadia	father (quoting term)	父親	1502018
ᶠadiazeagodhi	siblings of father's brothers	堂兄弟	1502075
ᶠakhadji	little finger	小指	1301129
ᶠalele	middle finger	中指	1301131
ᶠalili	stepmother (address term)	後母（對稱）	1502021
ᶠalili	stepmother (quoting term)	後母（指稱）	1502022
ᶠani	husband's mother (address term)	婆婆（對稱）	1502025
ᶠani	husband's mother (quoting term)	婆婆（指稱）	1502026
ᶠanimo	thumb	大姆指	1301128
ᶠaphu	father's sister's husband	姑父	1502033
ᶠaphu	husband's father (address term)	公公（對稱）	1502023
ᶠaphu	husband's father (quoting term)	公公（指稱）	1502024
ᶠapo	elder brother (address term)	哥哥（對稱）	1502057
ᶠapo	elder brother (quoting term)	哥哥（指稱）	1502058
ᶠapo	elder sister's husband	姐夫	1502064
ᶠashadia	where?	哪兒	2700040
ᶠbalala	butterfly	蝴蝶	204014
ᶠbantəji	small hand basket	提籃	703067
ᶠbikodra	beast	禽獸	201001

ᶠbikodra	beasts	走獸	201000
ᶠbiniphu	bad smell	臭	2003004
ᶠbuyu	the leg	腿	1301184
ᶠbzucər	intestinal worm	蛔蟲	204054
ᶠbzudra	honey	蜂蜜	204012
ᶠbzuloho	wasp	黃蜂	204013
ᶠbzupu	honeycomb, beehive	蜂窩	204011
ᶠchetsulobu	to get onto a cart	上車	1003018
ᶠchetsuzadia	to dismount from a cart	下車	1003019
ᶠchibu	liver	肝	1301150
ᶠchitsa	those	那些	2700028
ᶠchudjo	to measure (rice)	量（米）	904014
ᶠdhudiodju	to grow	長大	1401009
ᶠdiadjimopha	greater half	大半	2600006
ᶠdiakhu	distant (in relationship)	疏	1502006
ᶠdiaku	far	遠	2401039
ᶠdihlɛ	this month	這個月	2300048
ᶠdiodju	to be grown up	大了	1401010
ᶠdjuca	to cook soup	煮湯	406096
ᶠdjudjə	address	地址	1501013
ᶠdjumi	local place names	地名	803000
ᶠdrodro	to increase	增加	2600012
ᶠdruliga	to chew the cud	反芻	200011
ᶠdzibashiphi	landowner	地主	1700031
ᶠdzɨdzɨ	gong	鑼	1103060
ᶠdzingume	foster son	養子	1502081
ᶠdzringa	to thresh	打穀子	306025
ᶠdzudzuva	to foam	冒泡	102071
ᶠdzuva	place	地方	2401001
ᶠdzuva	the earth	地	102001
ᶠdzuva, ᶠmi	earth, fire	地理、火	102000
ᶠdzuvaphu	ground	地上	102003
ᶠdzuvuliɛ	earthquake	地震	102004
ᶠfukər	to gore	（牛）鬥角	203006
ᶠg'ūdjə	head	頭	1301029
ᶠg'etsu	to hang oneself	上吊	1401024
ᶠG'oacihlɛ	last month	上個月	2300049
ᶠG'oatha	very long (in time)	很久	2600003
ᶠg'odjəchu	to shave the head	剃頭	1303030
ᶠg'odjədjudju	to shake the head	搖頭	1302002
ᶠg'odjəkər	to have a haircut (female)	剪頭髮（女）	1303029
ᶠg'odjəkər	to have a haircut (male)	剪頭髮（男）	1303028
ᶠg'odjəkuku	to droop the head	低頭	1302004
ᶠg'odjəlotshu	to raise the head	抬頭	1302003

ᶠg'odjəndjo	to turn the head	回頭	1302005
ᶠg'odjətangər	to nod	點頭	1302001
ᶠg'opərngu	pigtail	辮子	1303025
ᶠhɛ	gold	金子	102072
ᶠhɛdru	verdigris	銅綠	102075
ᶠhidru	rainy day	下雨天	101070
ᶠhĩdru	it rains	下雨	101037
ᶠhĩdru	to get drenched by the rain	淋雨	101038
ᶠhĩlulu	raindrop	雨點	101044
ᶠhimidjudju	sunrise	日出	2300078
ᶠhiminigu	daytime	白天	2300071
ᶠhopərqa	to crack firecrackers	放鞭炮	1202003
ᶠhũtsa	what?	什麼	2700038
ᶠikiɨ	shop selling (cooking) oil	油房	902017
ᶠkapi	to pull	拉	1302107
ᶠkərbulu	shoulder	肩膀	1301109
ᶠkərpər	to crack	裂	102005
ᶠkhi	shit	大便	1301162
ᶠkhozukɔ	crossbar at the top of a Chinese bucket	桶杷子	703064
ᶠkhozula	hand bucket	提桶	703063
ᶠkhu	to split	劈	703012
ᶠkhumdju	shower	驟雨	101042
ᶠkhuzu	pail	桶	703062
ᶠkotshʉ	to ask	問	1001012
ᶠkudjɨligundjo	all year round	一年到頭	2300019
ᶠkug'u	beginning of the year	年初	2300017
ᶠkukɛr	horn	角	200009
ᶠkumər	end of the year	年底	2300018
ᶠlamo	to get old	老了	1401011
ᶠlaqo	crow	烏鴉	202015
ᶠlimər	youngest child	老幺	1600020
ᶠlĩndjophukohʉ	ivory	象牙	703084
ᶠlitrhi	to lose money in business	賠錢	901010
ᶠlo	tael	兩	904018
ᶠlodre	dragon	龍	200012
ᶠlohomandji	bald-headed	禿頭	1301036
ᶠluku	cave	山洞	102028
ᶠluku	hole	窟窿	102029
ᶠlutratra	to tell fortune	算命	1201042
ᶠmakotshʉ	"may I ask"	請問	1204037
ᶠmamiamtso	half-cooked	半生不熟	406091
ᶠmashatshʉ	to be silent	不做聲	1001017
ᶠmatsa	cloudy day	陰天	101069

ᶠmazusubədji	windfall	橫財	901054
ᶠmərcihlɛ	next month	下個月	2300050
ᶠmərgocilu	the last one	最後一個	2600041
ᶠmi	fire	火	102098
ᶠmikhu	smoke	烟	102106
ᶠmikhulaha	to smoke	燻	102107
ᶠmimaka	to burn	燒	102099
ᶠmimakalihᵾ	on fire, to catch fire	着火	102100
ᶠmindje	flame	火焰	102108
ᶠmitrhi	elder brother's wife	嫂子	1502059
ᶠmitrhihami	wives of brothers	妯娌	1502056
ᶠmizufu	to go with the wind	順風	103002
ᶠmnaka	god	老天爺	1201001
ᶠmnakha	sky	天空	101001
ᶠmnakhazrime	horizon	天邊	101004
ᶠmo	livestock	牲口	203001
ᶠmodjugu	macadam road	馬路	801013
ᶠmuərzupa	lightning	閃電	101062
ᶠmufu	ten heavenly stems	天干	2300020
ᶠmusu	wind	風	101027
ᶠmusudadji	the wind blows	刮風	101029
ᶠmutsaliqo	weather	天氣	101067
ᶠmuvo	thunder	雷	101064
ᶠmuvomərmər	it thunders	打雷	101065
ᶠmuvoukhi	to be struck by a thunderbolt	雷劈	101066
ᶠmuzukata	against the wind	頂風	103003
ᶠmyabu	tears caused by smoke, etc.	眼水	1301013
ᶠmyachohū	eyebrow	眉毛	1301042
ᶠmyachohū	eyelash	睫毛	1301047
ᶠmyadjiku	eyelid	眼皮	1301044
ᶠmyadjikudjici	single eyelid	單眼皮	1301045
ᶠmyadjikunyici	double eyelid	雙眼皮	1301046
ᶠmyakandju	chin	下巴	1301100
ᶠmyalu	eyes	眼睛	1301043
ᶠmyalumərmər	to close the eyes	閉眼	1302011
ᶠmyalupo	to open the eyes	開眼	1302010
ᶠmyalutsᵾmər	to knit the eyebrows	皺眉	1302008
ᶠmyando	dawn	天亮、黎明	2300076
ᶠmyando	the day breaks	天亮了	101002
ᶠmyasubulu	eyeball	眼珠	1301049
ᶠnanakayaku	world	世界	103022
ᶠndro	hail	冰雹	101060
ᶠndruahyomuchi	to dive	潛水	103012
ᶠndruchi	boiling water	開水	405001

ᶠndrudzər	against the current	逆水	103010
ᶠndrudzuva	climate	水土	101072
ᶠndruhota	to drown	溺	103011
ᶠndrukobo	water gate	水閘	103015
ᶠndrumər	lower course of a river	下流	102111
ᶠndrungu	upper course of a river	上流	102110
ᶠndruqaqanbər	with the current	順水	103009
ᶠndrutogo	embankment	水壩	103016
ᶠndruvudjumici	to submerge	丟在水裡	103024
ᶠndzrivakapa	drought	天旱	101071
ᶠndzrutshudju	(water) boils	水開了	406095
ᶠndzu	to sit	坐	1302178
ᶠndzundjandzu	to seat at a dinner table	入座	1204030
ᶠngu	silver	銀子	102073
ᶠniphi	to swallow	吞	1302043
ᶠnoni	year after next	後年	2300014
ᶠnonyisho	day after day after tomorrow	大後天	2300060
ᶠnosho	day atrer tomorrow	後天	2300059
ᶠnosohŭgu	day after tomorrow evening	後天晚上	2300068
ᶠnuakotsho	person from another province	外省人	1600037
ᶠnuha	ancestor	祖先	1502001
ᶠnuvu	to worship god	拜神	1201003
ᶠnyi	to rest	休息	1401013
ᶠnyuhla	deity	神	1201002
ᶠnzochie	temporary bridge	架橋	801025
ᶠnzonbər	to cross a bridge	過橋	801022
ᶠnzushubi	swamp	濕地、沼澤	102006
ᶠpapa	vulva (baby term)	女生殖器（兒語）	1301170
ᶠpapa	vulva (common term)	女生殖器（常語）	1301169
ᶠpapa	vulva (euphemistic term)	女生殖器（隱語）	1301171
ᶠpəratsutsu	young in age	（年紀）小	1401008
ᶠpsuvər	this year	今年	2300012
ᶠpulili	to roll	滾	703045
ᶠrafu	to hatch	孵卵、抱小鷄	203037
ᶠramomo	cockscomb	鷄冠	203029
ᶠrapo	cock	公鷄	203026
ᶠrapudri	young cock	小公鷄	203028
ᶠrasho	capon	閹鷄	203027
ᶠshidjudju	menstruation	月經	1301175
ᶠshitsha	(food) fresh	新鮮	2003003
ᶠshivu	(pork) liver	（豬）肝	402020
ᶠshuba	to have lice	生蝨子	1402063
ᶠshudzubzu	nail	釘子	703035
ᶠshuji	wire	鐵絲	703075

ᶠshunzo	suspension bridge	吊橋	801024
ᶠsodziyokho	schoolmate	同學	1503007
ᶠsohũ	tomorrow evening	明天晚上	2300067
ᶠsomi	teacher	老師	1700026
ᶠsoni	next year	明年	2300013
ᶠsukagədjə	to advance, develop (business, wealth, etc.)	發達	901055
ᶠsukər	to prosper by becoming wealthy	發財	901053
ᶠsutsho	outsider	外人	1600032
ᶠtandzu	"please have a seat"	請坐	1204046
ᶠthanshi	temporarily	暫時、暫且	2800018
ᶠtidjochucilusuhe	to order food in a restaurant	叫菜	902036
ᶠtitsa	these	這些	2700027
ᶠtrashidele	auspicious	吉祥	1201059
ᶠtshidju	to boil	煮（用水煮）	406072
ᶠtsipha	to twinkle	閃鑠	101021
ᶠtukutsho	aboriginal	本地人	1600036
ᶠvasu	carrying pole	扁担	703041
ᶠvie	snow	雪	101057
ᶠvuchire	wine shop	酒坊	902024
ᶠvudjandja	to measure (cloth)	量（布）	904015
ᶠvulamu	trade	買賣	901001
ᶠvũngasukajɨ	funnel	漏斗	703068
ᶠXodjə	backbone	背骨	1301157
ᶠXodjə	ribs	肋骨	1301203
ᶠyandri	to smoke	抽烟	405010
ᶠyiki	oil	油	404002
ᶠyohokosu	host	主人	1204014
ᶠyokokotsho	family	家眷、家人	1502096
ᶠyokolibu	to go home	回家	1002015
ᶠyoqo	home	家	1501012
ᶠyoqolamu	native village	老家	1501011
ᶠyuhũ	yesterday evening	昨天晚上	2300069
ᶠzavu	daughter's husband	女婿	1502086
ᶠzriga	brother's son	姪兒	1502087
ᶠzrimi	girl	女孩子	1600004
ᶠzudiadju	flood	大水	102039
ᶠzudzudjamo	to flood	泛濫	102041
ᶠzug'odza	ford	渡口	102066
ᶠzukuozako	to sink	沈	102043
ᶠzɯnyi	yesterday	昨天	2300061
ᶠzuvudje	waterfall	瀑布	102046
ᶠzuvulie	wave	波浪	102051
ᶠzuzaqo	to flow	（水）流	102037

ᶠzuzri	(water) to wash	（水）冲	102038
ᴴbi	fragrant	香	2003002
ᴴbu	insects	爬虫、昆虫	204000
ᴴbzūbu	bee	蜜蜂	204008
ᴴchərmichu	to shamanize	跳神	1201033
ᴴchi	dog	狗	203020
ᴴchi	to sell	賣	901004
ᴴdia	to enter	進	2402011
ᴴdjuguafoɟo	path	小徑	801020
ᴴdzuduzhua	to melt	溶解	101059
ᴴfu	(wind) to blow	（風）吹	101028
ᴴfu	to blow	吹	1302047
ᴴg'djandzro	to feel dizzy	頭暈	1402011
ᴴg'django	to have headache	頭痛	1402010
ᴴg'ər	to claw	抓	200007
ᴴgakuʙu	peak	山頂	102015
ᴴgakudjamər	foot of a hill	山脚	102017
ᴴgakudjiti	halfway up a mountain	山半腰	102016
ᴴhatamudo	to call, to designate	稱呼	1501007
ᴴhɛ	to buy	買	901003
ᴴhɛ	to take a wife	娶	1203006
ᴴhɛchire	gold shop	金店	902032
ᴴhĩdiaᶠdzumudru	heavy rain	大雨	101040
ᴴhĩLatsʉtsʉ	drizzle	小雨	101041
ᴴikhachire	teahouse	茶舘	902034
ᴴji	boy	男孩子	1600003
ᴴkhu	year	年	2300010
ᴴki	copper	銅	102074
ᴴkotsoii	to rinse the mouth	漱口	1303015
ᴴku	wild goose	雁	202027
ᴴlinbuchu	elephant	象	201010
ᴴlo	to come	來	2402007
ᴴmgo	disease	病	1402001
ᴴmgogə'djə	serious illness	大病、重病	1402003
ᴴmyalukobu	eyesight blurred	眼花	1402012
ᴴnahũ	night falls	天黑了	101003
ᴴngolu	to visit a doctor	看醫生	1403002
ᴴphi	to spit	吐口水	1302048
ᴴragubini	(ham) stale smell	（火腿）臭	2003006
ᴴshu	louse	蝨子	204049
ᴴshushubuyu	to enjoy coolness	乘涼	103021
ᴴsolupulilisuchez i	tricycle	三輪車	1003012
ᴴsulu	wheat	麥子	303013
ᴴthu	hour	鐘頭、小時	2300091

ʰthu	o'clock	點鐘	2300092
ʰtrhi	newly open	開張	901021
ʰtrhu	hulled rice	大米	303008
ʰtshocigumta	everyone, all	人人	2700012
ʰtshomo	corpse	僵屍	1401027
ʰvərmi	bride	新娘	1203012
ʰvərtsho	groom	新郎	1203011
ʰvərtshʉ	to take a husband	嫁	1203007
ʰvərtshʉsucinyi	wedding day	結婚的日子	1203008
ʰvu	bear	熊	201015
ʰvuchire	wine shop, a restaurant	酒舘	902035
ʰvutandzri	to pledge in wine	勸酒	1204032
ʰya	cigarette	紙烟	405009
ʰyugu	millet	小米	303020
ᴸabudjata	cricket	蟋蟀	204019
ᴸabumyaci	firefly	螢火蟲	204018
ᴸaco	beard	胡子	1301097
ᴸaco	mustache	胡鬚	1301098
ᴸadjudju	close (in relationship)	親	1502005
ᴸadzɿ	wife's mother (address term)	岳母	1502042
ᴸakərtsha	elbow	手臂肘	1301115
ᴸalele	index finger	食指	1301130
ᴸamimu	to start	開始	2402003
ᴸandjondjo	near	近	2401040
ᴸandjundju	around	附近	2401024
ᴸanya	heron	蒼鷺	202032
ᴸaomodiodji	father's elder brother (address term)	伯父（對稱）	1502028
ᴸaomodiodji	father's elder brother (quoting term)	伯父（指稱）	1502029
ᴸatsʉtsʉmopha	smaller half	小半	2600007
ᴸavomo	paternal uncles	叔伯	1502027
ᴸavu	paternal grandfather (address term)	爺爺	1502012
ᴸavu	paternal grandfather (quoting term)	祖父	1502013
ᴸavu	wife's father (address term)	岳父	1502040
ᴸavudhimi	siblings of father's sisters, of mother's brothers and sisters, cousins	表兄弟	1502076
ᴸaya	elder sister	姐姐	1502063
ᴸayagodhi	sisters	姐妹	1502061
ᴸayamo	husband's elder sister	大姑子	1502069
ᴸayi	paternal grandmother (address term)	奶奶	1502014

ᴸayi	paternal grandmother（quoting term）	祖母	1502015
ᴸazumo	married woman	女人（已婚）	1600012
ᴸbachər	whip	鞭子	703056
ᴸbachərmbo	to whip	鞭打、抽	703057
ᴸbadjibabuta	how much（asking for price）	多少錢	901040
ᴸbadjihabuta	to settle a restaurant bill	算帳	902037
ᴸbazri	capital	本錢	901007
ᴸbazridjabu	to pay tax	納稅	802014
ᴸbazrikondjo	to gain/to earn money	賺錢	901008
ᴸbazriyahɛ	to balance sale with capital	還本	901011
ᴸbi	to chant sacred books	念經	1201026
ᴸbucadji	pencil	鉛筆	1102017
ᴸbushokonɨ	widower	鰥夫	1600009
ᴸbuyeye	caterpillar	毛蟲	204015
ᴸbyako	cucumber	黃瓜	304024
ᴸbzu	to float	浮	102042
ᴸche	deer	鹿	201012
ᴸchɨ	to shoulder	挑	1302051
ᴸchibu	river bank	河岸	102065
ᴸchichire	shop selling salt	鹽店	902020
ᴸchidji	posthumous child	遺腹子	1600023
ᴸchidju	twin	雙胞胎	1600021
ᴸchiekuqa	soft core of the young antler of the deer	茸	200010
ᴸchiku	anus	肛門	1301206
ᴸchimu	there	那兒	2700030
ᴸchʉ	to bite	咬	1302031
ᴸci	one	一	2600019
ᴸcihaka	overnight	隔夜	2300087
ᴸcinika	every other day	隔一天	2300086
ᴸdadjicimər	a dollar	一塊錢	903006
ᴸdadjicitu	a dime	一毛錢	903007
ᴸdadjihĩ	a cent	一分錢	903008
ᴸdam	from	從、打	2402006
ᴸdhingutaco	to introduce	介紹	1204006
ᴸdiadjaga	movies	電影	1103081
ᴸdiadjagalu	to watch the movie	看電影	1103082
ᴸdiathatha	to point	指	1302066
ᴸdiɛnhua	telephone	電話	1001032
ᴸdiɛnhuabahĩ	to answer a telephone call	聽電話	1001035
ᴸdiɛnhuaga	to telephone	打電話	1001033
ᴸdiɛnhuandhi	to receive a telephone call	接電話	1001034
ᴸdiomu	above	上面	2401015

ˡdje	leopard	豹子	201004
ˡdjevivi	sand	沙	102013
ˡdjevivie	sandy beach	沙灘	102060
ˡdjie	wolf	狼	201005
ˡdjigichire	bookshop	書店	902031
ˡdjigidjinyu	to sign	簽字	901046
ˡdjigiphuko	to dismiss school	放學	1101008
ˡdjigisobu	to go to school	上學	1101007
ˡdjilamadji	to write the wrong characters	寫錯字	1101053
ˡdjilumu	whole	整個	2600004
ˡdjimopha	half	一半	2600005
ˡdjinimu	whole day	整天	2300073
ˡdjohū	body hair	毛	1301002
ˡdjosu	wheel	輪子	703044
ˡdjovi	wheat flour	麵粉	303018
ˡdju	to go	去	2402008
ˡdju	wild pepper	花椒	404029
ˡdjudju	to retreat	退	1404027
ˡdjugu	road	路	801007
ˡdjugubər	to walk on foot	走路	801008
ˡdjuguqhaqha	forked road	三叉路	801010
ˡdjuguqolumi	entrance to a road/street	路口	801012
ˡdjugushishi	to build a road	築路	801009
ˡdjuguvivi	crossroad	十字路	801011
ˡdravibyo	landslide	山崩	102019
ˡdri	soil, earth	土（乾的）	102007
ˡdridri	dragonfly	蜻蜓	204016
ˡdringu	buffalo	水牛	203004
ˡdrithadri	a little while	一會兒	2700051
ˡdritri	to fertilize	施肥	306008
ˡdrivapopo	slope of a hill	山坡	102018
ˡdrog'ashu	posters, notices	招貼	901036
ˡdroG'ogocilu	the first one	頭一個	2600040
ˡdrogi	to plow the field	種地	306011
ˡdrokhadji	ring finger, the 3rd finger	無名指	1301132
ˡdromər	to weed	除草	306006
ˡduka	wing	翅膀	202003
ˡdzi	existential verb, to have	有	2500003
ˡdzikata	to choke with food	哽	1302044
ˡdzimimuta	forever	永遠、永久	2800020
ˡdzolu	bullet	子彈	1404020
ˡdzrikavi	dust	灰塵	102093
ˡɛ	duck	鴨子	203042
ˡə	goose	鵝	203044

˩fudrikalaŋya	to congeal	凝固	102114
˩fuluphe	onion	洋蔥	304059
˩g'əsri	beef	牛肉	402027
˩g'a	to creep	（藤）蔓延	300002
˩g'a	to fish out	撈	1302115
˩g'a	to win	贏	1103088
˩g'ushosu	cattle tender	放牛的	1700032
˩ga	song	歌兒	1103045
˩gahũ	to call	叫	1001018
˩gakuatsutsu	mound	小山	102020
˩gəti	to hiccough	打噎	1402021
˩gidjibi	bird	鳥	202001
˩gidjihũ	feather	羽毛	202004
˩godrimo	husband's younger brother	小叔子	1502068
˩godrimo	husband's younger sister	小姑子	1502070
˩gu	advertisement	廣告	901033
˩gug'uzre	bow	船頭	1003028
˩gugumi	body of a boat	船身	1003030
˩guluchi	thigh	大腿	1301185
˩gumərpo	stern	船尾	1003029
˩gumi	body	身體	1301001
˩gumi	body parts and functions	身體、生理	1301000
˩gumichi	to have fever	發燒	1402042
˩gutshilu	fist	拳頭	1301138
˩habuta	how much/how many (less than ten)	幾個？（十個以內）	2700046
˩habuta	how much/how many (more than ten)	多少？（十個以上）	2700047
˩hakhudjə	how long (in time)	多久	2700048
˩hanihɛ˩hanini	(to tell date) "what day is today?"	幾月幾號（今天幾號）	2300094
˩hanithu	(to tell time) "what time is it?"	問時候（幾點鐘）	2300095
˩hatha	time	時間	2300000
˩hathacithu	time	時候	2300001
˩hə	teeth	牙	1301086
˩həkərpu	to remove teeth	拔牙	1402019
˩hephudradzɨ	evening meal, dinner	晚飯	401005
˩hətshu	toothbrush	牙刷	1303011
˩hĩ	eight	八	2600026
˩hĩ	to stand	站	1302181
˩hĩbi	(pig) stomach	（豬）肚	402016
˩hĩbi	tripe	肚子	402022
˩hĩbishu	to have diarrhea	拉肚子	1402034
˩hĩbu	deaf	耳朵聾	1402016
˩hĩkũ	aperture of the ear	耳孔	1301062

ˡhimichi	fine day, nice day	晴天	101068
ˡhĩmpər	ears	耳朵	1301059
ˡhĩXo	ten	十	2600028
ˡhlɛ	month	月	2300044
ˡhlɛcini	first day of the lunar month	初一	2300054
ˡhlɛG'oa	beginning of the month	月初	2300051
ˡhlɛkadju	middle of the month	月中	2300052
ˡhlɛmər	end of the month	月底	2300053
ˡhũ	afternoon	下午	2300082
ˡhũkhu	nighttime	夜間	2300072
ˡhũkhu	sunset	傍晚	2300083
ˡhũngu	evening	晚上	2300084
ˡhũngudjiti	midnight	半夜	2300085
ˡhyolo	tangerine	柑	305009
ˡidji	uvula	小舌	1301085
ˡimasusushu	to talk in sleep	説夢話	1401017
ˡini	last year	去年	2300015
ˡkadji	gift, present	禮物	1204020
ˡkadju	central	中心	2401008
ˡkalu	hoof	蹄子	200008
ˡkhɔ	voice	聲音	1301202
ˡkhər	to gnaw at a bone	齦（骨頭）	1302034
ˡkhushɨ	to observe the New Year	過年	1202006
ˡkodjer	domestic animals	家畜	203000
ˡkotso	mouth	嘴	1301074
ˡkozra	animals	動物	200000
ˡkuzri	ropes, cordage	繩索	703058
ˡla	to hold with the hand	拿	1302070
ˡlabudjər	arm	手臂	1301114
ˡlag'ər	left-hand	左手	1301113
ˡlaga	to ascend	上	2402009
ˡlakadyumu	back of the hand	手背	1301120
ˡlakandhi	to stretch out the hand	伸手	1302060
ˡlakanganga	to clap the hands	拍手	1302061
ˡlakaphala	to wave the hand	揮手	1302056
ˡlakasoso	to shake hands	握手	1302064
ˡlakər	space between the thumb and forefinger	虎口	1301124
ˡlakupa	to be pregnant	懷孕	1301178
ˡlami	finger	手指頭	1301122
ˡlamidjiku	fingernail	指甲	1301127
ˡlamigodja	finger tips	指尖	1301126
ˡlamikərkər	spaces between fingers	手縫	1301125
ˡlamitshi	knuckles	手節	1301123

ˡlandridri	sparrow	麻雀	202017
ˡlanika	to count with the fingers	數手指頭	1302067
ˡlanisa	to snap the fingers	彈指	1302068
ˡlanisachie	to crack the knuckles	折指頭關節	1302069
ˡlantu	hammer	錘子	703015
ˡlapsu	palm	手掌	1301121
ˡlatsı̄	wrist	手腕子	1301118
ˡli	to return (money)	還（錢）	903016
ˡlibi	turnip	蘿蔔	304030
ˡliqho	the rain ceases	晴雨	101039
ˡlisho, ˡlingu	to answer	答	1001013
ˡlithi	testicles	睾丸	1301209
ˡlithidjika	scrotum	陰囊	1301208
ˡlo	roedeer	馴鹿	201013
ˡloavu	great-grandfather	曾祖父	1502010
ˡloayi	great-grandmother	曾祖母	1502011
ˡlochi	senior generation	長輩	1502009
ˡlopər	to jump	跳	1302203
ˡlotsrhi	to sit up	坐起來	1302180
ˡlu	to see	看	1302009
ˡlupu	stone	石頭	102010
ˡlupuʳdiaposu	rock	大石頭	102011
ˡma	bamboo	竹	301004
ˡmadrio	fleshy part of bird's tail	尾椎	202011
ˡmadrudjʉ	bamboo-shoot	竹笋	301005
ˡmag'a	to lose	輸	1103089
ˡmakudzabudzru	to wag the tail	搖尾	200005
ˡmamu	to become a soldier	當兵	1404007
ˡmandohər	to disappear	不見了	2500005
ˡmandu	"excuse me"	對不起	1204042
ˡmbər	urine	尿	1301161
ˡmbər	wife	妻子	1502051
ˡmər	tail	（牛）尾	402023
ˡmi	monkey	猴子	201016
ˡmiag	to descend	下	2402010
ˡmichie	junior generation	晚輩	1502079
ˡmidjudji	to write	寫字	1101049
ˡmidjumasʉ	illiterate	不識字	1101032
ˡmidjusʉ	literate	識字	1101031
ˡmimi	constipation	便秘	1402082
ˡmina	mole	痣	1301005
ˡmindzuti	to sit down	坐下	1302179
ˡmo	horse	馬	203016
ˡmodri	to inter, to bury	埋葬	1203041

ˡmoloji	male	男人	1600006
ˡmoloji	young man	小伙子	1600005
ˡnakhi	pitch dark	黑	101025
ˡnbər	to cross	過	2402014
ˡnchi	gall bladder	胆	1301151
ˡndhuguphu	travelling expenses	路費	1002008
ˡndjigi	letter	信	1001024
ˡndjigi	newspaper	報紙	1001036
ˡndjigibu	to mail a letter	寄信	1001030
ˡndjigindji	to write a letter	寫信	1001025
ˡndjo	copula, existential	存現	2500000
ˡndo	to roar (as lion)	吼	201026
ˡndo	to shout	喊	1001019
ˡndrə	to drip	滴	101045
ˡndu	fox, wildcat	野猫	201008
ˡndupadrɨ	dike	堤防	103017
ˡndzru	water	水	102032
ˡndzrudimu	surface of water	水面	102033
ˡndzrugota	to freeze	結冰、凍	102035
ˡndzrukolo	bottom of water	水底	102034
ˡndzrundzru	ice	冰	102036
ˡndzᵾbər	four seasons	四季	2300002
ˡnga	five	五	2600023
ˡngamakotacibᵾsɨ	"allow me to pass"	借光	1204044
ˡngatsᵾ	eggplant	茄子	304032
ˡnggu	nine	九	2600027
ˡnguchi	to navigate	航海	103018
ˡngumidju	calf	牛犢子	203007
ˡngunyanya	milk	牛奶	405008
ˡni	two	二	2600020
ˡniho	male organ (baby term)	男生殖器（兒語）	1301167
ˡniho	male organ (common term)	男生殖器	1301165
ˡniho	male organ (euphemistic term)	男生殖器（隱語）	1301166
ˡniho	penis	陰莖	1301207
ˡnikadji	a little, some (quantity)	一點兒	2700050
ˡnipsidjə	lips	嘴唇	1301076
ˡnondzu	"how are you"	你好	1204036
ˡnu	bean	豆子	300044
ˡnyadzɨ	morning	早晨	2300079
ˡnyamba	mucus from the nose	鼻涕	1301068
ˡnyambachi	to snore	打鼾	1301073
ˡnyambadjudju	to have a running nose	流鼻涕	1301069
ˡnyanngashi	nosebleed	鼻血	1402080
ˡnyi	to lend, to borrow (money)	借（錢）	903013

ˡpər	year old	歲	1401030
ˡphomitshʉ	to wash face	洗臉	1303001
ˡphuhũ	to make a quotation	要價	901038
ˡphumi	face	臉	1301041
ˡpsʉ	measure of 10 feet	丈	904024
ˡqa	firecrackers	炮仗	1202002
ˡqadjihɛsu	customer	雇客	901048
ˡqaqandjozre	battlefield	戰場	1404011
ˡqədjidji	to unload goods	上貨	901027
ˡqədjila	to load goods	下貨	901028
ˡqədjitrhi	to open a shop	開舖子	901020
ˡqədjitrhizrɛ	shop	商店	901019
ˡqhu	six	六	2600024
ˡsadjudju	to breathe	呼吸	1301023
ˡsakhʉdjə	rope	麻繩	703060
ˡsakhʉdjəmbo	to twist ropes	打繩	703061
ˡshi	flesh	肉	1301009
ˡshi	to be surnamed	姓	1501002
ˡshichie	kneecap	膝蓋	1301186
ˡshichire	meat shop	肉店	902021
ˡshie	blood	血	1301011
ˡshiedjudju	to bleed	流血	1301012
ˡshikodjər	stick	棍子	703054
ˡshikozrembo	to beat (with a stick)	棍打	703055
ˡshini	year before last	前年	2300016
ˡshinyi	day before yesterday	前天	2300062
ˡshiqa	foot	脚	1301190
ˡshivivi	sawdust	鋸木屑	703090
ˡshizrika	bone	骨	1301006
ˡshugu	tomorrow	明天	2300058
ˡsi	seven	七	2600025
ˡso	three	三	2600021
ˡsodji	student	學生	1700027
ˡsoshica	to graduate	畢業	1101025
ˡtadjidji	"don't laugh at me -- my ignorance"	別見笑	1204043
ˡtahũ	this evening	今天晚上	2300066
ˡtali	additionally	另外	2800006
ˡtamu	here	這兒	2700029
ˡthobo	pine	松樹	301015
ˡthomoliko	fruits	水果	305000
ˡthozu	flea	跳蚤	204051
ˡtrhi	son's wife	媳婦	1502083
ˡtrhi	to press down	按	1302095

ˡtrhɨ	to betray one's country	賣國	802006
ˡtritrɨ	claw	爪子	200006
ˡtrutshɨ	to wash rice	淘米	406002
ˡtsər	cults	鬼神	1201000
ˡtshodjugu	sidewalk	人行道	801014
ˡtshokapisuchez i	rickshaw	人力車	1003008
ˡtshomaphio	enemy	敵人	1404010
ˡtshoXo	people	人民	802003
ˡtshugu	medicine	藥	1403009
ˡtshugu	medicine and cure	醫藥	1403000
ˡtshukuta	throat	喉嚨	1301107
ˡtsɨdjər	saliva	唾液	1301081
ˡtsolubyanga	mosquito	蚊子	204025
ˡtsondjukalala	bachelor	單身漢	1600008
ˡtsusri	mutton	羊肉	402029
ˡvahũ	shoat, piglet	小豬	203011
ˡvashibinɨ	(meat) rotten	（肉）臭	2003005
ˡvatamu	"do not stand on ceremony"	別客氣	1204045
ˡvatapa	to tend pigs	養豬	206011
ˡvatsrisu	pig tender	放豬的	1700033
ˡvɛ	flower	花	300024
ˡvər	guest	客人	1204015
ˡvərmu	to be a guest	作客	1204024
ˡvərndo	to invite guests, to give a party	請客	1204022
ˡvərpu	to see a visitor off	送客	1204023
ˡvudji	relatives	親戚	1502002
ˡvudjiadjudju	close relatives	近親	1502003
ˡvudjidiakhu	distant relatives	遠親	1502004
ˡvuzrechire	piece goods store	布庄	902029
ˡXogani	15th day of the lunar month	十五	2300055
ˡXohanilu	ten odd	十多個、十來個	2600037
ˡya	to lick with blade of tongue	舐	1302036
ˡyadiakhər	armpit	夾肢窩	1301110
ˡyahamu	all	所有、全部	2600001
ˡyaka	hand	手	1301111
ˡyakha	tares	稗子	303015
ˡyangərngər	to doze	打瞌睡	1301028
ˡyedjekərkərnita	to tug under the arm	腋下夾	1302054
ˡyimu	buckwheat	蕎麥	303014
ˡyo	sheep	羊	203014
ˡyobyokotsho	in-group	自己人	1600031
ˡyochy	vegetables	蔬菜	304000
ˡyokosu	to make friends	交朋友	1204005
ˡyokoyo	individually	各自	2700017

ᴸyokoyomu	the clouds disperse	雲散	101048
ᴸza	to pierce	穿	703014
ᴸzagəma	husband's elder brother	大伯子	1502067
ᴸzaiyagodhi	uterine brothers	同胞兄弟	1502055
ᴸzalidia	to descend from a hill	下山	103006
ᴸzayegodhishu	sworn brothers	結拜兄弟	1503004
ᴸzi	four	四	2600022
ᴸziko	uterus	子宮	1301172
ᴸzo	to rub in	擦	1302093
ᴸzrakərkər	crack	縫	102031
ᴸzraku	ravine, pit	山坑	102026
ᴸzraluku	gorge	山澗	102027
ᴸzriba	foam, froth	泡沫	102097
ᴸzubu	son's son	孫子	1502091
ᴸzubumi	son's daughter	孫女	1502092
ᴸzumiphiadjudju	unmarried young woman	姑娘	1600011
ᴸzupzudja	(animals) to give birth to the young	（動物）産子	200001
ᴿahɨ	below	下面	2401018
ᴿalayu	finch, oriole	黃鶯	202022
ᴿama	mother (address term)	媽媽	1502019
ᴿama	mother (quoting term)	母親	1502020
ᴿayi	father's younger brother's wife	婶母	1502032
ᴿayimi	old maid	老處女	1600013
ᴿayimi	old woman	老太婆	1600018
ᴿbahĩ	to hear	聽	1302020
ᴿbanyo	wild boar	野豬	201014
ᴿbapsɨ	sole of the foot	脚底	1301195
ᴿbi	fowl	飛禽	202000
ᴿbi	peach	桃兒	305002
ᴿbibaba	swallow	燕子	202014
ᴿbintu	marrow	髓	1301007
ᴿbodjo	praying mantis	螳螂	204034
ᴿbotho	lake	湖	102063
ᴿbu	to pop	爆	406077
ᴿbupa	to peck	啄	202007
ᴿbyakozi	melon seed	瓜子	403029
ᴿchacha	magpie	喜鵲	202016
ᴿchə	goat	山羊	203015
ᴿchedju	(mosquito) to bite	（蚊子）叮	204026
ᴿchieku	hoe	鋤頭	703048
ᴿchimər	hunting dog	獵狗	203022
ᴿchimi	bitch	母狗	203021
ᴿchithang	pond	池塘	102067

ᴿchiya	single child	獨生子	1600022
ᴿchuhɛ	to buy rice	買米、糴米	902015
ᴿchuhɛdji	shop selling rice	米棧	902014
ᴿchutri	to sell rice	賣米、糶米	902016
ᴿcidzɨ	to whole life	一生、一輩子	1401002
ᴿdasho	this morning	今天早上	2300064
ᴿdawa	moon	月亮	101011
ᴿdawaᴴzo	moonlight	月光	101015
ᴿdioma	language	話	1001001
ᴿdiomasu	to gossip	聊天	1103029
ᴿdjaku	navel	肚臍	1301148
ᴿdjapər	dust	末子	102096
ᴿdjapər	umbilical cord	臍帶	1301149
ᴿdjigilu	to read a book	看書	1101036
ᴿdjigimidju	store name	字號	901030
ᴿdjigipi	to study	念書	1101033
ᴿdjigiso	to teach	教書	1101027
ᴿdjiqa	skin	皮	1301003
ᴿdjiqata	wrinkle	皺紋	1301004
ᴿdjivika	mud playing	玩泥沙	1103002
ᴿdjo	to be born	出生	1401004
ᴿdjochɨ	to start serving a banquet	上菜	1204031
ᴿdjolɛlamog'olɛshoko	life, sickness, and death	生老病死	1400000
ᴿdjosuhatha	birthday	生日	1203026
ᴿdjosushinyiko	to celebrate birthday	做生日	1203027
ᴿdju	back	背	1301205
ᴿdju	expenses	開消	901012
ᴿdju	straw	草	703073
ᴿdju	waist	腰	1301146
ᴿdjubikuku	to clean the bottom	揩（屁股）	1303018
ᴿdjudja	stomach	胃	1301145
ᴿdjudju	to exit	出	2402012
ᴿdogadzɨ	noon meal, lunch	午飯	401004
ᴿdohɛjɨ	bright	亮	101022
ᴿdri	star	星	101016
ᴿdrove	powder	粉	102095
ᴿdruva	cloud	雲彩	101047
ᴿdruvaluta	rosy clouds, rosy sunset	晚霞	101049
ᴿdya	fox	狐狸	201006
ᴿdzəbi	hill	山	102014
ᴿdzɨ	grains	穀物	303000
ᴿdzɨ	seed	種子	300003
ᴿdzichire	eating house, restaurant	飯舘	902033
ᴿdzɨdzɨ	to unite	團結	802015

ᴿdzigadhɨ	people from the same native village	同鄉	1503005
ᴿdzɨlumopha	one and a half	一個半	2600008
ᴿdziphi	herd	群	200013
ᴿfu	green onion	蔥	304058
ᴿfuji	flute	笛子	1103054
ᴿfujifu	to play the flute	吹笛子	1103055
ᴿfukər	neighbor	鄰居	1503010
ᴿfukər	village	鄉村	801027
ᴿfulu	kidneys	腎	1301152
ᴿg'ūhudjə	brain	腦漿	1301038
ᴿg'əlu	to tend cattle	放牛	206008
ᴿg'u	the common yellow cattle	黃牛	203005
ᴿg'upʉ	comb	梳子	1303020
ᴿga	hawk	老鷹	202012
ᴿgan	rainbow	虹	101046
ᴿgədrɨ	younger sister (quoting term)	妹妹	1502065
ᴿgɛra	fog, mist	霧	101050
ᴿgodhi	younger brother (quoting term)	弟弟	1502060
ᴿgodji	brothers	兄弟	1502054
ᴿgohlu	chest	胸	1301139
ᴿgolu	tile	瓦	703077
ᴿgu	ship, boat	船	1003027
ᴿgucɨ	to row a boat	划船	1003033
ᴿguluvusʉtsoho	kiln	窯	703085
ᴿgumitshʉ	to take a bath	洗澡	1303003
ᴿgundzu	to go by boat	坐船	1003050
ᴿha	mouse	老鼠	201022
ᴿhadru	bat	蝙蝠	202033
ᴿhala	cat	貓	203024
ᴿhalamərmər	to mew	貓叫	203025
ᴿhanji	river	河	102064
ᴿhaphər	to pant	喘氣	1301026
ᴿhata	day	天	2300056
ᴿhe	pheasant	雉、野鷄	202030
ᴿhĩ	rain	雨	101036
ᴿhĩhĩ	to smell	聞	1302021
ᴿhĩmĩ	sun	太陽	101005
ᴿhĩmiᴸqhɛ	the sun sets	日落	101007
ᴿhĩmiᴿdzruzru	the sun rises	出太陽	101006
ᴿhĩmiᴿg'a	to sun	晒	101008
ᴿhĩsu	lacquer	漆	703079
ᴿhĩta	"don't trouble yourself to come out"	留步	1204047

ᴿhomolɛ	why?	爲什麼	2700044
ᴿhtshita	to hold in the mouth	含	1302042
ᴿhuhu	to stir fry, to fry	炒	406075
ᴿi	breakfast	早飯	401003
ᴿi	tongue	舌頭	1301077
ᴿi	shape	樣子	2004001
ᴿidhi	to stick out the tongue	吐舌頭	1302050
ᴿidji	concubine	偏房	1502053
ᴿig'ər	right-hand	右手	1301112
ᴿikha	tea	茶	405002
ᴿikhədjə	outside	外面	2401013
ᴿima	to dream	做夢	1401016
ᴿimi	legal wife	正房	1502052
ᴿishu	to go house hunting	找房子	902040
ᴿkaboatsutsu	stream	溪	102068
ᴿkabodre	ditch	溝渠	103023
ᴿkala	to play	玩	1103001
ᴿkala	travelling	旅行	1002000
ᴿkalabu	to travel	出門、旅行	1002001
ᴿkalasukadji	toy	玩具	1103003
ᴿkani	to take in the fingers	拈	1302071
ᴿkapo	river-bed	河床	102112
ᴿkcichithusuchez i	bicycle	脚踏車	1003010
ᴿkha	basket	籃	703066
ᴿkhə	catty	斤	904017
ᴿkhərta	to stop the flow of water	截水	103013
ᴿkhərzahusi	to dredge a river	疏通水流	103014
ᴿkhichi	to expel intestinal gas	放屁	1301164
ᴿkhoyu	lane, an alley	巷	801018
ᴿkhoyutsukata	dead end street	死巷	801019
ᴿkobo	shop front	門面	901029
ᴿkolo	inside	裡面	2401011
ᴿkudro	surrounding	周圍	2401025
ᴿkulu	sweat	汗	1301014
ᴿkuludjudju	to sweat	流汗	1301015
ᴿla	tiger	老虎	201002
ᴿlaba	round dumpling	包子	403009
ᴿlaci	sexual intercourse (common term)	性交	1301176
ᴿlaci	sexual intercourse (euphemistic term)	性交（隱語）	1301177
ᴿlakhu	child	小孩子	1600002
ᴿlakhug'ulu	to watch the children	看（孩子）	1401007
ᴿlakhug'umər	to raise children	養孩子	1401006
ᴿlakhupa	pregnant woman	孕婦	1600015
ᴿlapər	fly	蒼蠅	204020

ᴿlapu	blister	泡	1301019
ᴿlaulo	"I have troubled you"	勞駕	1204038
ᴿlidia	to return	回	2402013
ᴿligu	ox	公牛	203002
ᴿlilidədji	father's elder brother's wife	伯母	1502030
ᴿlimi	cow	母牛	203003
ᴿlodia	to guard	守	1404025
ᴿlopər	to dance	跳舞	1103066
ᴿlophu	forehead	前額	1301040
ᴿlopu	top of the head	頭頂	1301030
ᴿlopuko	dandruff	頭垢	1301031
ᴿmafu	the wind stops	（風）停	101030
ᴿmərdia	later	後來	2800022
ᴿmərpo	tail	尾巴	200004
ᴿmi	matches	火柴	703071
ᴿmi	name	名字	1501003
ᴿmitrhi	to light a match	劃火柴	703072
ᴿmolu	husband	丈夫	1502050
ᴿmolushokoni	widow	寡婦	1600016
ᴿmomi	mare	母馬	203017
ᴿmotho	grave clothes	壽衣	1203032
ᴿmuphə	frost	霜	101056
ᴿmuta	every	每	2600002
ᴿmuyi	dried fungus	木耳	402055
ᴿnahu	obscure, dark	暗	101024
ᴿnahū	shadow	影	101026
ᴿnbər	pus	膿	1301021
ᴿnbərdjudju	to suppurate	釀膿	1301022
ᴿnbudzə	to have nocturnal emissions	夢遺	1301168
ᴿnda	to chop with an axe	砍	703018
ᴿndji	to recite incantations	念咒	1201039
ᴿndju	awl	錐	703028
ᴿndju	to sleep	睡覺	1401014
ᴿndodje	sperm, semen	精液	1301210
ᴿndro	origin	出身	1501010
ᴿndrodju	the hail falls	下雹子	101061
ᴿng'a	to roast	烤	406084
ᴿngahī	numeral on the face of the clock	五分鐘	2300093
ᴿngku	to inundate	淹	102115
ᴿngo	to prick	刺	703013
ᴿngodru	ass, donkey	驢	203018
ᴿni	to steam	蒸	406080
ᴿnikhu	before noon	上午	2300080

ᴿnikhu	noon	中午	2300081
ᴿnikondju	to take a nap	睡午覺	1401015
ᴿnimilupər	nervous, palpitating heart	心跳	1402028
ᴿnyacu	gun	槍	1404018
ᴿnyaga	nose	鼻子	1301065
ᴿnyagaluku	nostril	鼻孔	1301067
ᴿnyo	rice husk	糠	303011
ᴿnzo	bridge	橋	801021
ᴿpami	green frog	青蛙	205051
ᴿphichu	net	網	703088
ᴿphichuluku	mesh	網眼	703089
ᴿphohoto	mildew, mold	霉	102092
ᴿphu	porcupine	刺蝟	201019
ᴿphuganga	to make an offer	還價	901039
ᴿphusa	buddha	佛	1201023
ᴿqa	peck, a dry measure (316c. in.)	斗	904020
ᴿrabibər	to climb a hill	爬山	103004
ᴿrabibər	to mount a hill	上山	103005
ᴿragugu	to lay eggs	下蛋	203035
ᴿrakhər	valley	山谷	102025
ᴿrangu	egg	蛋	202010
ᴿranzɨ	spring	泉	102070
ᴿruta	opposite	對面	2401026
ᴿsa	to count as	算	1501009
ᴿsa	vapor, steam	水蒸氣	102109
ᴿsadzɨ	lining, to be alive	活	1401005
ᴿsalatsu	trumpet	喇叭	1103058
ᴿsalatsufu	to blow the trumpet	吹喇叭	1103059
ᴿshabzu	sugar	糖	404010
ᴿshi	wood	木頭	703076
ᴿshica	to end	完	2402005
ᴿshichu	body dirt	垢	1301016
ᴿshicinyi	day before day before yesterday	大前天	2300063
ᴿshihεsu	to buy meat	買肉	902022
ᴿshihũ	day before yesterday evening	前天晚上	2300070
ᴿshipo	tree	樹	300008
ᴿshipsupsu	leaf	葉	300021
ᴿshishi	to repair	修理	703092
ᴿshogo	destruction of a nation	亡國	802004
ᴿshoko	to die	死	1401022
ᴿshuchie	to hunt	打獵	206003
ᴿshugunadje	tomorrow morning	明天早上	2300065
ᴿsipia	board	板	703074
ᴿsuphie	peacock	孔雀	202026

ᴿtaha	to stay overnight	過夜	2300088
ᴿtani	today	今天	2300057
ᴿthi	to suck	吸	1302030
ᴿthoyie	pigeon	鴿子	202018
ᴿthoyie	turtledove	斑鳩	202020
ᴿtoli	rabbit	兔子	201021
ᴿtra	to deep-fry	炸	406079
ᴿtrhala	lion	獅子	201003
ᴿtrhihə	it sells well	好賣	901005
ᴿtsai	again	再	2800005
ᴿtsho	to push	推	1302106
ᴿtshoəkhrbər	son who ruins the family	敗家子	1600028
ᴿtshoko	life	生命	1401001
ᴿtshupʉ	lungs	肺	1301144
ᴿtshʉta	to advance	進	1404026
ᴿtshʉta	to attack	攻	1404024
ᴿtsoshitsolodro	first born	頭胎	1600019
ᴿtsʉphu	lungs	（豬）肺	402021
ᴿudzɿ	old man	老頭兒	1600017
ᴿutiti	intestines	腸	1301155
ᴿvako	pig	（公）豬	203008
ᴿvami	sow	母豬	203009
ᴿvaphu	badger	貉	201018
ᴿvasu	breeding boar, sire pig	種豬	203010
ᴿviehua	the snow melts	化雪	101058
ᴿvumi	axe	斧頭	703017
ᴿXota	to spurt	噴	1302046
ᴿXucio	pepper	辣椒	304061
ᴿyabu	some (number)	一些	2700049
ᴿyaki	mud	泥（濕的）	102008
ᴿyayu	potato	馬鈴薯	304003
ᴿyokho	friend	朋友	1503008
ᴿyokholamo	intimate friend	老朋友	1503009
ᴿyoko	to go into partnership	合伙	901006
ᴿzidzəphi	to spit	吐痰	1301084
ᴿzikər	phlegm	痰	1301083
ᴿzimi	daughter	女兒	1502085
ᴿzo	light	光	101020
ᴿzo	to owe (money)	欠（錢）	903014
ᴿzo	to shine	照	101009
ᴿzrabu	to wrap	包	1302151
ᴿzrakonyu	to peel with a peeler	削皮	306039
ᴿzraku	cliff	山巖	102022
ᴿzrandi	hill without vegetation	童山	102021

ᴿzrikunyu	to peel	剥皮	306038
ᴿzumi	brother's daughter	姪女	1502088
ᴿzumi	female	女人	1600010
ᴿzumie	woodpecker	啄木鳥	202025
ᴿzumilivatshə	woman who remarries	再婚的女人	1600014
	nature, natural phenomena	自然、自然現象	100000

参考文献

【邦文文献】（日本語50音順）

池田巧．2000．「西暦1900年に記録されたナムイ語の語彙―H. R. Davis 著 YÜN-NAN 載の西南中國の民族語彙研究」『東方學報』72：770-755.

池田巧．2002．「西南中国〈川西民族走廊〉地域の言語分布」崎山理（編）『消滅の危機に瀕した言語の研究の現状と課題』（国立民族学博物館調査報告39）pp. 63-114.

岡本雅享．1999．『中国の少数民族と言語政策』東京：社会評論社．

庄司博史．2003．「中国少数民族政策の新局面　特に漢語普及とのかかわりにおいて」『国立民族学博物館研究報告』27．4：683-724.

長野泰彦．1986．「チベット・ビルマ系諸語における能格現象をめぐって」『言語研究』90　pp. 119-148.

西田龍雄．1989．「チベット・ビルマ語派」亀井孝・河野六郎・千野栄一（編著）．『言語学大辞典』東京：三省堂．第2巻．pp. 791-822.

西田龍雄．1993．「川西走廊言語」亀井孝・河野六郎・千野栄一（編著）．『言語学大辞典』東京：三省堂．第5巻．pp. 197-198.

西田龍雄．2000．『東アジア諸言語の研究Ⅰ』京都：京都大学出版会．

西田文信．1999．「声調の音声的特徴に関する一考察」『開篇』19：159-173.

西田文信．2004a．「書評：*The Sino-Tibetan Languages*. Edited by Graham Thurgood and Randy J. LaPolla. Routledge Language Family Series, no. 3. London: Routledge, 2003. xxii, 727 pp. ＄295.00（cloth）'」『麗澤論叢』15：121-132.

西田文信．2004b．「書評：*Languages of the Himalayas: An Ethnolinguistic Handbook on the Greater Himalayan Region, Containing an Introduction to the Symbolic Theory of Language*.（Handbook of Oriental Studies. Section 2 South Asia, 10), George van Driem. Leiden, Brill Publishers, 2001, ISBN 90-04-10390-2, vol. 1, xxvi, 462 pp., viii, 916 pp., 2 vols, 193 illus.」『麗澤大学紀要』79：267-276.

西田文信．2006a．「ナムイ語動詞の他動性について」麗澤大学言語研究センター第22回セミナー．麗澤大学．2006年1月26日．

西田文信．2006b．「ナムイ語における漢語からの借用語について」『開篇』25：334-341.

西田文信．2006c．「中国四川省涼山イ族自治州における言語生活～ナムイ語話者を

例として~」言語政策学会第 8 回大会発表論文.早稲田大学.2006 年 6 月 18 日.
西田文信.2007.「ナムイ語表記法試案」『中国研究』14:81-91.
西田文信.2010.「ナムイ語の格標識」澤田英夫(編)『チベット=ビルマ系言語の文法現象 1:格とその周辺』東京外国語大学アジア・アフリカ言語文化研究所.pp. 29-42.
西田文信.2013.「ナムイ語の使用状況について—四川省涼山彝族自治州冕寧県連合郷における調査結果から—」太田斎先生・古屋昭弘先生還暦記念中国語学論文集刊行委員会編.『太田斎先生・古屋昭弘先生還暦記念中国語学論文集』東京:好文出版.pp. 374-382.
松岡正子.2005.「「西番」諸集団の社会—四川省木里県水洛郷の〈西番〉チベット族を事例として—」長谷川清・塚田誠之(編)『中国の民族表象 南部諸地域の人類学・歴史学的研究』東京:風響社.pp. 175-206.
松岡正子.2006.「川西南の「西番」における民族識別(2)西番族の歴史の記憶」『愛知大学国際問題研究所紀要』127:221-237.
松岡正子.2008.「ナムイ・チベット族の選択—集落の解体と山の神祭りという民族表象」塚田誠之(編)『民族表象のポリティクス:中国南部における人類学・歴史学的研究』東京:風響社.pp. 327-358.
松岡正子.2011.「四川における 1950~60 年代の民族研究(1)」『愛知大学国際問題研究所紀要』137:97-115.
松岡正子.2012.「四川における 1950~60 年代の民族研究(2)李紹明が語る「中国少数民族問題五種叢書」と政治民族学」『愛知大学国際問題研究所紀要』139:225-243.

【漢語文献】(漢語拼音表記順)

戴庆厦.2001.〈藏缅语族语言使动范畴的历史演变〉《中国语言学报》29. 1:1-10.
戴庆厦,黄布凡,傅爱兰,仁增旺姆,刘菊黄.1991.《藏缅语十五种》北京:燕山出版社.
戴庆厦,刘菊黄,傅爱兰.1989.〈关於我国藏缅语族分类问题〉《云南民族学院学报》1989 年 3 期.pp. 82-92.
戴庆厦.1994.〈藏缅语個体量词研究〉《藏缅语新论》北京:中央民族学院出版社.pp. 166-181.
戴庆厦(编).1998.《二十一世纪的中国少数民族语言研究》.太原:书海出版社.
戴庆厦.2006.〈瀕危语言研究在语言学中的地位〉《长江学术》2006 年 1 期.pp. 97-101.

費孝通. 1980.〈関於我国民族的識別問題〉《中国社会科学》第 1 号. pp. 147-62.
費孝通（編）. 1991.《中华民族研究新探索》. 北京：中央民族学院出版社.
格勒. 1988.《论藏族文化的起源形成与周围民族的关系》. 广州：中山大学出版社.
古涛，王德和. 2014.《纳木依藏族文化初探》成都：四川大学出版社.
和即仁. 1991.〈"摩些"与"纳木依"语源考〉.《民族语文》1991年 6 期. pp. 60-63.
何耀华. 1983.〈冕宁县联合公社藏族社会历史调查〉《雅砻江下游考察报告》成都：中国西南民族研究学会编. pp. 1-37.
何耀华. 1988.《中国西南历史民族学论集》昆明：雲南人民出版社.
何耀华. 2004.〈川西南藏族历史初探〉《凉山藏学研究》第 4 号. pp. 14-15.
黄布凡. 1988.〈川西藏区的语言关系〉《中国藏学》1988年第 3 期. pp. 142-150
黄布凡. 1991.〈羌语支〉马学良（编）《藏缅语概论》北京：北京大学出版社. 第 1 卷. pp. 208-369.
黄布凡主编. 1992.《藏缅语族语言词汇》北京：中央民族学院出版社.
黄布凡. 1994.〈藏缅语动词的趋向范畴〉马学良（编）《藏缅语新论》北京：中央民族学院出版社. pp. 133-151.
黄布凡，仁增旺姆. 1991.〈纳木依语〉戴庆厦，黄布凡，傅爱兰，仁增旺姆，刘菊黄.《藏缅语十五种》北京：燕山出版社. pp. 153-173.
黄成龙. 2014.〈藏羌彝走廊羌语支语言2013年研究动态〉《阿坝师范高等专科学校学报》2014年 2 期. pp. 5-8.
黄成龙. 2015.〈2014年羌语支语言研究前沿〉《阿坝师范高等专科学校学报》2015年 1 期. pp. 5-8.
黄成龙，李云兵，王锋. 2011.〈纪录语言学——一门新兴学科〉《语言科学》2011年第 3 期. pp. 259-269.
黄行. 2000.《中国少数民族语言活力研究》北京：中央民族大学出版社.
黄约布. 2004.〈浅谈川西南藏族的族源与族称〉《凉山藏学研究》第 1 号. pp. 16-17.
拉玛兹偓. 1994.〈纳木依语支属研究〉《民族语文》1994年 1 期. pp. 50-60.
李锦芳. 2005.〈中国濒危语言研究及保护策略〉《中央民族大学学报（哲学社会科学版）》32卷 3 期. pp113-119.
李锦芳. 2015.〈中国濒危语言认定及保护研究工作规范〉《广西大学学报（哲学社会科学版）》37卷 2 期. pp. 107-114.
李绍明. 1986.〈六江流域民族考察述评〉《中国西南民族研究学报（人文社会科学版）》1986年 1 期. pp. 38-43.
李绍明（编）. 2003.《尔苏藏族研究》北京：民族出版社.
李绍明，童恩正（主编）2008.《雅砻江流域民族考察报告》北京：民族出版社.

刘光坤. 1989.〈藏缅语族中的羌语支试析〉《西南民族大学学报》1989年3期. pp. 31-38.

刘辉强. 1983.〈納木依语概要〉《雅砻江下游考察报告（六江流域民族综合科学考察报告之一）》pp. 218-241.

刘辉强. 1996.〈锣锅底纳木依语〉《语言研究》1996年第2期. pp. 186-199.

刘辉强. 2002.〈談川西南"西番"人的識別〉胡文明（編）.《普米研究文集》昆明：云南民族出版社. pp. 14-18.

刘辉强, 尚云川. 2006.〈拯救羌语支濒危语言——尔苏语，纳木依语，贵琼语，扎巴语资料记录和保存〉《西南民族大学学报》27卷12期. pp. 11-12.

刘杨翎. 2013.〈纳木依符号的文字性质初探〉《龙岩学院学报》2013. 4：41-45.

龙西江. 1991a.〈凉山州境内'西番'及渊源探讨"（上）〉《西藏研究》第1期. pp. 26–39.

龙西江. 1991b.〈凉山州境内"西番"及渊源探讨"（下）〉《西藏研究》第3期. pp. 56–64.

马学良（主編）. 1991.《藏缅语概论》北京：北京大学出版社.

马学良, 胡坦, 戴庆厦, 黄布凡, 傅爱兰（编）. 1994.《藏缅语新论》北京：中央民族学院出版社.

冕宁县. 2011.《冕宁县2010年第六次全国人口普查主要数据公报》http://mn.lsz.gov.cn

冕宁县地方志编纂委员会（主編）. 1994.《冕宁县志》成都：四川人民出版社.

齐佳. 2007.〈在重音与声调的连续体上汉史兴语〉《东方语言学》2：143-152.

瞿继勇. 2011.〈语言的濒危与保护〉《焦作大学学报》25卷4期. pp. 32-35.

申淑潔. 2013.《四川省九龍縣納木義語調查與研究》南京師範大学碩士論文.

四川省民族研究所. 1982.《四川少数民族》成都：四川民族出版社.

孙宏开. 1962.〈羌语概况〉《中国语文》12期. pp. 561-571.

孙宏开. 1981.〈羌语动词的趋向范畴〉《民族语文》1981年1期. pp. 34-42.

孙宏开. 1982.〈羌语支属问题初探〉《民族语文研究文集》西宁：青海民族出版社. pp. 189–224.

孙宏开. 1983a.〈我国藏缅语动词的人称范畴〉《民族语文》1983年2期. pp. 17-29.

孙宏开. 1983b.〈川西民族走廊地区的语言〉中国西南民族研究学会编《西南民族研究》成都：四川民族出版社. 1卷. pp. 429-454.

孙宏开. 1983c.〈六江流域的民族语言及其系属分类——兼述嘉陵江上游，雅鲁藏布江流域的民族语言〉《民族学报》3：99-274.

孙宏开. 1988a.〈語言識別与民族〉《民族语文》1988年2期. pp. 9-17

孙宏开. 1988b.〈試論中国境内藏緬語的譜系分類〉［A Classification of Tibeto-Burman

Languages in China]. In Paul K. Eguchi. et al. eds. *Languages and History in East Asia : Festschrift for Tatsuo Nishida on the Occasion of His 60th Birthday.* Kyoto : Shokado. pp. 61-74.

孙宏开. 1988c.〈藏缅语量词用法比较—兼论量词发展的阶段层次〉《中国语言学报》1988 年 3 期. p. 339.

孙宏开. 1989.〈中国开展语言规划工作的基本情况〉*Journal of Chinese Linguistics*, 17.1 : 1-49

孙宏开. 1991.〈从词汇比较看西夏语与藏缅语族羌语支的关系〉《民族语文》1991 年 2 期. pp. 1-11.

孙宏开. 2000.〈藏缅语族羌语支语言及语言学研讨会述评〉《当代语言学》2 卷 2 期. pp. 121-123.

孫宏開. 2001.〈論藏緬語族中的羌語支語言〉*Language and Linguistics* 2．1 : 157-181.

孙宏开. 2011a.〈古代羌人和现代羌语支族群的关系〉《西南民族大学学报》32 卷 1 期. pp. 1-7.

孙宏开. 2011b〈羌语支在汉藏语系中的历史地位〉《云南民族大学学报（哲学社会科学版）》2011 年 6 期. pp. 133-138.

孙怀阳，程贤敏（主编）1999.《中国藏族人口与社会》北京：中国藏学出版社.

宋伶俐. 2006.〈川西民族走廊濒危语言概况〉《暨南学报（哲学社会科学版）》28 卷 5 期. pp. 137-141.

谢建猷. 1992.〈木里多语社区〉中国民族语言学会（编）.《民族语文研究新探》成都：四川民族出版社. pp. 47-58.

徐菊芳（主编）. 1991.《藏缅语音词汇》北京：中国社会科学出版社.

徐中舒. 1993.《汉语大字典（缩印本）》成都：四川辞书出版社.

扬福泉. 2006.〈纳木依与"纳"族群之关系考略〉《民族研究》3 期. pp. 52-59，108.

尹蔚彬. 2016.《納木茲語語法標註文本》北京：社會科學文獻出版社.

藏缅语语音和词汇编写组. 1991.《藏缅语语音和词汇》北京：中国社会科学出版社.

张全昌. 1962.〈四川"西番"识别调查小结〉四川省民族委员会（编）《四川民族史志》

章晓清，符昌忠. 2011.〈青少年语言强化与濒危语言的保存〉《广东技术师范学院学报》32 卷 8 期. pp. 77-80.

赵丽明·宋兆麟编. 2011.《中国西南濒危文字图录（英汉对照）—清华百年西南濒危文字展选》北京：学苑出版社.

赵丽明（主编）. 2013.《纳木依藏族文献—中国西南地区少数民族濒危文字文献丛书》

桂林：广西师范大学.

赵丽明，张琰（编）．2014．《纳木依藏族帕孜文献—中国西南少数民族地区濒危文字文献调查研究丛书》桂林：广西师范大学．

【欧文文献】（アルファベット順）

Alkhenvald, Alexandra Y. 2000. *Classifiers: A typology of noun classification devices.* Oxford: Oxford University Press.

Baber, E. Colbone. 1882. *Travels and researches in Western China.* Supplementary papers Vol. 1., Royal Geographical Society.

Bates, Elizabeth and Brian MacWhinney. 1989. *The crosslinguistic study of sentence processing.* Cambridge, New York: Cambridge University Press.

Benedict, Paul King. 1972a. *Sino-Tibetan: A Conspectus.* Cambridge: Cambridge University Press.

Benedict, Paul K. 1972b. The Sino-Tibetan tonal system. In J. Barrau, et al. eds., *Langues et techniques, nature et société*, Paris: Klincksieck, pp. 25–34.

Benedict, Paul K. 1973. Tibeto-Burman Tones with a Note on Teleo-Reconstruction. *Acta Orientalia* 35: 127–138.

Bisang, Walter. 2006. Linguistic areas, language contact and typology: Some implications from the case of Ethiopia as a linguistic area, In Matras, Yaron, April McMahon and Nigel Vincent (eds.), *Linguistic areas. Convergence in historical and typological perspective.* Hampshire: Palgrave MacMillan. pp. 75–98.

Blair, Frank. 1990. *Survey on a Shoestring—A Manual for Small-Scale Language Surveys.* A Publication of the Summer Institute of Linguistics and The University of Texas at Arlington.

Bouquiaux, Luc and Jacqueline M. C. Thomas. 1992. *Studying and Describing Unwritten Languages.* Translated by James Roberts. A Publication of the Summer Institute of Linguistics.

Bradley, David. 1997, Tibeto-Burman languages and classification. In David Bradley, ed. *Papers in Southeast Asian linguistics No. 14: Tibeto-Burman languages of the Himalayas.* Canberra: Pacific Linguistics. pp 1–72.

Chirkova, Katia. 2008. Essential characteristics of Lizu, a Qiangic language of Western Sichuan. *Workshop on Tibeto-Burman Languages of Sichuan. November 21–24, 2008.* Institute of Linguistics, Academia Sinica. pp. 191–233.

Chirkova, Katia. 2009. Shixing, a Sino-Tibetan language of South-West China: A grammatical sketch with two appended texts". *Linguistics of the Tibeto-Burman Area*, 32. 1 : 1-90.

Chirkova, Katia. 2012. The Qiangic Subgroup from an Areal Perspective : A Case Study of Languages of Muli. *Language and Linguistics* 13. 1 : 133-170.

Comrie, Bernhard. 1976. *Aspect*. Cambridge : Cambridge University Press.

Comrie, Bernhard. 1993. *Tense*. Cambridge : Cambridge University Press.

Davies, Major H. R. 1909. *YÜN-NAN : The Link Between India and the Yangtze*. Cambridge : at the University Press.

DeLancy, Scott. 1999. Relativization in Tibetan. *Topics in Nepalese Linguistics*. eds. By Yadava, Yogendran P. and Warren W. Glover. Kathmandu : Royal Nepal Academy.

Ding, Picus Sizhi. 1998. *Fundamentals of Prinmi（Pumi）: A Tibeto-Burman Language of Northwestern Yunnan*. Ph. D. thesis. Canberra : Australian National University.

Ding, Picus. 2014. *A Grammar of Prinmi : Based on the Central dialect of northwest Yunnan, China*. Languages of the Greater Himalayan Region 14. Leiden : Brill.

Dixon, R. M. W. 1994. *Ergativity* New York : Cambridge University Press.

Dixon, R. M. W. 2009. *Basic Linguistic Theory, 1 : Methodology*. Oxford : Oxford University Press.

Dixon, R. M. W. 2009. *Basic Linguistic Theory, 2 : Grammatical Topics*. Oxford : Oxford University Press.

Dixon, R. M. W. 2012. *Basic Linguistic Theory Volume 3 : Further Grammatical Topics*. Oxford : Oxford University Press.

Driem, George Louis van. 1987. *A Grammar of Limbu*. Berlin : Mouton de Gruyter.

Driem, George Louis van. 1993a. *A Grammar of Dumi*. Berlin : Mouton de Gruyter.

Driem, George Louis van. 1993b. Language change, conjugational morphology and the Sino-Tibetan Urheimat, *Acta Linguistica Hafniensia*, 26 : 45-56.

Driem, George Louis van. 1997. Sino-Bodic. *Bulletin of the School of Oriental and African Studies*. 60. 3 : 455-488.

Driem, George Louis van. 1998. *Dzongkha*. Leiden : Research School for Asian, African and Amerindian Studies.

Driem, George Louis van. 2001a. *Languages of the Himalayas. An Ethnolinguistic Handbook of the Greater Himalayan Region*. Leiden : Koninklijke Brill.

Driem, George Louis van. 2001b. *Taal en Taalwetenschap*. Leiden : Onderzoeksschool voor Aziatische, Afrikaanse en Amerindische Studies.

Driem, George Louis van. 2007. A holistic approach to the fine art of grammar writing : The Dallas Manifesto. Novel Kishore Rai, Yogendra Prasad Yadav, Bhim N. Regmi and Balaram Prasain, (eds.) *Recent Studies in Nepalese Linguistics.* Kathmandu : Linguistic Society of Nepal. pp. 93-184

Fei, Xiaotong. 1997. Investigating Ethnicity : My Studies and Views of Ethnic Groups in China, *Bulletin of the National Museum of Ethnology*, 22. 2 : 461-479.

Gibbons, J. P. 1987. *Code-switching and code choice : A Hong Kong case study.* Clevedon : Multilingual Matters.

Hodgson, Brian Houghton. 1853. Sifan and Horsok Voabularies. *Journal of the Asiatic Society of Bengal.* 22 : 121-151.

Hodgson, Brian Houghton. 1874. *Essays on Languages, Literature, and Religion of Nepal and Tibet.* London.

Hulst, H. van der. 1999. Word Accent. In H. van der Hulst (ed.), *Word Prosodic Systems in the Languages of Europe.* Berlin : Mouton de Gruyter. pp. 3-115.

Hulst, H. van der and N. Smith. 1988. The Variety of Pitch Accent Systems : Introduction. In H. van der Hulst & N. Smith (eds.), *Autosegmental Studies on Pitch Accent* 9-24. Dordrecht : Foris.

Jacques, Guillaume and Alexis Michaud. 2011. Approaching the historical phonology of three highly eroded Sino-Tibetan languages : Naxi, Na and Laze. *Diachronica.* 28. 4 : 468-498.

Jiang, Li. 2015. *A Grammar of Guìqióng : A Language of Sichuan (Brill's Tibetan Studies Library, Volume 5/Languages of the Greater Himalayan Region, Volume 15)* Leiden : Brill.

Ju, Namkung. ed. 1996. *Phonological Inventories of Tibeto-Burman Languages* (STEDT Monograph 3). Berkeley : University of California Press.

Kibrik, A. E. 1977. *The Methodology of Field Investigations in Linguistics.* The Hague-Paris : Mouton.

Kitamura, Hajime, Nishida, tastuo and Yasuhiko Nagano (eds.). 1994. *Current Issues in Sino-Tibetan Linguistics.* Osaka : National Museum of Ethnology.

de Lacouperie, Terrien. 1887. *The Languages of China before the Chinese.* London.

Ladefoged, Perter and Ian Maddieson. 1996. The Sounds of the World's Languages. Oxford : Blackwell Publishers Inc.

Lama, Ziwo Qiu-Fuyuan. 2012. *Subgrouping Of Nisoic (Yi) Languages : A Study From The Perspectives Of Shared Innovation And Phylogenetic Estimation.* Doctoral Dissertation. University of Texas at Arlington.

LaPolla, James Rady. 1995. Ergative Marking in Tibeto-Burman. Yoshio Nishi, James A. Matisoff, & Yasuhiko Nagano (eds). *New Horizons in Tibeto-Burman Morphosyntax* (Senri Ethnological Studies 41) Osaka : National Museum of Ethnology. pp. 189–228.

Lass, Roger. 1984. *Phonology. An Introduction to Basic Concepts*. Cambridge : Cambridge University Press.

Li, Charles Na and Sandra A. Thompson. 1989. *Mandarin Chinese* : A Functional Reference Grammar. Berkeley and Los Angels : University of California Press.

Libu Lakhi, Tsering Bum, and Charles Kevin Stuart. 2010a. C*hina's Namuyi Tibetans : Life, Language, and Folklore Volume One*. Asian Highlands Perspectives. 2 A

Libu Lakhi, Tsering Bum, and Charles Kevin Stuart. 2010b. *China's Namuyi Tibetans : Life, Language, and Folklore Volume Two*. Asian Highlands Perspectives. 2 B

Libu Lakhi, Huimin Qi, Charles Kevin Stuart, and Gerald Roche. 2010. *Namuyi Tibetan Songs, Engagement Chants, and Flute Music*. Asian Highlands Perspectives. 2 C

Matisoff, James Alan. 1975. 'Rhinoglottophilia : the mysterious connection between nasality and glottality, In *Nasálfest. Papers from a symposium on nasals and nasalization*. Edited by Charles A. Ferguson, Larry M. Hyman and John J. Ohala eds. Language Universals Project, Department of Linguistics, Stanford University. pp. 265–287.

Matisoff, James Alan. 1991. Sino-Tibetan linguistics : Present state and future prospects. *Annual Review of Anthropology*. 20 : 469–504.

Matisoff, James Alan. 1994. Regularity and variation in Sino-Tibetan. In Kitamura, Hajime, Nishida, tastuo and Yasuhiko Nagano (eds.), *Current Issues in Sino-Tibetan Linguistics*, Osaka : National Museum of Ethnology. pp. 36–58.

Matisoff, James. Alan. 2003. *Handbook of Proto-Tibeto-Burman*. Berkeley, Los Angels and London : University of California Press.

Mazaudon, M. 1973. *Phonologie du tamang. Étude phonologique du dialecte tamang de Risiangku*. (*Langue tibéto-birmane du Népal*). Paris : Centre National de la Recherche Scientifique, Société d'Études Linguistiques et Anthropologiques de France (Langues et civilisations à tradition orale, 4)

Mazaudon Martine, 1974. Notes on Tone in Tibeto-Burman, *Linguistics of the Tibeto-Burman Area* 1. 1 : 27–54.

Mazaudon Martine, 1977. *Tibeto-Burman Tonogenetics, Linguistics of the Tibeto-Burman Area* 3 : 2.

Mazaudon Martine, 1980. Mutation consonantique et développement des systèmes de tons dans les langues tibéto-birmanes. In H. Walter ed. *Dynamique, Diachronie, Panchronie en Phonologie, Journée d'étude de Paris V*. pp. 35–46.

Michailovsky, Boyd. 1975. 'A case of Rhinoglottophilia in Hayu'. *Linguistics of the Tibeto-Burman Area*. 2. 2 : 293.

Moseley, Christopher (ed.). 2010. *Atlas of the World's Languages in Danger*, 3 rd edition. Paris, UNESCO Publishing.

Nettle, Daniel and Suzanne Romaine. 2000. *Vanishing voices : The Extinction of the World's Languages*. Oxford : Oxford University Press.

Nishi, Yoshio, James A. Matisoff, Yasuhiko Nagano. 1995. *New Horizons in Tibeto-Burman Morpho-Syntax* (Senri Ethnological Studies 41). Osaka : National Museum of Ethnology

Nishida, Fuminobu. 2005a. A Vocabulary of Nàmùyì. *Reitaku University Journal*. 80 : 213-223.

Nishida, Fuminobu. 2005b. A Sociolinguistic Study of the Namuyi language in Sichuan, China. *Reitaku Journal of Interdisciplinary Studies*. 13. 1 : 13–21.

Nishida, Fuminobu. 2005c. On pitch accent in the Nàmùyì language. Paper presented at the 11th Himalayan Language Symposium, Chulalongkorn University, Bangkok. 6 - 9, December, 2005.

Nishida, Fuminobu. 2006d. An outline of Nàmùyì grammar (1). *Reitaku University Journal*. 82 : 67-91.

Nishida, Fuminobu. 2006e. 〈su〉 Nominals in Namiyi. Paper presented at the 12th Himalayan Language Symposium, Tribhuvan University, Kathumandu. 27-29 November, 2006.

Nishida, Fuminobu. 2013. Phonetics and Phonology of Dzolo dialect of Nàmùyì. *Artes liberals*. 92 : 21-54.

Nishida, Fuminobu. 2015. On Transitivity of Namuyi. Otomo, Nobuya. ed. *Studies on European and American languages and cultures*, 2 : 135-149.

Nishida, Tatsuo. 1994. A personal view of the Sino-Tibetan language family. *Current Issues in Sino-Tibetan Linguistics*, Osaka : National Museum of Ethnology. pp. 1 –22.

Nordhoff, Sebastian, Hammarström, Harald, Forkel, Robert, and Martn Haspelmath. eds.

2013. Namuyi. *Glottolog 2. 2.* Leipzig : Max Planck Institute for Evolutionary Anthropology.

d'Ollone, et. al. 1912. *Langues des peoples non chinois de la chine.* Paris : E. Leroux.

Olson, James. S. 1998. *An Ethnohistorical Dictionary of China.* Westport : Greenwood Press.

Opgenort, Jean Robert. 2004. *A grammar of Wambule. Grammar, Lexicon, Texts and Cultural Survey of a Kiranti Tribe of Eastern Nepal.* Leiden : Koninkijke Brill.

Pannu, J. 1994. Code-mixing in a trilingual speech community ; Indian adolescents in Hong Kong M. A. thesis, City University of Hong Kong.

Payne, Thomas E. 1997. *Describing Morphosyntax : A Guide for Filed Linguists.* Cambridge : Cambridge University Press.

Pennington, M., Balla, J., Detaramani, C., Poon, A. & Tam, F. 1992. Towards a model of language choice among Hong Kong tertiary students : A preliminary analysis. Research Report No. 18, Department of English, City University of Hong Kong.

Plaisier, Heleen. 2006. *A Grammar of Lepcha.* Leiden : Koninklijke Brill.

Ramsey, Robert, S. 1987. *The Languages of China.* Princeton University Press.

Rose, Phil. 1996. Aerodynamic Involvement in Intrinsic F 0 perturbations-Evidence from Thai-Phake. In Paul McCormak & Alison Russel eds. *Proceedings of the 6 th Australian International Conf. on Speech Science and Technology.* Australian Speech Science and Technology Association, pp. 593-598.

Rutgers, Roland. 1998. *Yamphu : Grammar, Texts and Lexicon.* Leiden Research School for Asian, African and Amerindian Studies.

Shearer, Walter and Sun, Hongkai. 2002. *Speakers of the non-Han languages and dialects of China.* Lewiston : Edwin Mellen Press.

Sprigg, Richard Keith. 1987. Rhinoglottophilia revisited : observations on the mysterious connection between nasality and glottality. *Linguistics of the Tibeto-Burman Area.* 10. 1 : 44-62.

Sun, Hongkai. 1989. A Preliminary Investigation into the Relationship between Qiong Long and the Languages of the Qiang Branch of Tibeto-Burman. *Linguistics of the Tibeto-Burman Area* 12. 1 : 92-109.

Sun, HongKai. 1990. Languages of 'ethnic corridor' in Western Sichuan. (translation of Sun 1983a by Jackson T. -S. Sun) *Linguistics of the Tibeto-Burman Area.* 13.

1 : 1-31.

Sun, HongKai. 1992. On nationality and the recognition of Tibeto-Burman Languages. *Linguistics of the Tibeto-Burman Area.* 15. 2 : 1-19.

Sun, HongKai. 1999. On the Himalayan languages of the eastern Himalayan area in China. *Linguistics of the Tibeto-Burman Area.* 22. 2 : 61-72.

Tsunoda, Tasaku. 2005. *Language Endangerment and Language Revitalization.* Berlin : Mouton de Gruyter.

Turin, Mark. 2006. *A Grammar of the Thangmi Language.* Leiden : Koninklijke Brill.

Vaux, Bert and Justin Cooper. 1999. *Introduction to Linguistic Field Methods*, Muenchen : Lincom Europa.

Waterhouse, David M. 2004. *The origins of Himalayan studies : Brian Houghton Hodgson in Nepal and Darjeeling, 1820-1858.* London ; New York : Routledge Curzon.

Weidert, A. 1987. *Tibeto-Burman Tonology.* Amsterdam and Philadelphia : John Benjamins publishing company.

Yang, Zhenhong. 2009. An Overview of the Mosuo Language. *Linguistics of the Tibeto-Burman. Area* 32. 2 : 1-43.

Zang, Xiaowei (ed.) 2016 *Handbook on Ethnic Minorities in China.* Cheltenham : Edvard Elgar Publishing Ltd.

あとがき

　本書は筆者がこれまで調査してきた四川省涼山彝族自治州冕寧県連合郷（東経101°42′10″〜101°50′30″　北緯28°8′0″〜28°19′58″）にて2004年から2013年にかけて断続的に収集してきナムイ語の言語データを文法便覧の形で提示したものである。

　本記述言語学的研究は、単に一言語の研究にとどまらず、これまでわずかしか存在しなかった川西走廊諸語の言語学的資料として、川西走廊諸語の比較言語学的研究、または言語学の諸理論の研究にも貢献するものであると考える。

　第一章「序論」では、本論文での議論を展開するにあたっての基本的な事項の説明や定義を行う。本論文で扱うナムイ語の系統的位置づけや話者の置かれた社会状況などについて概説した。

　第二章「音論」では、ナムイ語の音声記述・音素体系を記述し、音声、音素、超分節音素について分析結果を提示した。特に4つのトーン及び語声調（word tone）の振る舞いについては詳細に記述した。

　第三章「名詞形態論」では、先ず形態論レベルの現象を記述した。ナムイ語における形態論的現象には、接辞による派生、複合、繰り返し（reduplication）による派生がある。接辞による派生、複合、繰り返しによる派生を扱った。続いて用いる品詞分類と分類の基準を示した後、名詞や名詞句に関連する文法現象についての議論、あるいは、名詞句に付く助詞の記述を行う。まず名詞句の構造を記述し、名詞の下位範疇の一つである代名詞について論じ、やはり名詞の下位範疇の一つである数詞および助数名詞について論じた。また様々な格標識を記述する。

　第四章「動詞形態論」では、ナムイ語の基本的語順を示し、さらに、本論文で用いる様々な概念の定義を行った。引き続き、動詞や動詞句に関連する文法現象についての議論、あるいは、動詞に付く助詞の記述を行った。ナムイ語は膠着語でSOVの語順を有する。しかしながら、述

語が文末に立つという厳格な文法的制約に違反しない限り、その他の構成要素の順序はかなり自由であることが解明された。動詞語幹の中にはチベット語系諸語とは明らかに系統を異にするものが存在し、また述語形式（助動詞）や助詞の中にはチベット＝ビルマ諸語の古い形式と同定できるものもあることが判明した。

　第五章「複雑な構造」では構成素順序、疑問文、否定文、存在構文および所有構文、トピック＝コメント構文などを概観した。

　最後の付録は参考資料である。筆者の収集になる当該方言で最も典型的なテキスト1篇を選んで挙げてある。つづいてナムイ語＝中国語＝英語の対照基礎語彙集を付した。当該言語の資料はこれまで公刊されているものが少ないため、歴史言語学的研究にも資するよう、中国語及び英語からも引けるように3種類の順序で提示した。

　本書を纏めるにあたって本当に沢山の方にお世話になった。先ず、中華人民共和国四川省涼山彝族自治州冕寧県連合郷の方々にお礼申し上げる。2004年に初めて現地を訪れて以来、県政府及び県政府の方々には多大なるご高配を賜ってきた。特に李小翠さんの献身的なご協力には改めて心よりお礼申し上げる。

　これまで様々な局面で言語に関するご指導を賜った諸先生方、就中、一般言語学・中国語学・粤語並びに電脳の仕組みをご教示下さり筆者の最初の留学の機会を与えて下さった故辻伸久先生、東南アジアの諸言語を語族を超えて観察することの重要性を教えて下さった三上直光先生、中国語学の肥沃な世界とその奥深さをお教え下さった古屋昭弘先生、音響音声学及び最新の音韻論を懇切丁寧にご指導下さった日比谷潤子先生、世界の諸言語の多様性・言語類型論と古典チベット語をご指導頂いたAnatole Lyovin先生、ヒマラヤ諸語の多様性に目を向けるきっかけを作って下さったGeogre van Driem先生、また研究全般でお世話になっている陳國平先生にこの場を借りてこれまでのご学恩に心より感謝申し上げる所存である。最初の調査に同行して頂いた松岡正子先生にも心より御礼申し上げる。

あとがき

　また、東北大学文学研究科でご指導いただいた千種眞一先生、後藤斉先生、斎藤倫明先生にも感謝申し上げる。

　東北大学出版会事務局長小林直之様には企画の段階から大変お世話になった。満腔の謝意を表する次第である。

　なお、本書は平成30年度科学研究費補助金（研究成果公開促進費：18HP5078）を受けている。

　最後に父重信、母三枝子、弟克信に心からお礼を申し上げたい。

西田文信

【著者略歴】

西田　文信（にしだ　ふみのぶ）

1973年群馬県生まれ。慶應義塾大学文学部文学科中国文学専攻卒業。ハワイ大学人文科学研究科言語学科修士課程修了。香港城市大學人文・社會科學研究院中文・翻譯及語言學學科博士課程単位取得満期退学。博士（文学）。

香港城市大學兼職講師、ライデン大学言語学研究所客員研究員、秋田大学国際交流センター准教授、岩手大学人文社会科学部准教授、ベルン大学言語学研究所客員研究員等を経て東北大学高度教養教育・学生支援機構教育内容開発部門言語・文化教育開発室准教授。

専門は言語学（記述言語学・歴史言語学、特に漢語諸方言及びTrans-Himalayan諸語）、言語教育。主著に『ゾンカ語基礎1500語』（大学書林，2016年）、『旅の指さし会話帳ブータン』（情報センター出版局、2013年）、『ニューエクスプレススペシャル日本語の隣人たちⅡ』（白水社、2013年、共著）、『地球の歩き方広東語＋英語』（ダイヤモンド社、2010年）。

ナムイ語文法の記述言語学的研究

A descriptive linguistic study of Namuyi

©Fuminobu NISHIDA 2019

2019年2月21日　初版第1刷発行

編　者　西田　文信
発行者　久道　茂
発行所　東北大学出版会
　　　　〒980-8577　仙台市青葉区片平2-1-1
　　　　TEL：022-214-2777　FAX：022-214-2778
　　　　https://www.tups.jp　E-mail：info@tups.jp
印　刷　亜細亜印刷株式会社
　　　　〒380-0804　長野県長野市大字三輪荒屋1154
　　　　TEL：026-243-4858

ISBN978-4-86163-323-2　C3087

定価はカバーに表示してあります。
乱丁、落丁はおとりかえします。

JCOPY　〈出版者著作権管理機構　委託出版物〉

本書の無断複写は著作権法上での例外を除き禁じられています。複写される場合は、そのつど事前に、出版者著作権管理機構（電話 03-5244-5088、FAX 03-5244-5089、e-mail:info@jcopy.or.jp）の許諾を得てください。